Essay Index

A Psychological Approach to Fiction

Studies in Thackeray, Stendhal,
George Eliot, Dostoevsky, and Conrad

A Psychological Approach to Fiction

Studies in Thackeray, Stendhal, George Eliot, Dostoevsky, and Conrad

By Bernard J. Paris

INDIANA UNIVERSITY PRESS

Bloomington & London

Published in Canada by Fitzhenry & Whiteside Limited,
Don Mills, Ontario
Manufactured in the United States of America

Library of Congress Cataloging in Publication Data

Paris, Bernard J
    A psychological approach to fiction.

    Includes bibliographical references.
    1.   Fiction—19th century—History and criticism.
I.   Title
PN3499.P3   809'.3'83   73-15239
ISBN 0-253-34650-9

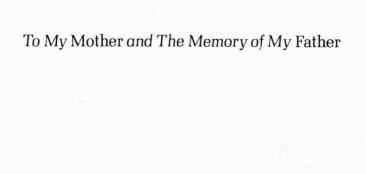

To My Mother *and The Memory of My* Father

Contents

Preface

This is a psychological study of five novels—*Vanity Fair, The Red and the Black, The Mill on the Floss, Notes from Underground,* and *Lord Jim.* Its understanding of neurotic processes is drawn mainly from the writings of Karen Horney, and its conceptions of health are based on what Abraham Maslow has called Third Force psychology. Since these theories are not well-known among literary critics, I have provided a full exposition of them in the second chapter. This study is concerned neither with authors as historical persons nor with reader response. It treats each of the novels discussed as an autonomous work of art; and it uses psychology to analyze important characters and to explore the consciousness of the implied author. In the opening chapter, I try to show why it is both necessary and proper to study certain kinds of characters and implied authors by a psychological method.

The psychological approach developed here answers a number of needs in the criticism of fiction. The greatest achievement of many realistic novels is their portrayal of character, but we have as yet no critical perspective that enables us to appreciate this achievement and to talk about it with sophistication. Realistic novels are often flawed by incoherence and contradiction. In some, like *The Red and the Black* and *The Mill on the Floss,* there is a disparity between representation and interpretation, between the implied author as a creator of mimetic portraits and the implied author as analyst and judge. Movements from one neurotic solution to another are interpreted as processes of growth and education. The implied authors glorify unhealthy attitudes which are close to their own, while at the same time *showing* their destructiveness. In other novels, like *Vanity Fair*, the interpretations are not only inappropriate or inadequate to the experience dramatized, but they are also inwardly inconsistent. Such works are thematically unintelligible. The psychological approach employed here will help us to make sense of thematic inconsistencies, to account for disparities between representation and interpretation, and to evaluate the adequacy for life of the solutions adopted by characters and implied authors.

This study began with an attempt to discover the unifying structural principle of *Vanity Fair*. The more I thought about the novel, the more clearly I came to see that it lacks a coherent thematic structure, that the interpretations of experience inherent in its rhetoric are not consistent with each other. As I struggled to understand the novel, I suddenly remembered Karen Horney's statement that inconsistency is as sure a sign of neurotic conflict as a rise in temperature is of bodily disorder. A fresh reading both of Horney and of the novel bore out my hypothesis that the inconsistencies of *Vanity Fair* make sense when they are seen as manifestations of a neurotic psyche, the structure of which includes and is, indeed, made up of conflicting attitudes and impulses. I soon perceived also that the major characters— Becky, Dobbin, and Amelia—are subtle portraits of troubled persons whose inner lives and patterns of behavior are best understood in terms of Horneyan psychology.

I have subsequently seen that Horneyan theory has wide applicability to literature. Though her psychology (like any other) is far from providing a complete picture of human nature, Karen Horney deals astutely with the same patterns of intra-psychic and interpersonal behavior that form the matter (and often the structure) of a good many novels and plays. In addition to applying her theories to the characters and implied authors of five realistic novels, in Chapters III through VII, I suggest in my concluding remarks a variety of other possible uses.

The five novels to be discussed here were chosen not only because they are all helpfully illuminated by Horneyan psychology, but also because they offer an interesting variety of personality types, of modes of characterization, and of narrative techniques. Comparing the novels with each other will help us to determine the virtues and defects of various modes of narration and the kinds of insight for which realistic fiction is most properly a vehicle.

In the course of writing this book I have been fortunate enough to incur many debts. Theodore Millon first made me aware of Karen Horney; Max Bruck has helped me to become aware of myself. I have had the opportunity to discuss Horney's thought with Doctors Harold Kelman, Helen Boigon, Norman J. Levy, Isidore Portnoy, Ralph Slater, Bella S. Van Bark, and Joseph Vollmerhausen, all of whom are practitioners and teachers of her theory. Doctors Kelman, Boigon, and Portnoy have read Chapter II and have given me the benefit of their advice. Abraham Maslow was kind enough to read this chapter also, and to assure me that it is accurate.

Herbert Josephs has discussed Stendhal with me many times; he and Laurence Porter have read my chapter on *The Red and the Black* and have shared with me their expert knowledge of the French text. Denis Mickiewicz has checked my quotations and my reading of *Notes from Underground* against the Russian original. Portions of this work have been read by Michael Steig, Richard Berchan, Richard Benvenuto, Joseph Waldmeir, Sam Baskett, Lore Metzger, Barry Gross, E. Fred Carlisle, Avrom Fleishman, J. Hillis Miller, and Frederick Crews; I am grateful to all of them for their comments. Michael Wolf, George Levine, Mark Spilka, and Henry H.H. Remak have provided thoughtful criticisms of earlier versions of Chapters III, V, and VI in their capacity as readers for *Victorian Studies, Novel,* and *PMLA;* such service is not frequently enough acknowledged. Herbert Greenberg has offered me the kind of dialogue without which the mind does not grow and the spirit sags.

I am grateful to Michigan State University for a sabbatical leave and to the National Endowment for the Humanities for a Fellowship which gave me the time to write this book. A grant from the Norman J. Levy foundation permitted me to visit New York for conferences with the Horneyan psychiatrists named above. Typing, photocopying, and other clerical assistance have been paid for by All-University Research Grants from Michigan State University.

The portions of my study which have appeared in *Novel, Victorian Studies, The Centennial Review,* and *PMLA* are included here, in revised and expanded form, with the kind permission of the editors of these journals.

My deepest debts are to my wife, whose objections have taught me more than the praise of others, and to Alan Hollingsworth, who has believed in what I am doing more than anyone else and who has given me unfailing encouragement and support.

BJP

A Psychological Approach to Fiction

Studies in Thackeray, Stendhal,
George Eliot, Dostoevsky, and Conrad

Chapter I

The Uses of Psychology:

Characters and Implied Authors

Norman Holland finds it "hard to see how a psychology [can] deal with a work of art *qua* work of art," and observes that in practice psychoanalytic critics "do not."[1] Psychology cannot consider works of art in themselves, he argues, because psychology as such is concerned "not with literature, but with minds" (p. 293). "Any psychological system," therefore, "must deal, not with works of art in isolation, but with works of art in relation to man's mind" (p. 151). The "three possible minds to which the psychological critic customarily refers" are the author's mind, a character's mind, and the audience's mind. It is only the study of the audience's mind, Holland feels, that can lead "to a bona-fide method; the other two tend to confusion" (p. 294). I believe that there are two kinds of minds within realistic novels that can be studied in psychological terms: they are the minds of the implied authors and the minds of the leading characters.

Holland argues that "we should use psychology on our own real and lively reactions" to the work "rather than on the characters' fictitious minds" (p. 308). He feels that character study is useful and legitimate only when it is incorporated into our analysis of the audience's mind. Then it is seen to "identify 'latent impulses' of the characters which may be considered as stimuli to or projections of latent impulses of the audience" (p. 283). Character study is not legitimate when, as in most psychological criticism, it talks "about literary characters as though they were real people" (p. 296). Holland's strongest argument in support of this position is that "Homo Fictus and Homo Dramaticus do not so much what Homo Sapiens would do in similar circumstances, but what it is necessary for them to do in the logical and meaningful realities of the works of art in which they live" (pp. 305–306). The artist "hovers between *mimesis,* making like, and *harmonia,* the almost musical ordering of the events he depicts. . . . The psychoanalytic critic of character neglects the element of *harmonia,* the symbolic conceptions that must modify the mimetic" (p. 306). Other critics of literature have learned to avoid this mistake: ". . . as a plain matter of fact, most literary critics do not—any more—treat literary characters as real people" (p. 296).[2]

Holland is participating in what W. J. Harvey calls "the retreat from character" in modern criticism, a retreat which Harvey's book, *Character and the Novel,* is intended to halt. "What has been said about character" in the past forty years, Harvey observes, "has been mainly a stock of critical commonplaces used largely to dismiss the subject in order that the critic may turn his attention to other allegedly more important and central subjects— symbolism, narrative techniques, moral vision and the like."[3] In the criticism of realistic fiction this has been especially unfortunate, for "most great novels exist to reveal and explore character" (p. 23). There are many reasons for this retreat, Harvey continues, the most important of which is the rise of the New Criticism:

> The New Criticism was centrally concerned to apply close and rigorous analytical methods to lyric poetry; it is noticeable how ill at ease its practitioners have been when they have approached the bulky, diffuse and variegated world of the novel. What we might

> expect is in fact the case; the new critic, when dealing with fiction,
> is thrown back upon an interest in imagery, symbolism or struc-
> tural features which have little to do with characterization. (p. 200)

The danger that the critic of novels must now be warned against
is not the neglect of *harmonia*, but the neglect of *mimesis;* for
harmonia has had its due of late, and "a mimetic intention" was,
after all, "the central concern of the novel until the end of the
nineteenth century" (p. 205).

No study of character should ignore the fact that characters in
fiction participate in the dramatic and thematic structures of the
works in which they appear and that the meaning of their behavior is often to be understood in terms of its function within these
structures. The less mimetic the fiction, the more completely will
the characters be intelligible in terms of their dramatic and thematic functions; and even in highly realistic fiction, the minor
characters are to be understood more functionally than psychologically. But, as Harvey points out, the authors of the great
realistic novels "display an appetite and passion for life which
threatens to overwhelm the formal nature of their art" (pp. 187–
188). There is in such novels "a surplus margin of gratuitous life,
a sheer excess of material, a fecundity of detail and invention, a
delighted submergence in experience for its own sake" (p. 188).
The result is "that characterization often overflows the strict
necessities of form" (p. 188). This is especially true in the characterization of the protagonists, of "those characters whose motivation and history are most fully established, who conflict and
change as the story progresses . . ." (p. 56). What we attend to
in the protagonist's story "is the individual, the unique and
particular case. . . . We quickly feel uneasy if the protagonist
is made to stand for something general and diffused; the more
he *stands for* the less he *is*" (p. 67). Though such characters
have their dramatic and thematic functions, they are "in
a sense . . . end-products"; we often feel that "they are what

the novel exists for; it exists to reveal them" (p. 56).

The retreat from character of which Harvey complains has been in part a reaction against reading plays, stories, impressionistic novels, and other tightly structured or basically symbolic works as though they were realistic fiction. This has frequently resulted, ironically, in the study of realistic novels as though they were tightly structured or basically symbolic forms. In our avoidance of what Northrop Frye would call a low-mimetic provincialism, we have often failed to do justice to the low-mimetic forms themselves.

Fortunately, the most recent trend in literary criticism has been to emphasize the qualities that distinguish the literary modes and kinds from each other. In the study of narrative art, we are learning to appreciate a variety of forms and effects; and this, in turn, is enabling us to grasp the distinctive characteristics of each form with greater precision.[4] We are coming to see, among other things, that character is central in many realistic novels and that much of the characterization in such fiction escapes dramatic and thematic analysis and can be understood only in terms of its mimetic function. A careful examination of the nature of realistic fiction as modern criticism is coming to conceive it will show that in certain cases it *is* proper to treat literary characters as real people and that only by doing so can we fully appreciate the distinctive achievement of the genre.

The diversity of aesthetic theories and of critical approaches is in part a reflection of the multiplicity of values to be found in literature and in part a product of the varying interests and temperaments with which different critics come to literature. Not all approaches are equally valid: the most satisfying kind of criticism is that which is somehow congruent with the work and which is faithful to the distribution of interests in the work itself. The approach employed here attempts to stress values which are inherently important in realistic fiction and to make these values more accessible to us than they hitherto have been.

The primary values of fiction can be described in a variety of terms; I shall classify them as mimetic, thematic, and formal. Fiction is mainly concerned with the representation, the interpretation, and the aesthetic patterning of experience.[5] In different works and in different fictional modes the distribution of emphasis varies; and in some works one of these interests may be far more important than the others. When a work concerns itself seriously with more than one of these interests, it must bring its various impulses into harmony if it is to be organically unified.

From the middle of the eighteenth to the beginning of the twentieth century, the novel attempted, by and large, to realize all of these values; but its primary impulse seems to have been the mimetic one. Henry James is reflecting not only his own taste, but the essential nature of the genre when he characterizes the novel as "a picture" and proclaims that "the only reason for the existence of a novel is that it does attempt to represent life."[6] It is not its interpretation of life or its formal perfection but its "air of reality (solidity of specification)" that James identifies as "the supreme virtue of a novel" (p. 14). Arnold Kettle distinguishes between the moral fable, which is dominated by "pattern" or "significance" and the novel, in which "pattern" is subordinate to "life." Despite a frequently strong commitment to thematic interests, the great realists, says Kettle, "are less consciously concerned with the moral significance of life than with its surface texture. Their talent is devoted first and foremost to getting life on to the page, to conveying across to their readers the sense of what life as their characters live it really feels like."[7]

The view of realistic fiction that we are developing is confirmed by such classic works on the subject as Ian Watt's *The Rise of the Novel* and Erich Auerbach's *Mimesis*. Formal interests cannot be paramount in a genre that, as Watt describes it, "works by exhaustive presentation rather than by elegant concentration."[8] Like E. M. Forster, Watt sees "the portrayal of 'life by time' as the distinctive role which the novel has added to literature's more ancient preoccupation with portraying 'life by values' " (p. 22). The domain of the novel is the individual and his social relationships, and it tends to present its subject less in terms of ethical categories than in terms of chronological and causal sequences. The distinctive characteristics of the novel are, for Watt, its emphasis upon the particular, its circumstantial view of life, and its full and authentic reporting of experience (pp. 31–32).

To our statement that the novel's primary impulse is a mimetic one, we must add the qualification that the reality imitated is not general nature or the world of Ideas, but the concrete and temporal reality of modern empirical thought. The novel came into being in a world dominated by secularism and individualism, a world in which men were losing their belief in the supernatural and institutional bases of life. "Both the philosophical and the literary innovations," says Watt, "must be seen as parallel manifestations of a larger change—that vast transformation of Western civilization since the Renaissance which has replaced the unified world picture of the Middle Ages with another very different one—one which presents us, essentially, with a developing but unplanned aggregate of particular individuals having particular experiences at particular times and at particular places" (p. 31).

For Erich Auerbach the foundations of modern realism are, first, "the serious treatment of everyday reality, the rise of more extensive and socially inferior human groups to the position of subject matter for problematic-existential representation"; and, second, "the embedding of random persons and events in the general course of contemporary history, the fluid historical background."[9] Throughout *Mimesis* Auerbach is concerned with the contrast between the classical moralistic and the problematic existential ways of presenting reality. The distinction is basically between the representation of life in terms of fixed canons of style and of ethical categories which are a priori and static, and a stylistically mixed, ethically ambiguous portrayal which probes "the social forces underlying the facts and conditions" that it presents (p. 27). The problematic existential perception of reality, which *Mimesis* exists to celebrate, is one that is informed by the insights of Historicism. It is characterized by an awareness that "epochs and societies are not to be judged in terms of a pattern concept of what is desirable absolutely speaking but rather in every case in terms of their own premises"; by "a sense of historical dynamics, of the incomparability of historical phenomena and of their constant inner mobility"; and by a "conviction that the meaning of events cannot be grasped in abstract and general forms of cognition" (p. 391).

It is evident that in fiction employing the classical moralistic perspective, interpretation will outweigh and, indeed, govern representation, whereas in fiction written from a problematic existential point of view the mimetic impulse will be predominant. In many realistic novels, however, the classical moralistic perspective continues to exist alongside of, and often in disharmony with, the concrete, "serio-problematic" representation of life. Auerbach observes that Balzac, for example, "aspires to be a classical moralist" but that "this suits neither his style nor his temperament" (pp. 422–423). In his novels "the classically moralistic element very often gives the impression of being a foreign body." It expresses itself in the narrator's "generalized apophthegms of a moral cast," which are "sometimes witty as individual observations," but which are often "far too generalized" and are sometimes "plain 'tripe'" (p. 422).

Realism for Auerbach means essentially social realism—the presentation of events in terms of the network of historical relations in which they exist and a concern for all of the forces at work, not simply for a limited, class-determined set of causes. His distinction between the categorical and the historistic views of experience applies just as readily to the presentation of character as it does to the rendering of society, though Auerbach himself has little to say about psychological realism. Representation is the primary interest of realistic fiction, and the two chief objects of representation are character and social milieu. Some novels are profoundly concerned with both character and society; others focus primarily on social or on psychological reality. Novels in which psychological realism predominates tend to present society from the point of view of the individual; novels of social realism often take a sociological rather than a psychological view of character.

Though realistic fiction is more concerned with mimesis than it is with theme and form the latter are, nonetheless, very important elements in the majority of novels. Indeed, one of the basic problems of the novel as a genre is that it attempts to integrate impulses which are disparate and often in conflict. The problematic existential portrayal of reality defies, by its very nature, authorial attempts at analysis and judgment. The great realists see and represent far more than they can understand. And, as Northrop Frye observes, "the realistic writer soon finds that the requirements of literary form and plausible content always fight against each other."[10] Form derives from generic conventions, and ultimately from mythic patterns, which are inherently unrealistic; realistic content obeys the laws of probability, of cause and effect, and belongs to a different universe of discourse. The integration of theme, form, and mimesis is an extremely difficult task.

Critics of realistic fiction, even some of those who best understand its nature, come to it demanding formal and thematic perfections which very few novels can achieve. The novel "may have a distinctive representational technique," says Ian Watt, "but if it is to be considered a valuable literary form it must also have, like any other literary form, a structure which is a coherent expression of all its parts" (p. 104). The novel, Watt feels, must "supplement its realism of presentation with a realism of assessment." If the interpretive element is weak "we shall be wholly immersed in the reality of the characters and their actions, but whether we shall be any wiser as a result is open to question" (p. 288). Arnold Kettle recognizes that "there are writers, and great ones, whose books have more vividness than wisdom, more vitality than significance"; but he feels that "the central core of any novel is what it has to say about life." Novels with more life than pattern, or in which life and pattern are not integrated, are wanting in the quality of their perception (pp. 14–16).

It is my impression that if we come to novels expecting moral wisdom and coherent teleological structures we are usually going to be disappointed. Such expectations are frequently aroused by the works themselves, and it is natural for the reader to want them fulfilled; but the mimetic impulse that dominates most novels often works against total integration and thematic adequacy. Even so, the novel is a valuable literary form. As Watt himself says, "In the novel, more perhaps than in any other literary genre, the qualities of life can atone for the defects of art . . ." (p. 301). The novel's weaknesses are in many cases the defects of its virtues, and its virtues are very great indeed. Some novels, of course, are integrated: they are usually those in which the interpretive element either is almost nonexistent or is incorporated into the mimesis. Such novels have coherent teleological structures, but they do not provide the kind of wisdom that Kettle, Watt, and many other critics seem to be looking for.

It is because they contain highly individualized characters or extremely detailed pictures of society that many novels lack total artistic integration. In novels of psychological realism (on which we shall focus here) there is a character-creating impulse which has its own inner logic and which tends to go its own way, whatever the implied author's formal and thematic intentions may be. As critics we demand, indeed, that the central characters of realistic fiction be like real people, that they have a life of their own beyond the control of their author. The novelist, says Harvey, "must accept his characters as asserting their human individuality and uniqueness in the face of all ideology (including his own limited point of view)" (p. 25). In realistic fiction, proclaims Georg Lukács, "what matters is the picture conveyed by the work; the question to what extent this picture conforms to the views of the authors is a secondary consideration."[11] "A great realist," Lukács continues,

> . . . if the intrinsic artistic development of situations and characters he has created comes into conflict with his most cherished prejudices or even his most sacred convictions, will, without an instant's hesitation, set aside these his own prejudices and convictions and describe what he really sees, not what he would prefer to see. This ruthlessness towards their own subjective world-picture is the hall-mark of all great realists, in sharp contrast to the second-raters, who nearly always succeed in bringing their own *Weltanschauung* into "harmony" with reality. . . . (p. 11)

Lukács is chiefly concerned with the portrayal of social reality, but his observations apply also to the presentation of character:

> The characters created by the great realists, once conceived in the vision of their creator, live an independent life of their own; their comings and goings, their development, their destiny is dictated by the inner dialectic of their social and individual existence. No writer is a true realist—or even a truly good writer, if he can direct the evolution of his own characters at will. (p. 11)

The point I am trying to make has been most brilliantly developed by E. M. Forster, in his discussion of flat and round characters. "The novelist," he observes, "has a very mixed lot of ingredients to handle." He is telling a story ("life in time") which has a meaning ("life by values"). His story is "about human beings":

The characters arrive when evoked, but full of the spirit of mutiny. For they have these numerous parallels with people like ourselves, they try to live their own lives and are consequently often engaged in treason against the main scheme of the book. They "run away," they "get out of hand": they are creations inside a creation, and often inharmonious towards it; if they are given complete freedom they kick the book to pieces, and if they are kept too sternly in check, they revenge themselves by dying, and destroy it by intestinal decay.[12]

What Forster has described here is the dilemma of the realistic novelist. If his characters are truly alive they will have a motivational life of their own and will tend to subvert the main scheme of the book. If he keeps his characters subordinated to their aesthetic and thematic functions, however, they will be lifeless puppets and his book will be flawed in a different and more serious way.

In their excellent book on narrative literature, Robert Scholes and Robert Kellogg recapitulate and refine many of our most recent insights into the nature of realistic fiction. Their division of characters into three types—aesthetic, illustrative, and mimetic—provides the best taxonomy that we have to date and offers a convenient way of formulating the thesis which I have been developing.

Characters should be understood in terms of the kind of function that they perform. Aesthetic types—"villains, ingénues, *ficelles*, choral characters, *nuntii*, and so on"—serve mainly to create formal patterns and dramatic impact. They have little inner depth or moral significance. Illustrative characters are most important in works governed by the classical moralistic perspective:

Illustration differs from representation in narrative art in that it does not seek to reproduce actuality but to present selected aspects of the actual, essences referable for their meaning not to historical, psychological, or sociological truth but to ethical and metaphysical truth.

Illustrative characters

> . . . are concepts in anthropoid shape or fragments of the human psyche masquerading as whole human beings. Thus we are not called upon to understand their motivation as if they were whole human beings but to understand the principles they illustrate through their actions in a narrative framework. (p. 88)

Behind realistic fiction there is a strong "psychological impulse" that "tends toward the presentation of highly individualized figures who resist abstraction and generalization, and whose motivation is not susceptible to rigid ethical interpretation" (p. 101). When we encounter a fully drawn mimetic character "we are justified in asking questions about his motivation based on our knowledge of the ways in which real people are motivated" (p. 87).

There are aesthetic and illustrative types in realistic novels, of course, and in the central characters there is often a mixing of and a tension between illustrative, mimetic, and aesthetic functions. But in novels of psychological realism the main characters exist primarily as mimetic portraits whose intricacies escape the moral and symbolic meanings assigned to them. Many aspects of their characterization which are of little formal or thematic interest become very significant when we see them as manifestations of the characters' inner being, as part of the author's unfolding of character for its own sake.

The great gift of the psychological realists, then, even of the most intellectually proficient and ethically sensitive of them, is not in the interpretation but in the representation of the experience of their characters. Their characters may have important functions in the thematic and formal structures of the works in

which they exist, but thematic and formal analysis cannot begin
to do justice to the psychological portraiture which is often the
greatest achievement of these works, and it frequently blinds us
to the fact that the experience represented does not always sustain the dramatic and thematic effects for which the work is striving.

Ortega y Gasset contends that all of the

> . . . psychological knowledge accumulated in the contemporary
> mind . . . is to no small degree responsible for the present failure
> of the novel. Authors that yesterday seemed excellent appear
> naive today because the present reader is a much better psycholo-
> gist than the old author.[13]

This is true only if we judge the old authors primarily in terms
of their analyses and assessments of their characters' behavior.
Given the fact that the old authors were not necessarily gifted as
analysts and moralists, that their value judgments were bound to
be influenced by their own neuroses, and that the psychological
theories available to them were inadequate to their insights, it
was inevitable that their interpretations would be inferior to their
representations of experience and that the beneficiaries of a
more advanced psychological science would feel superior to
them. If we do justice to their representations of character, however, we will see that they were excellent psychologists indeed,
and that we need all of the resources of modern knowledge to
understand and appreciate their achievement.

II

When Norman Holland speaks of the author's mind as one of
the "three possible minds to which the psychological critic customarily refers," he is thinking of the author as an historical
person; and what he objects to is the study of the man through
a psychological analysis of his works. One of the most valuable

contributions that Wayne Booth has made to the criticism of fiction is his insistence upon the distinction between the author as an historical person and the author as the writing self, the official scribe. Whatever may be the relation between the author as he is implied by the novel we are reading and the author as he was (or is) in life, outside of his creation, our concern as literary critics is primarily with the implied author, who exists completely in the book. Our examination of the nature of realistic fiction has shown that it is appropriate to study mimetic characters as though they were real people, to analyze their behavior in psychological as well as in formal and thematic terms. A consideration of the nature of the implied author will show that in many works his mind, too, can be fully understood only if it is studied by a psychological method.

The nature of the writing self is inferred mainly from his representation, interpretation, and aesthetic patterning of experience. So far we have been concerned with the implied author primarily in his mimetic function. We shall now consider him as the interpreter of the experience he portrays, as the creator of the novel's rhetorical structure; and we shall explore more fully the relationship between theme and mimesis in realistic fiction.

In a novel which is organically unified the impulses toward representation, interpretation and aesthetic patterning are harmonized; and the implied author emerges as a deeply integrated and coherent being. But there are many novels, including some great ones, which fail to achieve such organic unity. The implied author is not always in harmony with himself. There is frequently a disparity between representation and interpretation: the implied author's attitudes toward the experience that he represents, conveyed through a variety of rhetorical devices, are not always appropriate to the novel's total body of represented life. In some novels the thematic affirmations, though they are not validated by the work as a whole, are nonetheless consistent with themselves; there is a thematic structure which is coherent and intelligible in its own terms. There are other works, however, in which the implied author is inconsistent in his interpretations of the experience that he dramatizes; not only is there a disparity between representation and interpretation, but there is thematic confusion as well. One of the most valuable ways of studying a novel whose implied author is inwardly divided is to combine psychological with thematic analysis. Grasping the structure of the implied author's psyche can help us greatly to appreciate the values of such a novel and to make sense of its disparities and confusions.

It may seem that in emphasizing the importance of mimesis in realistic fiction I have unduly neglected theme. Some of the very critics whom I have cited to show the dominance of the mimetic impulse lay heavy stress upon interpretation as an essential ingredient of good fiction. The "good novel," says Arnold Kettle, "does not simply convey life; it says something about life. . . . It brings significance" (p. 13). If the novel "was to challenge older literary forms," Ian Watt proclaims, "it had to find a way of conveying not only a convincing impression but a wise assessment of life" (p. 288). According to Brooks and Warren, a piece of fiction, "to be good . . . must involve an idea of some real significance for mature and thoughtful human beings."[14] Theme is important not only for its moral value, for the "attitude" it suggests "toward life and the business of living" (p. 81), but also because it satisfies our psychological need "to have things put in order" (p. 273). "Just as we instinctively demand the logic of cause and effect, the logic of motivation, in fiction, so we demand that there be a logic of theme—a thematic structure into which the various elements are fitted and in terms of which they achieve unity" (p. 274). Theme is, therefore, a "structural necessity": "If we want a story, we are forced by our very psychological make-up to demand a theme: *No theme, no story*" (p. 274).

Let me say at once that my contention is not that theme is unimportant, but that its importance has been overestimated by many critics, including those quoted. The most challenging discussion of thematic values to occur in recent criticism is Wayne Booth's *The Rhetoric of Fiction,* and a consideration of some of Booth's leading contentions will help us at once to do justice to theme and to put it in its proper place.

Booth's central thesis seems to be that, despite the modern emphasis on showing and on objectivity, interpretation is an essential ingredient of all fiction. "The emotions and judgments of the implied author," he proclaims, "are . . . the very stuff out of which great fiction is made" (p. 86). In some cases the author as commentator is a person of great wisdom, charm, and intelligence whose companionship is one of the chief rewards of the book. In all cases, the author's ordering of his materials and his attitudes toward his characters and their world give the story its shape, tone, and significance. A story's dramatic impact derives not so much from the matter as from the treatment, from the author's control through his rhetoric both of emotional distance and of the reader's attitude toward his persons.

One of Booth's major efforts is to show that the author is always present as an interpreter, that "he can never choose to disappear," that his "judgment is . . . always evident to anyone who knows how to look for it" (p. 20). Even when, under the influence of the doctrine of objectivity, the author seeks to efface himself, his "voice is still dominant in a dialogue that is at the heart of all experience with fiction. With commentary ruled out, hundreds of devices remain for revealing judgment and molding response" (p. 272). The author is present "in every speech given by any character who has had conferred upon him . . . the badge of reliability," in "every distinctive literary allusion or colorful metaphor," in "every pattern of myth or symbol; they all implicitly evaluate" (p. 19). His "very choice of what he tells will betray him to the reader" (p. 20).

Given his insistence that the author cannot choose to disappear, it is surprising to discover, as we read on, that Booth feels the central problem of modern fiction to be the disappearance of the author. *The Rhetoric of Fiction* is, among other things, an attack upon works in which interpretation is either absent or obscure, and a plea for a return to the clear thematic ordering of fictional materials. Obviously, Booth cannot be right in claiming both that the author cannot disappear and that the author has disappeared. His confusion may stem from a tendency to regard the writing self as a whole and the implied author as interpreter as identical or inseparable. As he shows quite convincingly, there *are* works that have little or no thematic import, in which one of the most striking facts about the implied author is that he does not analyze and he does not judge. In such works the implied author has not disappeared—we can infer many things about him from his mimetic and formal concerns—but he is not significantly present as an interpreter of experience, and the works cannot be said to have a thematic structure.

As his argument proceeds, Booth moves from descriptive to prescriptive criticism. He begins by insisting that interpretation *is* always present, and concludes by insisting that it *should* always be present, even though it is not, for both moral and aesthetic reasons. A story will be "unintelligible," he feels, unless the reader is made clearly "aware of the value system which gives it its meaning" (p. 112). He believes, moreover, that the aesthetic effect of "even the greatest of literature is radically dependent on the concurrence of beliefs of authors and readers" (p. 140), that "the implied author of each novel is someone with whose beliefs on all subjects I must largely agree if I am to enjoy his work" (p. 137). The author, therefore, must not only make his beliefs known; but he must also "make us willing to accept that value system, at least temporarily" (p. 112). The reader must co-operate in the aesthetic transaction by willingly suspending his own attitudes, but "the work itself . . . must fill with its rhetoric the gap made by the suspension of my own beliefs" (p. 112).

There is much that I agree with in Booth's observations so far: the implied author as interpreter *is* an important feature of much fiction, we *do* have a powerful craving for thematic intelligibility, and it *is* necessary to identify with the perspective of the implied author if we are to experience a work according to its own inner logic. Booth's development of these ideas, to which I have done scant justice here, leaves all students of fiction in his debt. What I disagree with is his contention that interpretation is or should be a major ingredient of all fiction. This position, which violates his own injunction against general rules, is a reflection, I suspect, of Booth's strong personal preference for novels that have complex and accessible thematic structures.

Booth not only wants interpretation to be there and to be clear and to be persuasive while we are reading the novel; he also wants it to be true, both for the world of the book and for life in general. His essential plea is for every novel to have a reliable narrator, or some equivalent rhetorical device. At first this seems to be primarily a concern for "the reader's need to know where, in the world of values, he stands—that is, to know where the author *wants* him to stand" (p. 73). A reliable narrator is defined as one who "speaks for and acts in accordance with the norms of the work (which is to say, the author's norms)", and an unreliable narrator is one who "does not" (pp. 158–159). Later, however, in discussing the possibility of a nihilistic novel, Booth argues that in such a work "all forms of reliable narration will be inappropriate. If the world of the book is without meaning, how can there be a reliable narrator? What is he to be reliable about? The very concept of reliability presupposes that something objectively true can be said about actions and thoughts" (p. 299). It is evident that the narrator of such a novel could be a reliable transmitter of the facts of consciousness and of the implied author's attitudes; but reliability for Booth has come to mean correctness of judgment in the light of universal values. The function of the writing self is to "plumb to universal values," (p. 395), to see "into permanency" (p. 70) and to convey his wisdom clearly and persuasively to the reader through the use of such rhetorical devices as reliable narration: ". . . the artist must . . . be willing to be both a seer and a revelator" (p. 395). Booth celebrates those narrators who "originally succeeded and still succeed by persuading the reader to accept them as living oracles. They are reliable guides not only to the world of the novels in which they appear but also to the moral truths of the world outside the book" (p. 221).

I am wholly in sympathy with Booth when he insists that novels be inwardly intelligible (see p. 392) and when he shows the importance of a skillful rhetoric to works which depend for their effects upon the control of distance and of the reader's attitudes toward characters and events. In the discussion of *Vanity Fair* which follows, we shall see how this work is aesthetically impaired by its lack of a coherent thematic structure, of a reliable narrator in Booth's first sense of that term. I am sympathetic, too, with his demand that the judgments passed be "defensible in the light of the dramatized facts" (p. 79). Our analyses of *The Red and the Black* and *The Mill on the Floss* will consider the problems which arise when there is a disparity between representation and interpretation. But I am very reluctant to say, with Booth, that great literature is "radically dependent on the concurrence of beliefs of authors and readers" (p. 140), or that I must "largely agree" with the beliefs of the implied author "on all subjects . . . if I am to enjoy his work" (p. 137). The great work, for Booth, is one to which "we surrender our emotions for reasons that leave us with no regrets, no inclination to retract, after the immediate spell is past" (p. 131). If a book "is to maintain our respect," he feels, we must continue to entertain its thematic affirmations "as among the intellectually and morally defensible views of life" (p. 139).

There are serious difficulties in this position. By demanding a kind of truth that is rarely found in fiction, it leads us to reject the vast majority of novels. As Booth himself observes, "One of our most common reading experiences is, in fact, the discovery on reflection . . . that the beliefs which we were temporarily manipulated into accepting cannot be defended in the light of day" (p. 139). At times Booth speaks as though all novelists were wise; what they must do is to communicate their values effectively. At other times he indicates that we do not often find authors with whose judgments we can agree, and his appeal is for men who write novels to be virtuous and for those who are not to lay down their pens. In any event, he feels that novelists *ought* to be prophets and that, in the face of a fragmented society, they should "build works of art that . . . help to mold a new consensus" (p. 393). Booth is right in saying that our estimate of the implied author's beliefs inevitably affects our feelings about a work, and the thematic pretensions of many novelists may lead us to expect from fiction the kind of truth which Booth demands; but we are making a mistake, surely, if we go to fiction for ethical guidance or make our enjoyment or judgment of it dependent primarily upon our agreement with the author's values.

There is nothing in the gift, temperament, or technique of the novelist which makes him also a sage; and if we go to fiction for analytical insight or for universal values, we are likely in our disappointment to miss the unique experiences and revelations that fiction *can* give. If, as Booth says, the novelist has an obligation to plumb to universal values and to make his moral orderings clear, then he will usually fail; for as an interpreter of experience the novelist is usually no wiser or more consistent than other men. The real trouble with the narrative technique of much nineteenth century fiction is that the implied author as interpreter usually does not know what he is talking about. It may be partially in recognition of this fact that there has been such heavy stress in the twentieth century upon dramatization and objectivity.

III

Scholes and Kellogg distinguish between "two kinds of dynamic characterization: the *developmental,* in which the character's personal traits are attenuated so as to clarify his progress along a plot line which has an ethical basis . . . and the *chronological,"* in which the "plotting and characterization" are "highly mimetic" (p. 169). In the first mode of characterization, which is found in literature written from the classical moralistic perspective, character is presented rhetorically; in the second mode, which is typical of serio-problematic forms like the novel, character is presented psychologically. "For modern writers," Scholes and Kellogg observe,

> . . . a great problem has been to employ the developing knowledge of the human psyche without losing all those literary effects which rhetoric alone can achieve. The problem has been the achievement of new, workable combinations of psychology and rhetoric, and the great narrative artists have solved it in various ways. (p. 189)

As my discussion of Booth indicates, I agree with this formulation of the problem, but I do not believe that it has often been solved. In works which attempt to combine realism of presentation with realism of assessment, the assessments are usually confused, or inadequate, or both. This results in aesthetic flaws, for the work cannot be satisfactorily experienced in its own terms if there is no coherent thematic structure, and it cannot attain total integration if its attitudes are not sustained by its representation of life. Booth contends that failures of rhetoric are inevitable if the author has not plumbed to universal values, and this may be true—though I suspect that a work which reflects the reader's values will succeed well enough, with him, whether those values are universal or not. If interpretations that are faulty or that differ from the reader's impair the effectiveness of the work, the novel-ist might be wise to avoid interpretation altogether. If he does, however, he will be frustrating some of the strongest appetites with which, appropriately or not, many of us come to fiction—the appetites for clarity, for intellectually graspable meaning, for moral order. *"No theme,"* say Brooks and Warren, *"no story."* The writer of realistic fiction may be doomed to leave somebody, and perhaps everybody, dissatisfied.

It is appropriate to demand thematic adequacy and intelligibil-ity of those works which promise it; but it is not appropriate to make such demands, as Booth does, of works in which the ele-ment of interpretation is absent. It may be a mistake, as I have suggested, for the novel to attempt interpretation at all, though the history of the form made it inevitable that a strong rhetorical element would persist. As Booth points out, there is sometimes in fiction an "incompatibility of interests" (p. 134), and it may be that the rhetorical effects for which he asks are incompatible with the novel's dominant impulse toward representation. We will be unfair to works in which there are rhetorical or thematic failures if we do not recognize the subordination, in realistic fiction, of rhetoric to psychology, interpretation to mimesis.

I am not sure that it is ever appropriate to demand, as so many critics do, that fiction leave us "with an attitude to take toward things in general," that it give us "not only an evaluation of the particular experience which is the story, but a *generalized* evalua-tion."[15] This is to demand of art a health and a wisdom which have nothing to do with its intrinsic nature. It is to put art into competition with the intellectual disciplines from which so much modern criticism has tried to distinguish it and to invest artistic technique with a power of discovery which is almost magical. If an artist happens to be wise or healthy, his work may well embody a valid comment on human nature, the human condition, and human values; but wisdom and health are not essential to great art. Their presence supplies an illumination which is most welcome but which is not a distinctively aesthetic one.

The question of what kind of illumination art—or, in our case, realistic fiction—*does* supply is too large to be dealt with completely here; but it is central to our concerns, and I shall attempt to offer a partial answer. If we have realism of presentation without realism of assessment, says Ian Watt, "we shall be wholly immersed in the reality of the characters and their actions, but whether we shall be any wiser as a result is open to question" (p. 288). Immersion in the inner reality of characters provides a kind of knowledge which is not wisdom, though it may be the basis of wisdom, and which realistic fiction is especially fitted to supply. If we understand by phenomenology the formulation of "an experience of the world, a contact with the world which precedes all" judgment and explanation,[16] we can say that highly mimetic fiction gives us a phenomenological knowledge of reality. It gives us an immediate knowledge of how the world is experienced by the individual consciousness and an understanding of the inner life in its own terms. It enables us to grasp from within the phenomena which psychology and ethics treat from without.

As Wayne Booth has observed, when we read novels in which there are deep inside views "that . . . give the reader an effect of living thought and sensation" (p. 324), we tend to abandon judgment and analysis. When we are immersed in the "indomitable mental reality" (p. 323) of a character, we adopt his perspective and experience his feelings as though they were our own. This kind of experience, which is one of the great gifts of fiction, is acceptable to Booth only when the character's perspective is, in his view, an ethically acceptable one. It is very dangerous, he feels, if the character's values are destructive, for then the reader is liable to be corrupted by his identification with unhealthy attitudes. I feel that Booth has overestimated both the danger which the reader is in and the effectiveness of rhetoric as a corrective, and that he has underestimated the value of deep inside views, though he admits that they "can be of immeasurable value in forcing us to see the human worth of a character whose actions, objectively considered, we would deplore" (p. 378). Robbe-Grillet's *The Voyeur* "does, indeed, lead us to experience intensely the sensations and emotions of a homicidal maniac. But is this," Booth asks, "really what we go to literature for?" (p. 384). My answer is, Yes.

We go to literature for many things, and not the least of them is the immediate knowledge that it gives of variously constituted human psyches. The novel makes its revelations not only through mimetic portraits of characters, but also, in many cases, through the picture that it creates of the implied author. As both Wayne Booth and Sheldon Sacks point out, when the implied author functions as interpreter, he often makes a multitude of particular judgments as his characters display their temperaments and confront their choices. This gives rise to "a much more detailed ordering of values" than we ever encounter in systematic philosophy. Even if we cannot accept the implied author's values as adequate either to his fictional world or to life outside, we have a marvellously rich portrayal of a particular kind of consciousness making ethical responses to a variety of human situations. Through the novel's rhetoric we become aware of the meaning which the characters' experience has for a mind like that of the implied author, and we enter thus into his subjective world.

What I am suggesting, then, is that if we view him as a fictional persona, as another dramatized consciousness, rather than as an authoritative source of values, the implied author, too, enlarges our knowledge of experience. What we have, in effect, is a deep inside view of *his* mind, a view which makes us phenomenologically aware of *his* experience of the world. When we see him as another consciousness, sometimes the most fascinating one in the book, it becomes more difficult to regret the technical devices by which he is revealed, even when they produce aesthetic flaws.

To see him in this way we must set aside the fictional conventions which encourage us to invest him with the authority which Wayne Booth would like him to have; but it is essential to do so if we are to appreciate many great narrators whose wisdom we must question and whose obtrusiveness we must otherwise regret.

As long as we regard the implied author as a kind of God whose will we must understand but never question, it seems quite inappropriate to analyze him psychologically. His contradictions are manifestations of a higher harmony which we have not yet grasped; and his judgments, being right, require no explanation. When we see him as a dramatized consciousness whose values can be as subjective and as confused as those of an ordinary man, psychological analysis becomes a necessity.

I have tried to show by an analysis of the genre that it is often appropriate to study the characters and implied authors of realistic novels by a psychological method. In the interpretations of individual novels that will follow our discussion of Third Force psychology, I hope to demonstrate that the approach employed here helps us to appreciate some of fiction's most important values and to resolve some difficult critical problems.

I am aware, however, that the very arguments by which I have attempted to justify a psychological approach may seem to preclude it. I have argued that one of the chief interests of realistic fiction is a mimetic characterization which gives us a phenomenological grasp of experience in its immediacy and ambiguity and that the value of such characterization lies precisely in its continual resistance to the patterns by which the author has tried to shape and interpret it. It may be objected that the values of such characterization are incommensurate with any kind of analysis and that to intellectualize them is to destroy them. My reply must be that any criticism, whether it be psychological or not, is bound to operate with categories and abstractions which, if they are allowed to replace the values of literature, will destroy them.

Criticism can make literature more accessible to us, but we must use it as a means to rather than as a substitute for the aesthetic encounter.

A common complaint about the psychological analysis of character is that it does violence to the literary values of fiction by reducing the novel to a case history, the character to his neurosis. We must recognize that literature and criticism belong to different universes of discourse. As Northrop Frye says, "the axiom of criticism must be, not that the poet does not know what he is talking about, but that he cannot talk about what he knows."[17] The function of criticism is to talk about what the artist knows, and to do that it must speak in the language of science and philosophy rather than in the language of art. But if we are aware of what we are doing this does not convert art into science or philosophy. Criticism points to a reality which is far more complex and of a different nature than itself; the values of which it speaks can be experienced only in the aesthetic encounter. All criticism is reductive. Psychological analysis is our best tool for talking about the intricacies of mimetic characterization. If properly conducted, it is less reductive than any other critical approach.

It is extremely valuable to bring literature and psychology together. The psychologist and the artist often know about the same areas of experience, but they comprehend them and present their knowledge in different ways. Each enlarges our awareness and satisfies our need to master reality in a way that the other cannot. The psychologist enables us to grasp certain configurations of experience analytically, categorically, and (if we accept his conceptions of health and neurosis) normatively. The novelist enables us to grasp these phenomena in other ways. Fiction lets us know what it is like to be a certain kind of person with a certain kind of destiny. Through mimetic portraits of character, novels provide us with artistic formulations of experience that are permanent, irreplaceable, and of an order quite different from the discursive formulations of systematic psychology. And, if we view him as a fictional persona, as a dramatized conscious-ness, the implied author, too, enlarges our knowledge of the human psyche.

Taken together, psychology and fiction give us a far more complete possession of experience than either can give by itself. Psychology helps us to talk about what the novelist knows; fiction helps us to know what the psychologist is talking about.

Chapter II

The Psychology Used: Horney,
Maslow and the Third Force

I have tried to show that much realistic fiction calls by its very nature for psychological analysis and that a psychological approach to such fiction will help us to understand the minds both of mimetic characters and of implied authors. The question now is, what psychology should be used? A psychology of personality is obviously called for; but the major personality theories tend to focus on different stages of psychological evolution, and no one theory will suffice for all occasions. I shall use Third Force psychology because it works very well with the novels I have chosen; but there are undoubtedly novels which are best understood in the terms of Freudian id or ego psychology, of Jungian, Reichian, or phenomenological psychology, or of some other theory or combination of theories.

Their conception of human nature has led the Third Force psychologists to see healthy human development as a process of self-actualization, and unhealthy development as a process of self-alienation. Maslow is their greatest student of self-actualization; Horney offers the most systematic account of self-alienation. Horney's main concern is with what happens when, under the pressure of an adverse environment, the individual abandons his real self and develops neurotic strategies for living. Since

fictional characters and implied authors are much more frequently self-alienated than self-actualizing, it is Karen Horney's
theories which are most immediately relevant to our study of
fiction.

I have found it important, nevertheless, to devote much space
to Maslow. Horney was much more a clinician than a theorist of
human nature, though her clinical practice gave her a deep feeling for the constructive forces inherent in man. Her understanding of neurosis was built upon ideas concerning the "real self,"
the process of "self-realization," and the nature of health which
she did not have time to develop (her next book was to have been
on the "real self"). Maslow's treatment of these crucial matters
is, I think, very much in harmony with Horney's thinking and is
in many ways an extension of it. Horney's focus was upon sickness, upon the forces which block healthy growth. Maslow has
attempted a direct study of the process of self-actualization as it
occurs in the healthiest people and of the kinds of experiences
which characterize the highest stages of psychological evolution.
In addition, Maslow has synthesized the findings of many other
workers; he is the leading spokesman for Third Force psychology
as a whole. I shall present its basic ideas about human nature and
the nature of health largely through his vocabulary.

The exposition of Third Force psychology which follows will
be divided into three parts: I shall examine, first, its conceptions
of human nature, the human condition, and human values; next,
its treatment of self-actualization; and, finally, its analysis of self-
alienation. Since these concerns are overlapping and conceptu-
ally interdependent, no strict division will be possible. Some
ideas which are introduced early may not become entirely clear
until they are developed more fully in later sections.

Though I was drawn to Third Force psychology chiefly because
of its heuristic and explanatory power, I have come to find its
picture of man more sophisticated and more persuasive than that
of any other psychology. Jung observed that "every psychology

... has the character of a subjective confession,"[1] and this observation holds true for the psychologies we choose as well as for
those we construct. I do not expect anyone to be persuaded by
Third Force psychology who is not already receptive to its premises. Its value as a tool of analysis is, however, a less subjective
thing; and I hope that even those who disagree with some of its
premises will find that it does fit the experiences we shall be
examining (if only as phenomenological description) and that it
does illuminate the novels.

I. Human nature, the human condition, and human values

It is its view of human nature, more than any other part of its
theory, which unifies Third Force psychology as a movement and
distinguishes it from the other two major movements (Freudian-
ism and behaviorism) in modern psychology. This psychology
contends, in essence, that man is not simply a tension-reducing
or a conditioned animal, but that there is present in him a third
force, an "evolutionary constructive" force, which urges "him to
realize his given potentialities."[2] Each man has "an essential
biologically based inner nature" which is "good or neutral rather
than bad" and which should be brought out and encouraged
rather than suppressed. This inner nature "is weak and delicate
and subtle and easily overcome by habit, cultural pressure, and
wrong attitudes toward it"; but, "even though weak, it rarely
disappears. . . . even though denied, it persists underground
forever pressing for actualization."[3]

This view of human nature is based on the Third Force psychologists' experience with psychotherapy and on their study of
exceptionally healthy people. Psychotherapy has shown that
there is a drive toward self-realization, however weak, which
makes change possible; that cure involves helping the individual
first to get in touch with and then to live from his essential inner
nature; and that this inner nature, when uncovered, turns out to

be a source of spontaneous virtues and intrinsic values rather than a thing to be feared and repressed. The study of exceptionally healthy people has shown that the views of human nature which we find in most philosophies, theologies, and psychologies are based on the observation of imperfectly developed people (who constitute the vast majority) and that they do not characterize the essential nature of man. Third Force psychologists have asked not only what are most men like, but also what is man like, what is the essential nature of the species as it is represented by its most fully developed individuals?

One of the most interesting Third Force contributions to our understanding of man's essential nature is Abraham Maslow's theory of the hierarchy of basic needs. According to this theory, all men have needs for physiological satisfaction, for safety, for love and belonging, for self-esteem, and for self-actualization. These needs are not always experienced consciously; indeed, they tend to be more unconscious than conscious. The needs are hierarchical in that they exist in an order of prepotency; the physiological needs are the most powerful, and so on. The needs at the upper end of the hierarchy (higher needs) are much weaker than the lower needs, though they are no less basic.[4] The needs are basic in the sense that they are built into the nature of all men as a function of their biological structure and they must be gratified if the organism is to develop in a healthy way. Though the particular form in which they are expressed and the possibility of their satisfaction depends upon the surrounding culture, they exist prior to culture as part of the hereditary nature of the individual.

Because they are biologically based, Maslow calls the basic needs instinctoid. They are not like the instincts of animals—"powerful, strong, unmodifiable, uncontrollable, unsuppressible" (MP, 128); they are weak, especially the higher ones, and are "easily repressed, suppressed . . . masked or modified by habits, suggestions, by cultural pressure, by guilt, and so on"

(MP, 129). Though weak, they are in a sense also very strong; for they are "inconceivably stubborn and recalcitrant. . . . Consciously or unconsciously they are craved and sought forever. They behave always like stubborn, irreducible, final, unanalyzable facts that must be taken as givens or starting points not to be questioned" (MP, 125).

Each individual presses by nature for the fulfillment of all of these needs, but at any given time his motivational life will be centered upon the fulfillment of one of them. Since a higher need emerges strongly only when the needs below it have been sufficiently met, the individual tends to be occupied with the basic needs in the order of their prepotency. When he is at a given stage in the hierarchy, the needs which have already been met tend to cease functioning as motivators and the needs which are higher in the hierarchy are felt but weakly. The person living in an environment which is favorable to growth will move steadily up the hierarchy until he is free to devote most of his energies to self-actualization, which is the full and satisfying use of his capacities in a calling which suits his nature. The higher needs tend to emerge not only with the fulfillment of the lower needs, but also with the maturing of the organism.

The hierarchy of basic needs, then, establishes the pattern of psychological evolution. If the individual is not adequately fulfilled in his lower needs, he may become fixated at an early stage of development; or, if he passes beyond, he may be subject to frequent regressions. Frustration of a basic need intensifies it and insures its persistence; gratification diminishes its strength as a motivating force. People who have been very well satisfied in their lower needs early in life may develop a "frustration tolerance" which permits them to experience later deprivation without regressing. The more fully evolved person may regress, however, if he is deprived of a lower need in a severe way or for an extended period of time.

Maslow cautions us against understanding the dynamics of the hierarchy of basic needs in too crude or mechanical a way. Most behavior is multi-motivated; in any given instance there may be several or all of the basic needs at work, though they will not all be equally powerful. Most members of our society are partially satisfied and partially unsatisfied in all of their basic needs at any given time. There are decreasing percentages of satisfaction, however, as we move up the hierarchy of prepotency. Under especially favorable conditions we may have episodes of higher need motivation, and under particularly unfavorable conditions we may regress to a lower level of needing. Behavior is not solely determined by inner needs; the cultural setting and the immediate situation are also important determinants. The hierarchy of prepotency will determine what we want, but not necessarily how we will act.

Movement from one stage of psychological evolution to another has profound effects upon our attitudes toward the basic needs and their satisfiers. They are:

Independence of and a certain disdain for the old satisfiers and goal objects, with a new dependence on satisfiers and goal objects that hitherto had been overlooked, not wanted, or only casually wanted. . . . Thus there are changes in interests. That is, certain phenomena become interesting for the first time and old phenomena become boring, or even repulsive. This is the same as saying that there are changes in human values. In general, there tend to be: (1) overestimation of the satisfiers of the most powerful of the ungratified needs; (2) underestimation of the satisfiers of the less powerful of the ungratified needs (and of the strength of these needs); and (3) underestimation and derogation of the satisfiers of the needs already gratified (and of the strength of these needs). This shift in values involves, as a dependent phenomenon, reconstruction in philosophy of the future, of the Utopia, of the heaven and hell, of the good life, and

of the unconscious wish-fulfillment state of the individual in a
crudely predictable direction. (MP, 108–109)

These observations are extraordinarily useful in helping us to
understand conflicts and changes in values and differences
among the various psychological theories.

People at different stages of psychological evolution are bound
to have different philosophies of life and to emphasize different
values. Those at the lower stages of the evolutionary process will
be unable to understand the values of those at the higher stages,
while those at the higher stages are likely to underemphasize the
importance of some of the lower needs. Those who are still
growing psychologically will inevitably change their philosophic
orientation and will realize, on the basis of past experiences of
change, that their present position is most likely an incomplete
one. People who are fixated at a certain stage of growth will tend
to interpret everything in terms of the values appropriate to that
stage and to believe that all other values are illusory. Values come
from human needs; when they are felt in a healthy way, all of the
basic needs are sources of legitimate values. Any value system
which is based on only one or a few needs, however, is bound to
be incomplete and to involve a distortion of human nature. An
adequate conception of human nature and human values can be
derived only from the perspective of the most fully evolved people, though, as we have seen, this perspective is likely to underemphasize the importance of the lower needs. Perhaps there
is no one perspective which does not involve some distortion.

Each of the major psychological theories tends to focus on
some part of the hierarchy of needs rather than upon the whole
hierarchy. Jungian and Maslovian psychologies focus on the upper end of the hierarchy and are scanty in their treatment of the
lower needs. Freudian id psychology and behaviorist psychology
are strong in their treatment of the lower needs but weak in their
handling of the higher needs. Horney, Fromm, Rogers, the

Freudian ego psychologists, and the existential psychologists focus on the middle of the hierarchy. Horney is mainly concerned with the neurotic processes which occur as a result of the frustration of the needs for safety, love, and self-esteem.

An awareness of the partial nature of most psychologies helps us to assess both their achievements and limitations and puts us on guard against the problems to which such incompleteness may lead. A psychology which is devoted to the observation and explanation of certain aspects of human nature may provide excellent insight into the phenomena which it studies; but it is liable to serious error and distortion if it attempts to account for higher or lower needs mainly in terms of the needs on which it is focused. Many psychologies are weak in their picture of human nature because they attempt to derive the whole of man from the part which they know or which they feel can be studied best. The most frequent error, of course, is reductionism in which only the lower needs are seen as inherent motivators and the higher strivings are seen as derived from and therefore reducible to the lower ones. One of the most significant features of Third Force psychology is that it recognizes the higher needs to be just as much a part of our nature as the lower ones. It gives them an autonomous status and permits us to understand them and the values arising from them in their own terms.

As the preceding discussion has indicated, Maslow's conception of the hierarchy of basic needs and of its dynamics has a number of important implications for our understanding of human nature, the human condition, and human values. As Maslow sees him, man is a being whose psychological evolution is determined mainly by two factors: the structure of needs inherent in the human organism and the degree to which these needs are satisfied. Gratification of the basic needs produces health; it permits the individual to continue on his way toward self-actualization. Frustration of the basic needs produces pathology; it arrests the individual's development, alienates him from his real self, and leads him to develop neurotic strategies for making up his deficiencies. The frustration of nonbasic needs is not harmful; the person who is fairly well gratified in his basic needs can handle considerable frustration in other areas. Destructiveness, aggression, and a need to be omnipotent are not part of man's essential nature; they are defensive reactions to basic need deprivation. They are potentialities of his essential nature, however; for man is so constituted that he will sicken if his basic needs are not met, and he will then seek fulfillment in ways harmful to himself and to others. There are valuable as well as harmful frustrations. The individual must discover not only his potentialities, but also the limitations imposed by his nature, his place in the cosmos, and the social character of his existence.

There is no reason for frustrating any of the basic needs, for they are not, when experienced in the course of a healthy development, in conflict with civilization and man's higher values. The interests of the individual and of society are in conflict only under bad conditions; they are synergic under good conditions. The traditional distinctions between reason and impulse, spirit and body, man's higher and lower natures are based upon false dichotomies. The higher and lower needs are in conflict only when there is deprivation; in the most fully evolved people they are in harmony. In these people "desires are in excellent accord with reason. St. Augustine's 'Love God and do as you will' can easily be translated, 'Be healthy and then you may trust your impulses' " (MP, 233).

The Third Force psychologists seem optimistic (when compared, say, with Freud) in that they believe in the possibility of health and find the healthy man to be a relatively happy, harmonious, and creative being. It must be pointed out, however, that Maslow's self-actualizing people comprise no more than one percent of the population, and perhaps less. Because their instinctoid needs (especially the higher ones) are so weak and the voice of the real self is so faint, it is extremely difficult for human beings to be impulse aware, to know how they really feel and what they really want. Man is by nature a being who is easily self-alienated; he is a sensitive plant who requires such special and complex conditions for healthy growth that he rarely achieves a sound maturity. Raising a child to health is an extraordinarily difficult task, and the creation of a healthy society is incomparably more difficult.

It is difficult for man to know what he wants and difficult for him to get what he needs. When he gets what he needs, he will not be satisfied, for needing never ceases. Satisfaction of any one need produces no more than a momentary tranquillity; other and higher needs soon emerge and striving is renewed. The satisfaction of the lower needs does not result in stagnation, as many seem to fear. Rather it "elevates" the individual "to the point where he is civilized enough to feel frustrated about the larger personal, social, and intellectual issues" (MP, 119).

The more highly evolved individual, though always engaged in a process of becoming, will frequently have end (or "peak") experiences. These are experiences of being which are self-sufficient and intrinsically valuable. They are not means to any other ends but are the ends to which all other forms of gratification are the means. They are moments of complete fulfillment from which no higher strivings will emerge.[5] The highly evolved individual will have such experiences frequently; but they will not free him more than momentarily from the condition of wanting, for having had them will make him want them again.

Though suffering and limitation is the fate of all men, people at different stages of psychological evolution will, to some extent, experience different kinds of frustration and have different views of the human condition. We will be able to see this more clearly if we divide human problems into three kinds: personal, historical, and existential.[6] Personal problems are rooted in the life history of the individual; they are symptomatic of the interferences with his psychological evolution which have been produced by the frustration of his basic needs. Historical problems arise from the social, cultural, and economic development of a particular community. They are shared by all members of the community, but not all communities have the same problems. Personal problems are partly the result of historical problems; but temperament and the immediate family situation also play large roles in individual development. Not all members of the community are affected by their common environment in the same way. Historical problems are partly the result of individual problems, and they are perpetuated by the neuroses which they help to foster. Both personal and historical problems are accidental, variable, and, theoretically, at least, remediable. Existential problems arise out of the disparity between man's natural wants (for life, health, control of his destiny, etc.) and the unalterable cosmic and historical conditions of his existence. They are shared by all men, and they are irremediable.

The Third Force psychologists do not feel that man's existential problems are such as to prevent healthy development and a reasonably satisfactory existence. The historical problems of our society make a high degree of psychological evolution impossible for most men. Even our most mature people are significantly hampered by historical problems and have achieved considerably less than full humanness. Even so, the freedom, tolerance, prosperity, and diversity of our society, combined with our rapidly developing psychological insight and the emergence of effective psychotherapies, make our environment more favorable to self-actualization than most others which men have experienced.

Self-actualizing people are by no means free of conflict and suffering, but they suffer mainly from historical and existential rather than from personal problems. Their relative freedom from personal problems makes them more accurately aware of historical and existential problems than are most self-alienated people.

They tend to work in a patient, realistic way for the alleviation of historical problems and to approach existential problems with a combination of resignation and humor. Their positive experiences are so numerous and so rewarding that they feel generally accepting toward the human condition, without being at all blind to its tragedies. The fact that their lives are so full of possibilities leads them at times to feel the limitations of time, age, and death and the gap between aspiration and opportunity with special poignancy. Their awareness of the impoverished quality of most human lives fills them with an unmitigable sadness.

Self-alienated people usually see the possibilities for fulfillment as fewer and the frustrations of the human lot as greater than do self-actualizing people. In forming an estimate of the human condition they tend to generalize from their own experience, in which intrinsically satisfying end experiences are rare and suffering is frequent. Because of their insecurities and their compensatory strategies, they overreact to historical and existential problems. They then judge the magnitude of the problems by the intensity of their response. Because of their limited experience, their need to externalize, and their desire to avoid feelings of uncertainty, isolation, and inferiority, they tend to see their personal problems not as belonging to themselves, but as historical or existential in nature. They confuse neurotic anxiety with existential *Angst,* and neurotic despair with a philosophic sense of the absurdity of human existence.

We have already seen some of the implications of Third Force psychology for our understanding of human values. Values are derived from human nature and its needs. Those things are good which gratify basic needs and are thus conducive to healthy development; those things are bad which arrest or distort man's psychological evolution. What an individual values most will be largely determined by the most powerful of his ungratified needs. Just as there are higher and lower needs, there are also higher and lower values. An individual who has been gratified in both will place a greater value upon a higher need than upon a lower one.

Maslow's account of the relation of values to the stages of psychological evolution applies mainly to people who are engaged in a process of healthy growth and to the healthy component in the neurotic person's development. As we shall see when we discuss Horney, the neurotic person's values are determined not only by his ungratified basic needs, but also by his defensive strategies. Neurotic needs result from the frustration of basic needs, but they are not the same as basic needs. The neurotic person tends to value not so much what he needs in order to grow as what he needs in order to maintain his system of defense. Insofar as his defensive strategies are essential to his survival, his neurotic values have a certain functional legitimacy and must be respected. They are, however, in no way normative, as are the values which derive from the needs which are part of man's essential nature.

The "single ultimate value for mankind," the "far goal toward which all men strive," has been "called variously by different authors self-actualization, self-realization, integration, psychological health, individuation, autonomy, creativity," and "productivity." Though they use different terms, all Third Force psychologists agree that the highest value for a human being is to realize his potentialities, to become "fully human," everything that he *"can* become" (PB, 145). This is the highest good, the *summum bonum,* for all men, whether they realize it or not. This does not mean that all self-actualizing people will want the same things or have exactly the same values. Each person has a different self to actualize, and these constitutional differences generate differences in values. Men are most like each other in their lower needs and most idiosyncratic in their self-actualizing activities. This means that some values are species-wide (though they take different forms in different cultures), and some values are unique to the individual or are shared only by individuals with similar capacities and temperaments. Self-actualization, the fulfillment of both our species-wide and our unique natures, takes many different forms; but it is the *raison d'être* of all men. It is the reason for being also of our various social institutions, and the worth of these institutions is to be measured by their success or failure in fostering individual growth.

It should be evident by now that the Third Force psychologists reject many of the relativisms characteristic of our time. Some of them, like Maslow, feel that they have the solution to the modern crisis in values.[7] The values they propose are, of course, relative to human beings; but for human beings they are absolute.

The cultural anthropologists did a great service, they feel, by alerting us to our ethnocentricity; but cultural relativism goes too far when it derives all values from culture and proclaims itself unable to distinguish between good and bad cultures. In general, says Maslow, "the paths by which the main goals in life are achieved are . . . determined by the nature of the particular culture" (MP, 48). But the goals themselves are not culturally determined. "The fundamental or ultimate desires of all human beings do not differ nearly as much as their conscious every day desires" (MP, 67). The former are determined by the essential nature of man, the latter by the mores, patterns, and opportunities of the surrounding culture.

Cultures, too, operate according to the hierarchy of needs.[8] They are organized around the lower needs first, and only when these are adequately met can they respond to the higher needs of their members. Individuals who are products of a culture which is at an early stage of evolution will not be able to feel the higher needs very strongly, but the needs will continue to exist and will exert an upward pressure. Those individuals who, through especially fortunate circumstances or contact with a higher civilization, have evolved beyond their immediate culture often become progressive forces within their society.

Being, for the most part, therapists, the Third Force psychologists recognize the importance of understanding each individual
in his own terms and of accepting the fact that each individual's
value system has a certain logic and validity, for him. They do not
feel, however, that there is no way of choosing between differing
value systems and ways of being in the world. Though they employ a phenomenological perspective, they do not confine themselves to it. To understand all is not necessarily to abandon
judgment. Some values are healthy and some are neurotic; some
are conducive to a fuller realization of human potentialities, and
some result in a stunting of human growth. All values, neurotic
and healthy alike, derive from human wants; but neurotic wants,
unlike the basic needs of the healthy man, are destructive both
of self and of others. Frustration of the basic needs so alienates
the individual from his essential nature and so disturbs the course
of his development that he is no longer aware of his own best
interests or able to pursue them.

The value theory which Maslow proposes is essentially a hedo-
nism which differs from past hedonisms in its more complete
understanding of man's essential nature and in its more sophisticated approach to the problems of distinguishing between
higher and lower values, healthy and sick pleasures. No value
theory will be adequate, Maslow argues, "that rests simply on the
statistical description of the choices of unselected human beings.
To average the choices of good and bad choosers, of healthy and
sick people, is useless" (PB, 143). The values of healthy people
hold for all men, whether they believe in them or not; for "good
choosers can choose better than bad choosers what is better for
the bad choosers themselves" (PB, 143). Many men have had no
opportunity to choose higher over lower, healthy over sick pleasures. If both their natures and their cultures were highly enough
evolved to give them the opportunity for choice, they would
choose the pleasures of self-actualization over all else. One evidence for this is that people undergoing psychotherapy tend to

change their values in a predictable direction. Maslow feels that a naturalistic value system can be arrived at by observing what "our best specimens choose, and then assuming that these are the highest values for all mankind" (PB, 159).

Maslow contends, in effect, that there is an essential human nature, that we can identify the people in whom this nature has achieved its fullest growth, and that we can derive from the observation of these people an idea of what would be good (growth-fostering) for all men and of what all men would want if they were fully evolved. There are a number of difficulties in this argument. It is impossible to establish conclusively that there is an essential human nature; all value systems which are based on this premise begin with a leap of faith. It is impossible to demonstrate that one has actually identified the best specimens. Maslow derives his scientifically based, naturalistic value system from the observation of good choosers; but, as he himself recognizes, the good choosers must be chosen, and there is no way of establishing the credentials of the original choosers. The possibilities of projection are great; one may just be choosing those whose personalities and value systems are parallel to one's own or are the embodiment of a neurotic ideal. Just when we think that we have escaped from relativism, we realize that there is no way of validating, for those who are not already convinced, the criteria of psychological health, the criteria by which the good choosers are chosen. This, I think, is an existential problem.

II. Self-actualization

According to Maslow, "healthy people have sufficiently gratified their basic needs for safety, belongingness, love, respect and self-esteem so that they are motivated primarily by trends to self-actualization." He defines self-actualization as the "ongoing actualization of potentials, capacities and talents," as "fulfillment of mission (or call, fate, destiny, or vocation)." It involves "a fuller knowledge of, and acceptance of, the person's own intrinsic nature" and "an unceasing trend toward unity, integration or synergy within the person" (PB, 23).

This definition presents self-actualization as a process which occurs in the later stages of psychological evolution. Maslow's total conception of self-actualization is much broader than this, however. His study of peak experiences has led him to see that in such experiences "any person . . . takes on temporarily many of the characteristics" of self-actualizing individuals (PB, 91). Self-actualization can be defined, then, "as an episode, or a spurt in which the powers of the person come together in a particularly efficient and intensely enjoyable way. . . . He becomes in these episodes more truly himself, more perfectly actualizing his potentialities, closer to the core of his Being" (PB, 91). All people can have experiences of self-actualization. What distinguishes self-actualizing people "is that in them these episodes seem to come far more frequently, and intensely and perfectly than in average people" (PB, 92). Self-actualization, then, is "a matter of degree and of frequency rather than an all-or-none affair" (PB, 92).

The discussion of self-actualization to be presented here will not deal with all aspects of this complicated phenomenon; it will focus mainly upon the real self and upon some of the chief characteristics of self-actualizing people. Since all people may be self-actualizing at times, perhaps it would be more accurate to say that we shall discuss not simply self-actualizing people, but the ways in which all people relate to self, to others, and to the world when they are functioning in a self-actualizing rather than in a deficiency motivated or neurotic fashion.

It was not until her last book, *Neurosis and Human Growth*, that Karen Horney introduced the concept of the real self as a foundation stone of her system. Her "theoretical and therapeutic approach" had always rested upon "the belief in an inherent urge to grow" (NHG, 38); now she identified the real self as "the

'original' force toward individual growth and fulfillment, with
which we may again achieve full identification when freed of the
crippling shackles of neurosis" (NHG, 158). It is the real self for
which we are looking "when we say that we want to find ourselves" (NHG, 158).

In the course of his development the child is much influenced
by the things which he learns—skills, coping behaviors, social
roles, reward and punishment associations, and so forth. "But
there are also forces in him," says Horney, "which he cannot
acquire or even develop by learning. You need not, and in fact,
cannot, teach an acorn to grow into an oak tree, but when given
a chance, its intrinsic potentialities will develop. Similarly, the
human individual, when given a chance, tends to develop his
particular human potentialities" (NHG, 17).

Under favorable conditions, the individual "will develop . . .
the unique alive forces of his real self: the clarity and depth of his
own feelings, thoughts, wishes, interests; the ability to tap his
own resources, the strength of his will power; the special capacities or gifts he may have; the faculty to express himself, and to
relate himself to others with his spontaneous feelings. All this will
in time enable him to find his set of values and his aims in life"
(NHG, 17). Such a development, says Horney, "is far from uni-
form." It will be influenced by "his particular temperament,
faculties, propensities, and the conditions of his earlier and later
life . . . But wherever his course takes him, it will be *his* given
potentialities which he develops" (NHG, 13).

Under unfavorable conditions, when the people around him
are prevented by their own neurotic needs from relating to him
with love and respect, the child develops a "feeling of being
isolated and helpless in a world conceived as potentially hostile"
(NHG, 18). This feeling of "basic anxiety" makes the child fearful
of spontaneity, and, forsaking his real self, he develops neurotic
strategies for coping with his environment. The real self, though
abandoned or suppressed, remains alive, however; and it is possi-

ble, with the help of therapy or other favorable conditions, for the
individual to get back to it and to grow from it again. The neurotic person is, in greater or lesser degree, divorced from his real
self; but the real self remains as a possibility, a "possible self"
(NHG, 158).

The preceding paragraphs contain the best of Horney's relatively few direct statements about the real self. There is much that
we can infer about it from her analysis of self-alienation, of
course; and our later discussion of her theories of neurosis will
deepen our understanding of her conception of the real self. To
clarify our notion of the real self we can also draw upon the work
of Maslow, who has adopted Horney's term and whose theories
are in many ways an extension of her concept.

"One's personal biology," says Maslow, "is beyond question a
sine qua non component of the 'Real Self.' Being oneself, being
natural or spontaneous, being authentic, expressing one's identity, all these are also biological statements since they imply the
acceptance of one's constitutional, temperamental, anatomical,
neurological, hormonal, and instinctoid-motivational nature."[9]
Each person's real self "has some characteristics which all other
selves have . . . and some which are unique to the person" (PB,
179). All persons, except those who are extraordinarily stunted,
have the basic needs for physiological gratification, safety, love
and belonging, self-esteem, self-actualization, beauty, knowledge, and understanding. Each person has his own talents, capacities, tastes, temperamental predispositions, and physiological
peculiarities.

As we have seen, Maslow holds that the choices or values of
self-actualizing people (or of all people in their moments of self-
actualization) are normative for the species as a whole. He calls
these values Being-values (or B-values) and lists them as follows:
truth, goodness, beauty, wholeness, dichotomy-transcendence,
aliveness, uniqueness, perfection, necessity, completion, justice, order, simplicity, richness, effortlessness, playfulness, self-

sufficiency.[10] Maslow feels that the B-values are part of the real self; that is, all human beings by their nature have a potentiality for experiencing these as the highest values, they must have their desire for these values satisfied if they are to achieve full humanness, and they cannot violate these values without damage to themselves.

Following Horney and Fromm, Maslow affirms the existence of an "intrinsic conscience" which generates "intrinsic guilt" and which is also part of the real self. "The serious thing for each person to recognize vividly, poignantly, each for himself, is that every falling away from species-virtue, every crime against one's own nature, every evil act, *every one without exception records itself* in our unconscious and makes us despise ourselves" (PB, 4–5). Our intrinsic conscience, which has nothing to do with local customs or the Freudian super-ego, generates appropriate feelings of guilt whenever we violate the B-values or betray any aspect of our real selves.

The components of the real self, says Maslow, "are potentialities, not final actualizations. Therefore they have a life history and must be seen developmentally. They are actualized, shaped or stifled mostly (but not altogether) by extra-psychic determinants (culture, family, environment, learning, etc.)" (PB, 178). The real self is actualized only as a self-in-the-world; the way in which it is actualized and the degree to which it is actualized are determined largely by the nature of its world.

The actualization of the real self requires a culture which offers a course of activity which is congruent with the individual's inner bent and which permits him to realize the highest of his capacities. It requires, even more, a set of significant adults who are interested in the child as a being for himself and who will allow him to have his own feelings, tastes, interests, and values. The child is a weak and dependent being whose needs for safety, protection, and acceptance are so strong that he will sacrifice himself, if necessary, in order to get these things. If faced with

a choice between his own delight experiences and the approval
of others, he "must generally choose approval from others" (PB,
49); and he gradually loses the capacity to know how he really
feels and what he really wants.

The person who is able to develop in accordance with his real
self possesses a number of characteristics which distinguish him
from the self-alienated person. The child who is not permitted to
be himself and who does not live in a safe, relatively transparent
world develops a defensiveness which cuts him off both from
himself and from external reality. The opposite of defensiveness
is "openness to experience," and the self-actualizing person is
characterized above all by his openness to his own inner being
and to the world around him.

The self-actualizing person's openness to himself is manifested
in his greater congruence, his greater transparence, and his
greater spontaneity. A person is congruent, says Rogers, when
whatever feeling or attitude he is experiencing is matched by his
awareness of that attitude.[11] The congruent person knows what
he wants, feels, thinks, and values. In Maslow's terms, he is impulse aware; his "inner signals" are relatively loud and clear. He
is not self-deceived or torn by unconscious conflicts. He may not
have a direct intellectual cognition of his inner depths, but there
is no significant disparity between his conscious and unconscious
selves.

A person is transparent when his acts, words, and gestures are
an accurate indicator of what is going on inside of him. Transparency is synonymous with honesty, lack of pose, and genuineness.
A person must be congruent before he can be transparent; an
incongruent person invariably transmits confusing or misleading
signals. Transparency requires self-acceptance and a confidence
that one's real self will be accepted by other people or that one
can handle rejection. It requires great strength and courage.

Spontaneity involves both congruence and transparence; it involves an absence of inhibition both in experiencing and in ex-

pressing the real self. Healthy spontaneity should not be confused with the acting out of neurotic compulsions which often
goes on in its name. Such behavior does not flow freely from the
real self but is a product of defensiveness and involves a breaking
through rather than a freedom from inhibitions. Spontaneity cannot exist without a profound self-trust, and it is only the psychologically healthy person who can have such trust in himself.

There is no serious conflict between spontaneity and morality,
for people cannot be truly spontaneous unless they are self-
actualizing, and the self-actualizing person "is so constructed
that he presses toward . . . what most people would call good
values, toward serenity, kindness, courage, honesty, love, unselfishness, and goodness" (PB, 147). Most Third Force psychologists would agree with Horney that the way to become good
is to become healthy and that "our prime moral obligation" is not
to control ourselves, but "to work at ourselves" (NHG, 15).

The self-actualizing person is a superior ethical being partly
because he is living from his inner core, which is good, and partly
because he is extraordinarily open to others and to the total
situation in which he is acting. By a process of partly conscious
and partly unconscious calculation, he seeks that course of action
which permits the maximum fulfillment of all his needs, which
offers the highest degree both of self-realization and of social
good possible under the circumstances.

The world-openness of the self-actualizing person is manifested in his ways of perceiving and of relating himself to external
reality. When they are self-actualizing, people are relatively free
of urgent needs and fears, and they have, therefore, an unusual
ability to attend to the external world and to perceive it objectively. In Schachtel's terms, defensive people tend to be autocentric (subject-centered) in their perceptions, while self-actualizing
people tend to be allocentric (object-centered) in their approach
to reality.

In the autocentric mode of perception the world is divided into

"objects-of-use" and "objects-to-be-avoided." Things and people are seen in terms of how they will "serve a certain *need* of the
perceiver, or how they can be *used* by him for some purpose, or
how they have to be *avoided* in order to prevent pain, displeasure,
injury, or discomfort."[12] Autocentric perception corresponds
closely to what Maslow calls D-cognition, that is, "cognition organized by the deficiency needs of the individual" (PB, 69).

In the allocentric mode of perception (which corresponds to
Maslow's Being or B-cognition), the perceiver exposes himself to
the object with relatively few preconceptions and protective devices. The "allocentric attitude" is "one of profound interest in
the object, and complete openness and receptivity toward it, a
full turning toward the object which makes possible the direct
encounter with it and not merely a quick registration of its famil-
iar features according to ready labels" (M, 220–221). Interest is
in the whole object and the perceiver turns toward it with the
whole of his being.

Allocentric perception provides a far richer and more accurate
picture of the world than does the more usual autocentric mode.
It is more ideographic than conceptual and hence restores to
awareness those aspects of reality which our systematic knowledge has ignored. It gives us "the real, concrete world" rather
than the "system of rubrics, motives, expectations, and abstractions which we have projected onto" it (PB, 38). It permits us to
see other people as they are in and for themselves, holistically,
"as complicated, unique individuals" (PB, 33).

There is a close connection between allocentric perception and
what Maslow calls Being-love.[13] Those who see all human relationships as I-it relationships, in which people use each other as
objects and in which the subjectivity of the other is threatening
and must be denied, are describing as inherent in the general
human condition relationships as they exist between deficiency-
motivated, autocentrically oriented people. In the Being-love relationship the other person is seen allocentrically, as he is in and

for himself; and he is loved for what he is and because he is understood rather than for what he can give to the lover. The B-love relationship is a non-clinging relationship in which there is respect for the other's dignity and autonomy and a desire for the other's growth. B-love is not confined to one partner but is extended to all persons who are seen allocentrically; it is the central feature of all the relationships which Carl Rogers characterizes as "helping relationships." Being-love is what all men need, more than anything else, in order to grow (see PB, 41). One of man's profoundest cravings is to be allocentrically perceived by another: "We all want to be recognized and accepted for what we are in our fulness, richness and complexity. If such an acceptor cannot be found among human beings, then the very strong tendency appears to project and create a godlike figure, sometimes a human one, sometimes supernatural" (PB, 88).

Allocentric perception has an "enriching, refreshing, vitalizing" effect upon the perceiver (M, 177). But it is also a frightening experience, a venture into the unknown, which requires unusual inner strength and autonomy. The "immediate and live contact with the ineffable objects of reality," says Schachtel, "is dreadful and wonderful at the same time. It can be frightening, as though it were death itself" (M, 193). It is so fearsome because it threatens our defenses and disturbs our embeddedness.

Schachtel sees human development as, in part, a conflict between our tendencies toward embeddedness and our tendencies toward openness and growth. There is in every man's psychic evolution "a conflict between the wish to remain embedded in the womb or in the mother's care, eventually in the accustomed, the fear of separation from such embeddedness, and the wish to encounter the world and to develop and realize, in this encounter, the human capacities" (M, 151). In the course of healthy development "the embeddedness principle yields to the transcendence principle of openness toward the world and of self-realization which takes place in the encounter with the world"

(M, 157). Under unfavorable conditions, such as "anxiety-arous-
ing early experiences in the child-parent relationship, the embeddedness principle may remain pathologically strong, with the
result that the encounter with the world is experienced in an
autocentric way as an unwelcome impinging of disturbing
stimuli" (M, 157–158). Embeddedness and openness are always
matters of degree; the conflict between them is never finally
resolved: "Man always lives somewhere between these two poles
of clinging to a rigid attitude with its closed world and of leaping
into the stream of life with his senses open toward the inexhausti-
ble, changing, infinite world" (M, 199–200).

The self-actualizing man is distinguished, then, not only by his
courage to be himself, but also by his courage to be in the world.
All rubricizing, says Maslow, "is, in effect, an attempt to 'freeze
the world' " (MP, 271). The anxious man is "afraid that without
the support of his accustomed attitudes, perspectives, and labels
he will fall into an abyss or founder in the pathless" (M, 195). He
tries to "freeze or staticize or stop the motion of a moving,
changing process world in order to be able to handle it" (MP,
272). The self-actualizing man is able to recognize and live with
the fact that "the world is a perpetual flux and all things are in
process" (MP, 271). He trusts his real self enough to follow its
promptings without knowing exactly where they will lead, and he
trusts his ability to sustain his encounters with the world enough
to be open to an authentic experience of the out there.

III. Self-alienation

Though the concept of the real self did not become central in
Horney's thinking until her last book, she quite early began to
conceive of neurosis as a process of self-alienation, and of
therapy as a process of giving the individual "the courage to be
himself."[14] In order to "restore the individual to himself, to help
him regain his spontaneity and find his center of gravity in him-

self," therapy must "lessen his anxiety to such an extent that he can dispense with his 'neurotic trends' " (NW, 11). As Horney sees it, adverse conditions in his environment produce in the individual a feeling of basic anxiety, which he seeks to overcome by developing certain interpersonal and intra-psychic strategies of defense. These, however, by virtue of the inner conflicts they generate and the increased self-alienation they entail, tend to create new problems and to exacerbate the conditions they were devised to remedy. Neurotic development is characterized by a number of vicious circles in which the individual's efforts to protect himself lead to self-betrayal and a kind of psychic death.[15]

We shall trace here the process by which the self is lost and a false-self system is formed.[16] As we do so, let us keep in mind that the various aspects of the process tend to interact and to reenforce each other in extremely complicated ways and that in each self-alienated individual there is a unique combination of the patterns which Horney describes as typical of neurotic development.

Neurosis begins as a defense against basic anxiety. Basic anxiety is a "profound insecurity and vague apprehensiveness" (NHG, 18) which is generated by feelings of isolation, helplessness, fear, and hostility.[17] It involves a dread of the environment as a whole, which is "felt to be unreliable, mendacious, unappreciative, unfair, . . . begrudging . . . merciless" (NW, 75). As a result of this dread, the child develops self-protective strategies, which in time become compulsive. His "attempts to relate himself to others are determined not by his real feelings but by strategic necessities. He cannot simply like or dislike, trust or distrust, express his wishes or protest against those of others, but has automatically to devise ways to cope with people and to manipulate them with minimum damage to himself" (OIC, 219). He abandons himself in order to protect himself, but as the real self becomes weaker the environment becomes more threatening. Environmental threat weakens the self, the weakness of the

self increases the sense of threat, and a basic anxiety takes the
place of basic trust in self and in the world.

Basic anxiety involves a fear not only of the environment, but
also of the self. A threatening environment is bound to produce
in the child both an intense hostility and a profound dependency
which makes him terrified of expressing his hostility and compels
him to repress it. Because he "registers within himself the existence of a highly explosive affect"[18] he is extremely fearful of
himself, afraid that he will let out his rage and thus bring the
anger of others down upon him. The child's hostility is generated
not only by the unfairness of his treatment, but also by his knowledge, at some level, that he is being forced to abandon his real
self and, with it, his chance for a meaningful life. He hates those
who are compelling him to the sacrifice, and he hates himself, as
well, for his weakness.

The repression of hostility has very bad consequences. It rein-
forces the child's feeling of defenselessness; it leads him to blame
himself for the situation about which he is angry and to "feel
unworthy of love" (NP, 84); and it makes him extremely fearful
of spontaneity. It may lead to the development of a retaliation
fear, a fear that others will do to him what he wants (unconsciously) to do to them. Since the child needs to get rid of the
hostility which is so dangerous to him, he often projects his
hostile impulses onto the outside world, in which case he feels
himself in the hands of malign powers. This increases his fear of
the world and leads to an intensification of both anxiety and
hostility.

Basic anxiety affects the individual's attitudes toward both himself and others. He feels himself to be impotent, unlovable, of
little value to the world. Because of his sense of weakness he
wants to rely on others, to be protected and cared for, but he
cannot risk himself with others because of his hostility and deep
distrust. The invariable consequence of his basic anxiety "is that

he has to put the greatest part of his energies into securing reassurance" (NP, 96). He seeks reassurance in his relation to others by developing the interpersonal strategies of defense which we shall examine next, and he seeks to compensate for his feelings of worthlessness and inadequacy by an intra-psychic process of self-glorification. These strategies constitute his effort to fulfill his highly intensified needs for safety, love and belonging, and self-esteem.

There are three main ways in which the child, and later the adult, can move in his effort to overcome his feelings of helplessness and isolation and to establish himself safely in a threatening world. He can adopt the compliant or self-effacing solution and move *toward* people; he can develop the aggressive or expansive solution and move *against* people; or he can become detached or resigned and move *away from* people.[19] The healthy person moves flexibly, of course, in all three directions; he gives in, fights, or keeps to himself as the occasion and his basic needs demand. The neurotic person, however, "is not flexible; he is driven to comply, to fight, to be aloof, regardless of whether the move is appropriate in the particular circumstance, and he is thrown into a panic if he behaves otherwise."[20]

In each of the defensive moves "one of the elements involved in basic anxiety is overemphasized": helplessness in the compliant solution, hostility in the aggressive solution, and isolation in the solution of detachment. Since under the conditions which produce neurosis all of these feelings are bound to arise, the individual will come to make all three of the defensive moves compulsively. The three moves involve incompatible value systems and character structures, however; and a person cannot move in all three directions without feeling terribly confused and divided. In order to gain some sense of wholeness and ability to function, he will emphasize one move more than the others and will become predominantly compliant, aggressive, or detached.

Which move he emphasizes will depend upon the particular combination of temperamental and environmental factors at work in
his situation.

The other trends will continue to exist quite powerfully, but
they will operate unconsciously and will manifest themselves in
devious and disguised ways. The "basic conflict" will not have
been resolved, but will simply have gone underground. When the
submerged trends are for some reason brought closer to the
surface, the individual will experience severe inner turmoil, and
he may be paralyzed, unable to move in any direction at all.
Under the impetus of some powerful influence or of the dramatic
failure of his predominant solution, the individual may embrace
one of the repressed attitudes. He will experience this as conversion or education, but it will be merely the substitution of one
neurotic solution for another.

As we discuss the three inter-personal moves and the character
types to which they give rise, let us keep in mind the fact that we
will find neither characters in literature nor people in life who
correspond exactly to Horney's descriptions. As Horney herself
observes, "although people tending toward the same main solution have characteristic similarities they may differ widely with
regard to the level of human qualities, gifts, or achievements
involved."

> Moreover, what we regard as "types" are actually cross sections of
> personalities in which the neurotic process has led to rather ex-
> treme developments with pronounced characteristics. But there is
> always an indeterminate range of intermediate structures deriding
> any precise classification. These complexities are further en-
> hanced by the fact that, owing to the process of psychic fragmenta-
> tion, even in extreme instances there is often more than one main
> solution. "Most cases are mixed cases," says William James, "and
> we should not treat our classifications with too much respect."
> Perhaps it would be more nearly correct to speak of directions of
> development than of types. (NHG, 191)

If we keep these qualifications in mind, we shall find Horney's analysis of the process of self-alienated development and of the kinds of character structures to which it gives rise to be of great value for the appreciation of literature. If we forget them, we are likely to focus on identifying neurotic types, rather than upon grasping the complexity and the phenomenological reality of individual characters and implied authors, and our analysis will be nothing more than a reductive labeling.

The person in whom compliant trends are dominant tries to overcome his basic anxiety by gaining affection and approval and by controlling others through his need of them. He needs to feel himself part of something larger and more powerful than himself, a need which often manifests itself as religious devotion, identification with a group or cause, or morbid dependency in a love relationship. *"His salvation lies in others"* (NHG, 226). As a result, "his need for people . . . often attains a frantic character" (NHG, 226). His "self-esteem rises and falls" with the approval or disapproval of others, with "their affection or lack of it" (OIC, 54).

In order to gain the love, approval, acceptance, and support he needs, the basically compliant person develops certain qualities, inhibitions, and ways of relating. He seeks to attach others to him by being good, loving, self-effacing, and weak. He tries to live up to the expectations of others, "often to the extent of losing sight of his own feelings" (OIC, 51). "He becomes 'unselfish,' self-sacrificing, undemanding—except for his unbounded desire for affection. He becomes . . . over-considerate . . . over-appreciative, over-grateful, generous" (OIC, 51–52). He is appeasing and conciliatory and tends to blame himself and to feel guilty whenever he quarrels with another, feels disappointed, or is criticized. Regarding himself as worthless or guilty makes him feel more secure, for then others cannot regard him as a threat. For similar reasons, "he tends to subordinate himself, takes second place, leaving the limelight to others" (OIC, 52). Because "any wish, any striving, any reaching out for more feels to him like a dangerous or reckless challenging of fate," he is severely inhibited in his self-assertive and self-protective activities and has powerful taboos against "all that is presumptuous, selfish, and aggressive" (NHG, 218, 219). Through weakness and suffering he at once controls others and justifies himself. His motto is: "You must love me, protect me, forgive me, not desert me, *because* I am so weak and helpless" (OIC, 53).

The compliant defense brings with it not only certain ways of feeling and behaving, but also a special set of values. "They lie in the direction of goodness, sympathy, love, generosity, unselfishness, humility; while egotism, ambition, callousness, unscrupulousness, wielding of power are abhorred—though these attributes may at the same time be secretly admired because they represent 'strength' " (OIC, 54–55). Citing their possible neurotic origin does not necessarily mean, of course, that these values are no good or that they are always held for neurotic reasons. The compliant person, however, does not hold them as genuine ideals but because they are necessary to his defense system. He must believe in turning the other cheek, and he must see the world as displaying a providential order in which virtue is rewarded. He is not wholeheartedly committed to the Christian values which he professses, for there exist in him powerfully the very tendencies which he consciously abhors.

In the compliant person, says Horney, there are "a variety of aggressive tendencies strongly repressed." These aggressive tendencies are repressed because feeling them or acting them out would clash violently with his need to feel that he is loving and unselfish and would radically endanger his whole strategy for gaining love and approval. His compliant strategies tend to increase rather than to diminish his basic hostility, for "self-effacement and 'goodness' invite being stepped on" and "dependence upon others makes for exceptional vulnerability" (OIC, 55–56). But his inner rage threatens his self-image, his philosophy of life, and his safety; and he must repress, disguise, or justify his anger in order to avoid arousing self-hate and the hostility of others.

The meaning of life for the compliant person usually lies in the love relation. Love appears "as the ticket to paradise, where all woe ends: no more feeling lost, guilty, and unworthy; no more responsibility for self; no more struggle with a harsh world for which he feels hopelessly unequipped" (NHG, 240). If he finds a partner "whose neurosis fits in with his own, his suffering may be considerably lessened and he may find a moderate amount of happiness" (OIC, 62). As a rule, however, "the relationship from which he expects heaven on earth only plunges him into deeper misery. He is all too likely to carry his conflicts into the relationship and thereby destroy it" (OIC, 62). Because of his need for surrender and for a safe expression of his aggressive tendencies, the compliant person is frequently attracted to his opposite, the masterful, expansive person: "To love a proud person, to merge with him, to live vicariously through him would allow him to participate in the mastery of life without having to own it to himself" (NHG, 244). This kind of relationship generally develops into a "morbid dependency," in which "the dependent partner is in danger of destroying himself, slowly and painfully" (NHG, 243).[21] When the love relation fails him, the compliant person will be terribly disillusioned and will feel either that he did not find the right person or that nothing is worth having.

The person in whom aggressive tendencies are predominant has goals, traits, and values which are quite the opposite of those of the compliant person. Since he seeks safety through conquest, "he needs to excel, to achieve success, prestige, or recognition" (OIC, 65). What appeals to him most is not love, but mastery. He abhors helplessness and is ashamed of suffering. He seeks to cultivate in himself "the efficiency and resourcefulness" necessary to his solution (OIC, 167). There are three expansive types: the narcissistic, the perfectionistic, and the arrogant-vindictive. They all "aim at mastering life. This is their way of conquering fears and anxieties; this gives meaning to their lives and gives them a certain zest for living" (NHG, 212).

The narcissistic person seeks to master life "by self-admiration and the exercise of charm" (NHG, 212). He has an "unquestioned belief in his greatness and uniqueness" which gives him a "buoyancy and perennial youthfulness" (NHG, 194). "He has (consciously) no doubts; he *is* the anointed, the man of destiny, the prophet, the great giver, the benefactor of mankind" (NHG, 194). His insecurity is manifested in the fact that he "may speak incessantly of his exploits or of his wonderful qualities and needs endless confirmation of his estimate of himself in the form of admiration and devotion" (NHG, 194). He frequently gets into trouble because he "does not reckon with limitations" and he "over-rates his capacities" (NHG, 195). On the surface he is "rather optimistic" and "turns outward toward life," but "there are undercurrents of despondency and pessimism" (NHG, 196). Since life can never match his expectations, he feels, in his weaker moments, that it is full of tragic contradictions.

The perfectionistic person "feels superior because of his high standards, moral and intellectual, and on this basis looks down on others" (NHG, 196). He needs "to attain the highest degree of excellence"; and, because of the difficulties which this entails, he tends "to equate in his mind standards and actualities—*knowing* about moral values and *being* a good person" (NHG, 196). While he is this way deceives himself, he may insist that others live up to "his standards of perfection and despise them for failing to do so. His own self-condemnation is thus externalized" (NHG, 196). He feels that there is "an infallible justice operating in life" and that success is a proof of virtue (NHG, 197). Because there is a just order, his "virtues" entitle him to good treatment by others and by life. Through the height of his standards he compels fate. Ill fortune shakes him "to the foundations of his psychic existence. It invalidates his whole accounting system and conjures up the ghastly prospect of helplessness" (NHG, 197).

The arrogant-vindictive person is motivated chiefly by a need for vindictive triumphs. He is extremely competitive: ". . . he cannot tolerate anybody who knows or achieves more than he does, wields more power, or in any way questions his superiority. Compulsively he has to drag his rival down or defeat him" (NHG, 198). In his relations with others he is at once ruthless and cynical. He seeks to "exploit others, to outsmart them, to make them of use to himself" (OIC, 167). He trusts no one and is out to get others before they get him. He avoids emotional involvement and dependency and uses the relations of friendship and marriage as a means by which he can possess the desirable qualities of others and so enhance his own position. He wants to be hard and tough, and he regards all manifestation of feeling as sloppy sentimentality. Since it is important for a person "as isolated and as hostile" as he is not to need people, he "develops a pronounced pride in a godlike self-sufficiency" (NHG, 204).

The philosophy of the arrogant-vindictive type tends to be that of an Iago or a Nietzsche. He feels "that the world is an arena where, in the Darwinian sense, only the fittest survive and the strong annihilate the weak. . . . a callous pursuit of self-interest is the paramount law" (OIC, 64). Considerateness, compassion, loyalty, self-sacrifice are all scorned as signs of weakness; those who value such qualities are fools whom it is no crime to take advantage of, since they are just asking for it. The only moral law inherent in the order of things is that might makes right. Just as the compliant person must repress his hostile impulses in order to make his solution work, so for the aggressive person "any feeling of sympathy or attitude of compliance would be incompatible with the whole structure of living he has built up and would shake its foundations" (OIC, 70). It is because his own softer feelings are such a threat to him that he must deny them so completely. He despises the Christian ethic and is "likely to feel nauseated at the sight of affectionate behavior in others" (OIC, 69) because he must repudiate anything which threatens to rouse up his compliant tendencies.

The basically detached person worships freedom and strives to be independent of both outer and inner demands. He pursues neither love nor mastery; he wants, rather, to be left alone, to have nothing expected of him and to be subject to no restrictions. He has a *"hypersensitivity to influence, pressure, coercion* or *ties* of any kind"* (NHG, 266). He may react with anxiety to physical pressure from clothing, closed in spaces, long term obligations, the inexorability of time and the laws of cause and effect, traditional values and rules of behavior, or, indeed, anything that interferes with his absolute freedom. He wants to do what he pleases, when he pleases; but, since he is alienated from his spontaneous desires, his freedom is rather empty. It is a *freedom from* what he feels as coercion rather than a *freedom to* fulfill himself. His desire for freedom may take the form of a craving for serenity, which "means for him simply the absence of all troubles, irritations, or upsets" (NHG, 263).

The detached person handles a threatening world by removing himself from its power and by shutting others out of his inner life. He disdains the pursuit of worldly success and has a profound aversion to effort. He has a very strong need for superiority and usually looks upon his fellows with condescension; but he realizes his ambition in imagination rather than through actual accomplishments. He feels "that the treasures within him should be recognized without any effort on his part; his hidden greatness should be felt without his having to make a move" (OIC, 80). In order to avoid being dependent on the environment, he tries to subdue his inner cravings and to be content with little. He cultivates a "don't care" attitude and protects himself against frustration by believing that "nothing matters." He seeks privacy, shrouds himself "in a veil of secrecy" (OIC, 76), and, in his personal relations, draws around himself "a kind of magic circle which no one may penetrate" (OIC, 75). He may feel an "intolerable strain in associating with people" (OIC, 73), and he "may very readily go to pieces" (OIC, 90) if his magic circle is entered and he is thrown into intimate contact with others.

The detached person withdraws from himself as well as from others. "There is a general tendency to suppress all feeling, even to deny its existence" (OIC, 82). His resignation from active living gives him an "onlooker" attitude toward both himself and others and often permits him to be an excellent observer of his own inner processes. His psychological insight is divorced from feeling; he looks at himself "with a kind of objective interest, as one would look at a work of art" (OIC, 74).

The detached person tries to resolve the conflict between his aggressive and compliant trends by withdrawing from the field of battle. Unless his warring impulses have been very deeply repressed, however, he is more likely than the other two types to entertain the attitudes and to display the moves of the subordinated solutions. As a result, "his sets of values are most contradictory" (OIC, 94). He has a "permanent high evaluation of what he regards as freedom and independence" (OIC, 94); and he cultivates individuality, self-reliance, and an indifference to fate. But "he may at some time . . . express an extreme appreciation for human goodness, sympathy, generosity, self-effacing sacrifice, and at another time swing to a complete jungle philosophy of callous self-interest" (OIC, 94).

While inter-personal difficulties are creating the movements toward, against, and away from people, and the basic conflict, the concomitant intra-psychic problems are producing their own self-defeating defensive strategies. The destructive attitudes of others, his alienation from his real self, and his self-hatred make the individual feel terribly weak and worthless. To compensate for this he creates, with the aid of his imagination, an "idealized image" of himself: "In this process he endows himself with unlimited powers and with exalted faculties; he becomes a hero, a genius, a supreme lover, a saint, a god" (NHG, 22). The nature of the idealized image is determined by the individual's predominant solution to his basic conflict; it contains all the attributes which are exalted by the compliant, aggressive, or detached moves. The submerged trends may be glorified, too; but they remain in the background, are isolated through compartmentalization, or are seen, somehow, as "compatible aspects of a rich personality" (NHG, 23). In the course of neurotic development, the idealized image assumes more and more reality. It becomes the individual's "idealized self"; it represents to him "what he 'really' is, or potentially is—what he could be, and should be" (NHG, 23).

The idealized image is designed to enhance the individual's feeling of worth and to provide a feeling of identity, but it rather quickly leads to increased self-contempt and additional inner conflicts. As a person becomes aware of the disparity between his idealized image and his real attainments, he starts to rage against himself, "to despise himself and to chafe under the yoke of his own unattainable demands upon himself" (OIC, 112). Since he can feel worthwhile only if he *is* his idealized image, everything that falls short is deemed worthless; and there develops a "despised image" which is just as unrealistic as its idealized counterpart. "He wavers then between self-adoration and self-contempt, between his idealized image and his despised image, with no solid middle ground to fall back on" (OIC, 112). There are now four selves competing for his allegiance: the real (or possible) self; the idealized (or impossible) self; the despised self; and the actual self, which is what he realistically is at the moment.

The increased self-hate and inner conflict produced by the formation of the idealized image leads to further self-glorification (with its concomitant of intensified self-contempt) and to compulsive efforts to realize the idealized image, either in action or in imagination. Thus begins the "search for glory," as "the energies driving toward self-realization are shifted to the aim of actualizing the idealized self" (NHG, 24). The search for glory often takes the form of a quest of the absolute: "All the drives for glory

have in common the reaching out for greater knowledge, wisdom, virtue, or powers than are given to human beings . . .
Nothing short of absolute fearlessness, mastery, or saintliness
has any appeal" (NHG, 34–35).

Horney does not see the search for glory, the quest of the
absolute, the need to be God as an essential ingredient of human
nature. Because he has the ability to imagine and to plan, man
is always reaching beyond himself; but the healthy individual
reaches for the possible (he dreams a possible dream) and he
works to achieve his goals within the context of human and cosmic limitations. He is able to take satisfaction in his achievements
and to sustain his frustrations without rage, self-hate, or despair.
The neurotic individual, however, is either all or he is nothing.
Indeed, it is because he feels himself to be nothing that he must
claim to be all. He who can be a man does not need to be God.

For the neurotic individual, the search for glory is often the
most important thing in his life. It gives him the sense of meaning
and the feeling of superiority which he so desperately craves. He
fiercely resists all encroachments upon his illusory grandeur and
may prefer death to the shattering of his dream.

The creation of the idealized image produces not only the
search for glory but a whole structure of neurotic strategies which
Horney calls "the pride system." The idealized image leads the
individual to make both exaggerated *claims for* himself and *excessive demands* upon himself. He takes an intense pride in the attributes of his idealized self, and on the basis of this pride he makes
"neurotic claims" upon others. At the same time he feels that
he *should* perform in a way commensurate with his idealized
attributes.

The overall function of neurotic claims is to perpetuate the
individual's "illusions about himself, and to shift responsibility to
factors outside himself" (NHG, 63). "He is entitled to be treated
by others, or by fate, in accord with his grandiose notions about
himself" (NHG, 41). The general characteristics of neurotic

claims are that they are unrealistic, they are egocentric, they demand results without effort, they are vindictive, they are based on an assumption of specialness or superiority, they deny the world of cause and effect, and they are "pervaded by expectations of magic" (NHG, 62). The effects of neurotic claims are "a diffuse sense of frustration," a "chronic discontent," an intensification of the burdensomeness of any hardship, an attitude of envy and insensibility toward others, an uncertainty about rights, and a feeling of inertia (NHG, 57). Neurotic claims are extremely tenacious, partly because they are necessary to the preservation of the idealized image and partly because their failure threatens the individual with intense self-hate.

The individual's need to actualize his idealized image leads him not only to make excessive claims upon others, but also to impose stringent demands and taboos upon himself ("the tyranny of the should"). The function of the shoulds is "to make oneself over into one's idealized self: *the premise on which they operate is that nothing should be, or is, impossible for oneself*" (NHG, 68). Since the idealized self is for the most part a glorification of the compliant, aggressive, or detached solutions, the individual's shoulds are determined largely by the character traits and values associated with his predominant trend.

The different neurotic types not only have different (predominant) shoulds, but they also have different attitudes toward the inner dictates. The aggressive person tends to identify himself with his shoulds, to accept their validity, and to try "to actualize them in one way or another" (NHG, 76). He covers over his shortcomings with imaginative reconstruction of reality, with arrogance, or with arbitrary rightness. The compliant person also feels "that his shoulds constitute a law not to be questioned" (NHG, 76); but, though he tries desperately to measure up to them, "he feels most of the time that he falls pitiably short of fulfilling them. The foremost element in his conscious experience is therefore self-criticism, a feeling of guilt for *not* being the supreme being" (NHG, 77). The detached person, with his ideal of freedom and his hypersensitivity to coercion, tends to rebel against his shoulds, especially those of the aggressive and the compliant attitudes, which in him are rather close to the surface. He may rebel passively, in which case "everything that he feels he should do arouses conscious or unconscious resentment, and in consequence makes him listless" (NHG, 77). Or he may rebel actively and behave in ways that defy his demands and violate his taboos.[22]

Characteristics of the shoulds are their coerciveness, their disregard for feasibility, their imperviousness to psychic laws, and their reliance on will power for fulfillment and on imagination for the denial of failure. There is a good deal of externalization connected with the shoulds. The individual feels his shoulds as the expectations of others, his self-hate as their rejection, and his self-criticism as their unfair judgment. He expects others to live up to his shoulds and displaces onto others his rage at his own failure to live up to his standards. The chief effects of the shoulds are a pervasive feeling of strain, hypersensitivity to criticism, impairment of spontaneity, and emotional deadness. The shoulds are a defense against self-loathing, but, like other neurotic defenses, they aggravate the condition they are employed to cure. Not only do they increase self-alienation, but they also intensify self-hate, for they are impossible to live up to—partly because they demand perfection and partly because they reflect the individual's inner conflicts and are often contradictory in nature. The penalty for failure is the most severe feeling of worthlessness and self-contempt. This is why they have such a tyrannical power. "It is the threat of a punitive self-hate that lurks behind them, that truly makes them a regime of terror" (NHG, 85).

Neurotic pride is "the climax and consolidation of the process initiated with the search for glory" (NHG, 109). It substitutes for realistic self-confidence and self-esteem a pride in the attributes of the idealized self, in the successful assertion of claims, and in the "loftiness and severity" (NHG, 92) of the inner dictates. What the individual takes pride in will be determined largely by his predominant solution; anything can become a source of pride.

Pride is vitally important to the individual; but, since it is based on illusion and self-deception, it makes him extremely vulnerable. Threats to it produce anxiety and hostility; its collapse results in self-contempt. The individual is especially subject to feelings of shame (when he violates his own pride) and humiliation (when his pride is violated by others). He reacts to shame with self-hate and to humiliation with a vindictive hostility which ranges "from irritability, to anger, to a blind murderous rage" (NHG, 99).

There are various devices for restoring pride. They include retaliation, which re-establishes the superiority of the humiliated person, and loss of interest in that which is threatening or damaging. They include also various forms of distortion, such as forgetting humiliating episodes, denying responsibility, blaming others, and embellishing. Sometimes "humor is used to take the sting out of an otherwise unbearable shame" (NHG, 106). There is an effort to protect pride by a system of avoidances. This includes not trying, restricting wishes and activities, and remaining detached, at a safe distance from involvement.

The pride system is in large measure a defense against self-hate; but, as we have seen, it cannot work and only intensifies the problem which it is designed to solve. Self-hate is a neurotic phenonemon which must not be confused with intrinsic guilt or healthy self-criticism. The self-actualizing person will not always like himself, but he will not hate himself. He will handle feelings of guilt and inadequacy in a basically self-accepting and constructive way by recognizing his limitations as a human being and by doing everything he can to repair damage and to avoid future error. He will work at himself patiently, realistically, and without expecting miracles. The self-alienated person will resort to the strategies of self-glorification, neurotic claims, tyrannical shoulds, and neurotic pride in order to blot out his deficiencies and to maintain his self-esteem. It is these strategies, ironically, which are the major source of self-hate; for the neurotic's loathing for himself is generated not so much by impaired functioning or by intrinsic guilt as by the disparity between what his pride system compels him to be and what he can be. "We do not hate ourselves because we are worthless," says Horney, "but because we are driven to reach beyond ourselves" (NHG, 114).

Self-hate is essentially the rage which the idealized self feels toward the actual self for not being what it "should" be. As the real self emerges in the course of favorable development, there develops what Horney calls the "central inner conflict"—between the real self and the pride system—and "self-hate now is not so much directed against the limitations and shortcomings of the actual self as against the emerging constructive forces of the real self" (NHG, 112). Living from the real self involves accepting a world of uncertainty, process, and limitation. It means giving up the search for glory and settling for a less exalted existence. The proud self therefore senses the real self as a threat to its very existence and turns upon it with scorn. Though it occurs at a rather late stage in the development from self-alienation to self-actualization, the central inner conflict is a fierce one. The person who has centered his life for a long time on dreams of glory may never be able fully to free himself from his idealized image, with its concomitants of pride, claims, shoulds, and self-hate.

Self-hate is for the most part an unconscious process, since "there is a survival interest in *not* being aware of its impact" (NHG, 115). The chief defense against awareness is externalization, which may be either active or passive: "The former is an attempt to direct self-hate outward, against life, fate, institutions, or people. In the latter the hate remains directed against the self but is perceived or experienced as coming from the outside" (NHG, 115). Self-hate operates in six ways, through "relentless demands on self, merciless self-accusation, self-contempt, self-frustrations, self-tormenting, and self-destruction" (NHG, 117). There is often a pride in self-hate which serves to maintain self-glorification: "The very condemnation of imperfection confirms the godlike standards with which the person identifies himself" (NHG, 114–115).

Self-hate is the end result of the neurotic process. Horney sees it as "perhaps the greatest tragedy of the human mind. Man in reaching out for the Infinite and Absolute also starts destroying himself. When he makes a pact with the devil, who promises him glory, he has to go to hell—to the hell within himself" (NHG, 154). Only when self-hate abates can "unconstructive self-pity turn into a constructive sympathy with self" (NHG, 153). In order for this to happen the individual must have "a beginning feeling for his real self and a beginning wish for inner salvation" (NHG, 153).

Chapter III

The Psychic Structure of
Vanity Fair

In "every artistic creation," writes Ernst Cassirer, "we find a definite teleological structure." Every facet of the work "is part of a coherent structural whole."[1] Cassirer's remarks suggest that all works of art *are* organic wholes. Indeed, critics usually begin by assuming that in any work under examination there *is* an aesthetic structure in terms of which all of the components of the work can be understood—much as theologians assume that the cosmos is informed by a moral order in terms of which every event has a purpose and meaning. The work is held to have its own *telos,* its own purpose or intention, the discovery of which is the job of criticism. It is possible, of course, that a given work lacks unity, that there is in it no coherent system in relation to which all of its motifs have a function or meaning. What does the critic do when he cannot discover the work's internal organizing principle, when the work seems to have no coherent teleological structure?

Some critics hold acknowledged masterpieces in such awe that they find the flaw or limitation in themselves when they cannot make sense of a work—just as theologians, when baffled, blame the imperfection of human reason rather than the unintelligibility of the cosmos. Their position cannot be easily dismissed, for it is impossible to *prove* that a work of art does not have a coherent structure. The flaw may always be in our understanding. We never know.

It is my contention that *Vanity Fair* lacks organic unity. I have not been able to find a teleological structure in terms of which its various motifs are intelligible. Its thematic inconsistencies become explicable, however, when they are seen to be manifestations of a psychic structure in which there are unresolved neurotic conflicts. My thesis here is that the implied author of *Vanity Fair* is not in harmony with himself because he is troubled by inner conflicts. The neurotic personality seems chaotic and hopelessly inconsistent, but to the trained observer the inconsistencies make sense. They are intelligible in terms of a total psychological structure which includes, and is, indeed, made up of conflicting attitudes and impulses. *Vanity Fair,* I propose, while lacking a coherent aesthetic structure, is informed by another kind of structure—the structure of its implied author's psyche— in terms of which its inconsistencies are comprehensible.

The psychic structure of *Vanity Fair* cannot be understood in terms of any principle of order established within the novel itself; we can look, however, to Third Force psychology, and particularly to the theories of Karen Horney, for our principle of explanation. Before I can offer my psychological interpretation of the novel, I must first show why *Vanity Fair* does not make sense in its own terms; and in order to do this I shall present some of the difficulties I encountered when I tried by thematic analysis to discover the novel's over-all structure. After I have discussed the novel's inconsistencies and provided a psychological meaning scheme in terms of which these inconsistencies make sense, I shall show how the same meaning scheme can heighten our sensitivity to many other aspects of the novel. It will enable us to understand the real nature of the novel's pattern of contrasts, to grasp one of the main principles of its dramatic structure, and to appreciate the greatness of Thackeray's achievement in characterization, particularly in his creation of Becky, Dobbin, and Amelia.

When both the thematic and the psychological analyses are completed, I shall consider some of the implications of psychological analysis for our judgment of the novel's worth. Wayne Booth feels that those novels are seriously flawed in which there is no intelligible thematic structure, in which "the author professes to believe in values which are never realized in the structure as a whole" (*Rhetoric*, p. 75), or in which there is no reliable guide "to the moral truths of the world outside the book" (p. 221). *Vanity Fair* possesses all of these deficiencies; but the psychological approach employed here will, I believe, enable us to affirm its greatness in spite of them.

II

Vanity Fair seems to ask, What is worth pursuing in life: Wherein lies happiness? Its inner purpose, its *telos*, appears to be the exploration of these questions. Permeated as it is by the phraseology and tone of the book of *Ecclesiastes*, the novel seems to be concerned, above all, with the question of the Preacher, What is it good for the sons of men that they should do under the heaven all the days of their life? We come to feel, as we study the novel, that we will have grasped its theme, "the chief value to which *this* implied author is committed" (*Rhetoric*, p. 74), when we have discovered its dominant attitude toward this problem.

In the actions of which Becky and Amelia are the centers, two very different solutions are proposed and tested. Becky is the chief representative of all those characters in the novel who spend their lives pursuing money, power, and prestige; she values personal relationships only insofar as they are a means to social success. Amelia, on the other hand, is indifferent to social success; she is the chief representative, along with Dobbin, of those characters who devote themselves to love and friendship.

An effort to grasp the theme of *Vanity Fair* might profitably begin, then, by examining the attitudes that the novel establishes toward these conflicting value systems.

Vanity Fair's assault upon the identification of worth and happiness with money, power, or prestige is the source of most of its satire. Addressing a society that has been taught by the Protestant ethic to regard economic success as a mark of virtue and failure as a sign of social and spiritual undeservingness, the novel insists that the socio-economic order is not also a moral order. The distribution of rewards in society is not an index of true worth or a revelation of God's will. The social destinies of men seem, for the most part, to be unintelligible, accidental, and unfair.

The gifts and pleasures of Vanity Fair are of little worth not only because they are accidental, impermanent, and unsanctioned by God, but also because, even if we can have and hold them till death, they do not satisfy. The Marquis of Steyne, who possesses what all yearn for, tells Becky, " 'Everybody is striving for what is not worth the having!' " (Ch. 48).[2] Again and again Thackeray[3] presents the image of the poor or low born poring over the peerage or standing enviously outside of the great houses watching the sumptuous entertainments within; and invariably he reminds us that greatness and luxury have nothing to do with happiness. The prizes of the social lottery are like the baubles that we try to win at a fair. The atmosphere of the fair creates an illusion of joy and value, and the prizes of the lottery seem glittering and desirable. When we return home with our shabby winnings the emptiness and futility of our pursuits is borne in upon us.

Becky is the chief means by which we are introduced to the various shops and shows of the Fair. In the story of her climb from the bottom to the top of the ladder, almost every aspect of society is exposed. Not only is her success very fleeting, but even when she is at the height of her career, when she has "penetrated into the very centre of fashion" and seen "the great George IV face to face," she finds that this too is Vanity. "Her success excited, elated, and then bored her" (Ch. 51). In Becky we see the futility of social climbing; there is nothing, really, to climb to.

In Becky, too, we see most vividly the connection between snobbery (overvaluing money, power, and prestige) and dishonesty. Becky's lying, cheating, and hypocrisy are necessary to the fulfillment of her ambitions. The novel suggests more than once that the entire social structure depends for its stability upon the suspension of moral principles.

The worship of success involves the sacrifice not only of integrity, but also of meaningful personal relationships. Those who are playing the great game live in a world where all relationships are manipulative, where one is courted or cut according to his place or market value. Family relationships are perverted if there is money or a title to be inherited. The rich are fawned upon and served, but they are also terribly alone, for they cannot ever be sure that the object of others' affection is themselves and not their money. Though Thackeray sometimes suggests that the poor can be more loving toward each other than the rich, at other times he shows that acquisitiveness, envy, and resentment pervade all levels of society.

Of all the human relationships that the novel shows being disrupted or perverted by social competitiveness, the marital relation suffers most. Instead of being an offspring of love and a means to emotional fulfillment, marriage, in the world of *Vanity Fair,* is fundamentally a means by which money, power, and prestige are acquired and increased. Men and women are eager to unite themselves with partners whom they neither love nor respect, and with whom they are bound to be miserable, in order to make what society considers a good marriage. Much of the action of the novel, especially in the first half, centers around the conflict between the generations over marriage. The older generation, hoping to gratify its ambitions through the marriages of the younger, violently disapproves of romantic attachments which do not enhance the family's status. Rawdon and George both make "bad" marriages and, as a consequence, are disinherited.

Vanity Fair's bitterest complaint against the ways of the world is that they inhibit the free flow of feeling and lead to starvation of the affections. The inhabitants of Vanity Fair keep their feelings strictly disciplined lest they endanger fortune or respectability. The most intimate relationships, instead of being a refuge from the uncertainty and injustice of the social lottery, are subordinated to worldly interests. The novel's sentimentality seems, in part, to be a defense of spontaneity and feeling in a world dominated by calculation and the values of the market place.

We find in *Vanity Fair*, then, an attack upon the ways and values of society which is strongly reminiscent of the book of *Ecclesiastes*. The pursuit of money, power, and prestige is shown to be vanity and a striving after wind. Like the Preacher, Thackeray demands justice and is terribly aware of the absurdity of our earthly destinies. He attacks the gifts and pleasures of this world as transitory, flawed, uncertain, and unsatisfying. The pursuit of them is not only meaningless but destructive.

III

What, then, should we do under the heaven all the days of our life? The novel's condemnation of worldliness as destructive implies a norm by which worldliness is being judged; and the preceding analysis suggests that the things of worth which are sacrificed to the false values of the world are love, friendship, and emotional fulfillment. Gordon Ray finds that, even though Becky is in many ways the more impressive character, it is Amelia and the values surrounding her story that serve as a moral norm in *Vanity Fair:*

Life is redeemed for Thackeray only by affection, by love, by loyalty to the promptings of the heart. . . . Becky's career is admirably suited to illustrate the destructive operation of the standards of Vanity Fair, but Thackeray desired through Amelia's history to show what he would put in their place, the life of personal relations, the loyalty and selflessness inspired by home affections. This recurring contrast was essential to his purpose.[4]

As we have seen, there are many things in the novel that support this interpretation. But an equally impressive argument can be made, I think, that the novel presents *all* earthly pursuits as vain. There is certainly a strong contrast drawn between Becky's and Amelia's ways of life, but the contrast is between two equally imperfect and frustrated lives, and the novel seems to show that devotion to social success and devotion to love are both unrewarding. Hence the frequent charges of cynicism.

Vanity Fair is a novel of disenchantment. Those of its characters who become educated learn that they have been pursuing or valuing something unworthy of their effort or devotion. And it is not only the gifts and pleasures of social life that prove to be disappointing: love and friendship in the world of the novel are usually built upon illusion and are therefore liable to disenchantment and change.

George Osborne is utterly unworthy of Amelia's devotion; Amelia loves not George but an image created by her romantic imagination. When her engagement with George is broken off, Amelia is inconsolable and longs for death. Nine days after her marriage, she is already "looking sadly and vaguely back" (Ch. 26). Hers is the common lot: "always to be pining for something which, when obtained, [brings] doubt and sadness rather than pleasure. . . ." George's death leads Amelia to forget his faults and to idealize him further, and she spends the next eighteen years worshipping a false idol, deliberately constricting and sterilizing her existence as an act of homage to her "saint in heaven."

Meanwhile, Dobbin is blindly offering up eighteen years of his life to his idealized picture of Amelia. Eventually he sees and owns his delusion: "It was a fond mistake. Isn't the whole course of life made up of such? and suppose I had won her, should I not have been disenchanted the day after my victory?" (Ch. 67).

The mistakes of Amelia about George and of Dobbin about Amelia seem, indeed, typical of the whole course of life. Amelia is mistaken not only about George, but also, in different ways, about Dobbin and Becky. Dobbin's worship of George is almost as foolish as Amelia's. Amelia idealizes her son and little Rawdon idealizes his mother, at first. Rebecca deceives many, for a while, including Sir Pitt Crawley and Jos Sedley; but it is Rawdon, her husband, who is most under love's spell and who is most stricken by his disillusionment.

One of the chief characteristics of personal relations in *Vanity Fair* is their lack of reciprocity. The narrator cites the cynical Frenchman who said "that there are two parties to a love transaction: the one who loves and the other who condescends to be so treated" (Ch. 13); and *Vanity Fair* seems again and again to bear out this observation. In every relationship the one who loves is in the power of his less ardent partner; the pursuer is a slave of the pursued. This pattern prevails whether the relationship is between friends, lovers, or parents and children. *Vanity Fair* leaves us with the impression that true love and friendship may be worth having, but that they do not exist.

Amelia Sedley devotes herself to love and the home affections, and not one of her relationships is satisfactory. When her parents are kind to her, she is indifferent; when she succors them they are complaining and ungrateful. Amelia worships George, and George condescends to be so treated. As George treats her, so Amelia treats Dobbin: "It is those who injure women who get the most kindness from them—they are born timid and tyrants, and maltreat those who are humblest before them" (Ch. 50).

After George's death, Amelia devotes herself to her son; and he, of course, comes to tyrannize over her as has his father before him. When Georgy goes to live with his grandfather Osborne, he leaves "smiling as the mother breaks her heart. By heavens it is pitiful, the bootless love of women for children in Vanity Fair" (Ch. 50). When little Rawdon goes off to school, we have a repetition of the parting of Amelia and Georgy. His father is "sad and downcast"; little Rawdon is "happy enough to enter a new career, and find companions of his own age" (Ch. 52).

No less pitiful than the unreciprocated love of parents for their children is the bootless love of William Dobbin for Amelia. Amelia's dedication to her saint in heaven prevents her from reciprocating Dobbin's warmth, and so she retains her power over him. She reserves Dobbin for herself and uses him at her pleasure, but she is unresponsive to his love and unconcerned about his feelings. In Pumpernickel she finally decides that she can never marry him:

> She couldn't, in spite of his love and constancy, and her own acknowledged regard, respect, and gratitude. What are benefits, what is constancy, or merit? One curl of a girl's ringlet, one hair of a whisker, will turn the scale against them all in a minute. They did not weigh with Emmy more than with other women. (Ch. 66)

Again we get the feeling that irrationality and injustice are the prevailing qualities of the novel's world. We can no more expect virtue and merit to be fairly rewarded in love than we can expect our position in society to be commensurate with our deserts.

There are other important parallels between Thackeray's treatment of social vanities and his vision of inter-personal relationships. Love and friendship are no less transitory than fame and fortune. The pursuit of worldly success creates many barriers between people; but in our most intimate personal relationships some degree of hypocrisy is usually present. If it were not, "we should live . . . in a frame of mind and a constant terror, that would be perfectly unbearable" (Ch. 31). The members of families seem naturally to hate, abuse, or be disappointed in each other. Even the saintly William Dobbin is usually at odds with his sisters. Even if one could imagine a family in Thackeray that was utterly devoid of worldliness, it seems unlikely that the relations between brothers and sisters, parents and children, husbands and wives would be characterized by "loyalty and selflessness."

If I am correct in arguing that Becky's and Amelia's stories are variations on the theme of vanity, that social success and love relationships are equally unrewarding, then *Vanity Fair* presents a devastating indictment of human nature and the human condition. The novel as a whole seems to bear out the narrator's closing comment: "Ah! *Vanitas Vanitatum!* Which of us is happy in this world? Which of us has his desire? or, having it is satisfied?" Thackeray does not say that life is not worth living, but that it is universally frustrating and, therefore, no great prize. There *are* pleasures and satisfactions, which we should not despise, but they are imperfect and fleeting. The greatest folly seems to be to take any aspect of our earthly existence too seriously, to pursue any of the prizes of life too strenuously.

It does not seem to make much difference what the sons of men do under the heaven all the days of their life. Becky's aristocratic pleasures are transitory, but so are all other mortal delights. And *Vanity Fair* is not a novel in which virtue is rewarded and vice punished. It seems possible that Becky at the end is as satisfied (or as dissatisfied) with her existence as Amelia and Dobbin are with theirs. Out of the action of the novel there arises no moral perspective which shows any way of life to be preferable to another.

IV

Though much of *Vanity Fair* can be understood as an illustration of the vanity of human wishes, the preceding analysis does not provide a satisfactory explication of the novel as a whole.

Some of the motifs that we have discussed do not seem to hang together. For example: on the one hand, the novel condemns social ambition as destructive because it leads to the sacrifice of love, friendship, and emotional fulfillment. On the other hand, it shows that all earthly pursuits are vain, that those who devote themselves to personal relations are no less frustrated than those who seek success in the social lottery. A study of some of the novel's other motifs will reveal further difficulties in relating all of the motifs to each other and to a total teleological structure.

The author often professes to believe in values which are not realized in the novel as a whole. In the commentary, he extols love and alludes to cheery lasses and hearty families and happy husbands and wives (see the comment on Peter Butt and Rose in Chapter 9); but we look in vain to find examples of such fruition in love and family life in the dramatized portions of the novel. The burden of most of the novel is that the social order is not also a moral order, that our rewards are usually not commensurate with our deserts. But in an early passage, commenting on Becky's desire for revenge upon Miss Pinkerton, the narrator affirms the opposite:

> Miss Rebecca was not, then, in the least kind or placable. All the world used her ill, said this young misanthropist, and we may be pretty certain that persons whom all the world treats ill, deserve entirely the treatment they get. The world is a looking glass, and gives back to every man the reflection of his own face. Frown at it, and it will in turn look sourly upon you; laugh at it and with it, and it is a jolly kind companion; and so let all young persons take their choice. (Ch. 2)

The implication of this passage is that kindly, cheerful people will be well-treated by the world, whereas ill-disposed people will suffer. If this is true, then people who suffer deserve not our sympathy but our condemnation. I cannot arrive through thematic analysis at any explanation of this jarring passage. It is out of harmony not only with the action of the novel, but also with many other passages of commentary.

The commentary urges us "to love and pray!" (Ch. 14). The action, however, gives us little reason to believe in either love or prayer. And yet the religious motif is an important one in *Vanity Fair*. It could be argued that the whole point of showing how vain is the pursuit of both social success and love is to lead us to prayer and submission to the will of God. Since there are no values inherent in the nature and condition of man, the only source of values in the novel's cosmos is God. But God's values are inscrutable, his wisdom is "hidden and awful," and our only recourse is to submit to things as they are, realizing our ignorance and impotence.

For the most part the human condition is judged in terms of human cravings for rationality, justice, and fulfillment; and it is found to be terribly wanting. But when we examine the religious motif in *Vanity Fair* we find that the frustrations and miseries of the human lot are justified in that they scourge our pride and bring us to God in a spirit of proper humility. They make us realize that we find in this life neither "the summit of the reward nor the end of God's judgment of men" (Ch. 38). From this religious point of view, all of the evils of the human condition are not only justified, but are positively desirable. It is better to fail than to succeed, better to be ineffectual than to be competent, better to be wretched than to be satisfied (see Ch. 61). In the eyes of God everything that to us humans seems desirable is evil; all earthly joys are snares and delusions that lead us to sinful feelings of pride and self-sufficiency.

This religious motif is logically compatible with *Vanity Fair's* satire upon the vanity of human wishes, but it is quite out of keeping with the prevailing tone of the novel. Its presence is too intermittent and too superficial for it to act as a unifying principle in terms of which other motifs can be explained. *Vanity Fair* is not basically a religious novel. One of its frequent objects of satire, in fact, is Evangelical Christianity, as represented by Lady South-down and her daughter Lady Emily, authoress of "The Washer-woman of Finchley Common" (see Dobbin's repudiation of Ame-lia's other-worldly attitudes in Chapter 62). The religious position expounded in Thackeray's sermon on the death of Mr. Sedley (Ch. 61) is essentially that of the sect which he elsewhere attacks.

Nothing is more difficult to understand in *Vanity Fair* than the role of Becky Sharp. It is not hard to show, as John E. Tilford, Jr., has done, that to the author Becky is "a 'monster' all along" and that "in her thoughts, words, and actions he almost unremit-tingly makes her represent evil."[5] And yet, as many critics have testified, Becky is not only the most fascinating character in the novel, but also one who excites admiration and sympathy. It is this which makes it so hard to understand her function in the novel as a whole.

The first thing we must do is to try to understand why we are so often on Becky's side. The answer is fairly simple: the action is so structured that in about three-fourths of her conflicts Becky is the protagonist. The first several chapters of the novel are dominated by various forms of battle imagery, as Becky sets out on campaign for a respected place in society. Becky is alone and at a disadvantage, and our sympathies are almost always with her as she manages to outmaneuver her powerful enemies. We are for Becky not only because she is the underdog, but also because her enemies are often oppressive social institutions and attitudes which are the enemies of us all. When Becky deals unscrupu-lously with harmless people who are themselves victims—like Amelia, Briggs, or Raggles—we are against her. But for the most part we are in sympathy with her rebellion against an unjust society and with her desire to conquer it, even when she is cruel and her means are unethical.

Many of the episodes of Becky's story are brilliantly comic, and, as a result, our moral judgment of Becky is often suspended.

While we are, to a certain extent, empathically involved with Becky, we are completely detached from most of her victims, who are not persons at all but caricatures and grotesques. We laugh at the discomfiture of a Miss Pinkerton, a Jos Sedley, a Lady Bareacres, a General Tufto, or a Wagg; and we are not at all concerned with the means Becky uses to gain her triumphs. There is in *Vanity Fair* a world of comedy in which immoralities cancel each other out. Our sense of Becky's viciousness often gives way to sheer enjoyment of her cleverness, wit, and vitality. The comedy is, as I say, brilliant; but *Vanity Fair* is not essentially a comic novel; and the amorality of its comic episodes seems out of keeping with its prevailing concern for values.

As the novel draws to a close Becky becomes less and less the heroine of the comic action and more and more the antagonist in the moral drama. Rawdon and Jos, whose discomfiture or exploitation at Becky's hands we had earlier enjoyed, now become true victims, the objects of our sympathy. We are somewhat shocked by how dark the story becomes at the end, when Becky is suspected of murdering Jos, not because Becky seems incapable of such an action, but because it is a violation of the comic nature of their relationship as it has been depicted throughout the novel. We are surprised to find ourselves feeling pity and fear for Jos, whose sufferings have always been so ludicrous.

Most of the time, Becky is just doing what everybody does, and somehow she seems to have more justification for doing it than most. Many of her characteristics seem undesirable, but when we view Becky in her situation they seem just the weapons she needs to win her way in an unfriendly world. The gentle Amelia is, as Becky says, "no more fit to live in the world than a baby in arms" (Ch. 67) and must depend upon others for protection. The only character who can cope with the world in an honorable way is Dobbin, but he is an imperfect foil to Becky. Besides, his image is tarnished by virtue of the fact that he is a spooney; he is victimized not by the world, but by the world's victim, Amelia. It is not surprising, then, that while one critic feels that Becky is presented as a monster all along, another argues that the passage in Chapter 64 in which she is so described is not "quite fair to its subject, who must pay now belatedly for Thackeray's confusion.⁶

When our sympathies are with Becky, we tend to lose sight of the fact that it is her unhealthy ambition that exposes her to many of her humiliations. She participates in every vice and vanity of the society with which she is at war. In seeking her just place she perpetrates as many injustices as the system against which she is rebelling. Moreover, she is not rebelling against the system as a whole, but only against its treatment of her. She completely accepts the values of the establishment; what she wants is for the establishment to accept her. When we see this clearly, we begin to wonder how Becky can function in even a limited way as a protagonist in the novel's attack on society's snobbery and unfairness.

We are beginning to swing back to the dark view of Becky, and I could quickly demonstrate that she is really a monster all along. The problem, of course, is that she really *is* a monster all along, and, at the same time, she is the protagonist in much of the action. Until this truth is fully understood, debates among critics will be endless.

And, as we have seen, the problem of Becky is only one of a number of difficulties that we encounter when we attempt to comprehend the teleological structure of *Vanity Fair*. Amelia's story seems at once to show that "life is redeemed . . . only by affection, by love, by loyalty to the promptings of the heart," and to reveal how all personal relationships are blighted by their transitoriness, lack of reciprocity, and failures in knowledge and communication. The narrator's attitude toward Amelia is no less ambivalent than his attitude toward Becky; and, as many critics have shown, the sense of Amelia's thematic function that we get from the commentary is often at odds with Thackeray's portrayal of her character and actions. The narrator applauds Amelia and Dobbin as the true lady and gentlemen; but Amelia is weak, foolish, and exploitative, and Dobbin is her slave. There is much indignation in the novel at the absence of rationality, justice, and fulfillment in the human condition; but, as we have seen, in one of its religious motifs all of our humiliations are good, for they make us needful of God and acceptable to Him.

Since I am unable to discover an overall teleological structure within which such apparently conflicting motifs make sense, I can only conclude that *Vanity Fair* lacks organic unity. Thematic analysis has revealed the implied author's inconsistencies, but it can take us no farther. At this point we must have recourse to psychological analysis, for it alone can make sense of these inconsistencies and help us to grasp what is happening in the novel.

V

The inconsistencies in *Vanity Fair* seem to be manifestations of a basic conflict in which compliant tendencies predominate but are continually at war with a powerful, though submerged, aggressiveness. Since the implied author's aggressive trends constitute a threat to his conscious self-image and world view, they must somehow be made acceptable to his compliant value system. This is done through disguise and displacement. Sometimes his aggressive attitudes are so subtly expressed that it is easy to be unaware of their presence; at other times they are put into the service of compliant values. It is the latter device which accounts for a large part of Thackeray's satiric impulse, and the former which explains why Becky Sharp is so often a protagonist.

Although they are less important than either the aggressive or the compliant trends, tendencies toward detachment also figure prominently in the psychic structure of *Vanity Fair*. Detachment is an attempt to reduce inner conflict by putting feeling at a distance, by denying the importance of the warring impulses.

Detachment is manifested in *Vanity Fair* by the conclusion that all is vanity and by the narrator's irony, often unfocussed, which is the means by which the implied author negates what he has affirmed and protects himself from the consequences of commitment. Because of his irony Thackeray cannot be accused of believing in any of these foolish values. If he is accused of being cynical, however, he can always protest that he was only joking, that his heart is in the right place. The effectiveness of ironic detachment as a defense is evidenced by the fact that some critics defend Thackeray against charges of sentimentalism, cynicism, and inconsistency by pointing to his mocking tone.[7]

In our analysis of the novel's thematic structure we saw that Thackeray's presentation of Becky Sharp is inconsistent. Becky represents everything that the compliant value system deems loathsome, and there is no question but that she is strongly condemned in the novel. At the same time, however, she is the incarnation of the submerged half of Thackeray's personality. In her character structure, value system, and world view Thackeray has perfectly embodied the aggressive trends that he consciously repudiates but longs to express. Thackeray protects his compliant value system and his public image by his overt condemnation of Becky, but his tendencies to *move against* manifest themselves in his structuring of the action in such a way that Becky is the protagonist. They are expressed in so hidden and subtle a way that Thackeray can ignore them or can pretend innocence. But he is disturbed by them, nonetheless, and the more effectively Becky rules the action the more he is compelled to condemn her.

We can see Thackeray's conflicting tendencies at work in the well-known passage in Chapter 8 in which he announces his intention to step down from the platform and talk about his characters. The passage as a whole leaves us feeling bewildered and uncomfortable: it is at once earnest and ironical, humble and self-righteous, meek and full of rage, seemingly sincere and smacking of cant. The placing of this passage is very important, for it comes just after a mocking and irreverent letter by Becky Sharp. Having expressed some of his own aggressive attitudes in this letter, Thackeray becomes anxious and violently repudiates them. His aggressive impulses lead Thackeray to be bitingly satirical, but his compliant trends force him to retreat into the pose of the amiable humorist, the humble moralist, who does not mean to hurt anybody's feelings—unless they happen to be wicked and heartless. This is not the only place in which Thackeray intrudes as narrator because his anxiety about having expressed forbidden feelings makes him want to set the record straight. What we have in these cases is the compliant Thackeray repudiating the aggressive Thackeray who keeps getting expressed through the structuring of the action. The ironic tone of such passages derives from Thackeray's detachment. He often adopts this tone when he is in the grip of conflicting feelings, and in such cases his irony is fuzzy—we cannot say what he really means.

The aggressive elements in *Vanity Fair*'s psychic structure are so strong that they are often more vividly presented than the opposing compliant views. The looking glass passage which is so incongruent with the novel as a whole and even with the situation that evoked it is a perfect expression of the *moving toward* defense. The way to get along in the world is to be "kind and placable"; if we are good (compliant) there is nothing to fear, for everyone will like us and be good in return. If we are bad (aggressive) we will arouse the hostility of others and be punished. The world is really a safe and just place; if we suffer misfortune it is because we are bad, because we have frowned at the world. If we accept everything with good humor we will have no really serious troubles; but if we are bitter and rebellious, then watch out!

The compliant defense posits the world as fair, as responsive to kindness and placability, because that is the way the world must be if submission is to be a means to safety and power. In this scheme of things goodness is a means of controlling, of conquering. We see how this works when Amelia conquers Miss Pinkerton far more easily and effectively than does Rebecca. Because she is so "humble and gentle" Amelia is adored by all, and there is an orgy of grief at her departure from Miss Pinkerton's.

A similar scene occurs much later in the novel when Dobbin leaves Pumpernickel:

> Old Burcke, the landlord of the lodgings came out, then Francis with more packages—final packages—then Major William,—Burcke wanted to kiss him. The Major was adored by all people with whom he had to do. It was with difficulty that he could escape from this demonstration of attachment. (Ch. 66)

When Georgy, who had already "burst out crying in the face of all the crowd," howled again during the night, the maid "mingled her lamentations with his. All the poor, all the humble, all honest folks, all good men who knew him, loved that kind-hearted and simple gentleman" (Ch. 66). In these and a few other passages, which seem like intrusions of a fairy tale world into the sordid reality of *Vanity Fair,* we see the looking-glass passage borne out, the compliant defense working to perfection. If this is the way of the world, it is not only wrong, it is foolish to be like Becky rather than like Amelia.

What makes the looking-glass passage seem so incongruous, of course, is the fact that by far the greater part of the novel presents the aggressive solution's view of the world as a jungle in which everyone is out for himself and the weak go to the wall. As I have said, there are times when Becky's mode of operation seems justified by the nature of her situation. If society is unfair and almost everyone is trying to exploit you, why shouldn't you look out for yourself, use the weapons of the enemy, and get them before they get you? This is the philosophy of the aggressive type; it is Becky's philosophy; and in the context of the novel as a whole it seems to make a lot more sense than the idea of being kind and placable. It is the aggressive view of the world that unquestionably receives the more effective dramatic presentation.

Even more strongly than it is presented as justified, however, the aggressive pursuit of worldly success is presented as pointless and destructive. Much of the novel's satire is generated by Thackeray's righteous anger that the world is *not* as the looking glass passage describes it. Not only are the means to worldly success shown to be sordid; its ends are shown to be worthless. And this, I think, is not only because the compliant Thackeray cannot afford to desire these things, but also because the aggressive Thackeray has learned that they do not really satisfy.

Even though it manifests strong leanings toward aggressive values, then, *Vanity Fair* passionately rejects the philosophy of the *moving against* solution. It does so partly because a neurotic solution provides no genuine answers, but mainly because compliant trends are dominant in its psychic structure. It endorses most strongly that strategy for living which rejects competitiveness and seeks safety and a sense of worth and belonging through goodness, submissiveness, and self-effacement. It attacks the values of the social world as false and destructive because they lead to the sacrifice of love, friendship, and emotional fulfillment—the things to which the compliant solution looks for the meaning of life.

And yet, as we have seen, the stories of Becky and of Amelia are but variations on the theme of Vanity: Thackeray presents social success and love relationships as equally unrewarding. *Vanity Fair* is as inconsistent in its presentation of compliant values and characters as it is in its depiction of the aggressive types and their philosophy. Thackeray's ambivalence towards Amelia and Dobbin and the contempt for sentiment expressed by some of his aggressive characters suggest that his negative attitudes toward the compliant solution stem in part from his aggressive trends. But the main reason for his rejection of compliant values is that they, like their aggressive counterparts, do not work.

What the novel shows brilliantly is the inadequacy of these two kinds of neurotic solutions. But there is no awareness within the novel that this is its import. Every aspect of the novel's structure and tone reveals its striving to be a comment on man's essential nature and condition. There is no nonneurotic character or perspective present to serve as a moral norm and thereby to provide an internal revelation that its subject is sickness.

The concluding comment of the narrator that all is vanity and no one is happy in this world cancels out both of the novel's conflicting value systems and is perfectly appropriate to its actual presentation of life. Thackeray's sense of the hopelessness of all solutions contained within the novel, combined with his inability to see beyond them, leads him at the end to a position of detachment. It does not matter what we do under the heaven all the days of our life. Nothing is worth pursuing ardently and no one is to be taken seriously: "Come children, let us shut up the box and the puppets, for our play is played out." This statement, which is so jarring to our sense of the novel's moral and artistic earnestness, is perfectly in keeping with the resigned defense which protects us from our conflicts and from our feelings of futility and despair by viewing the human scene from a distance, with a detached amusement.

There is one aspect of the compliant solution which is not negated by the conclusion that all is vanity. As we have seen, it could be argued that Thackeray depicts the frustrations and miseries of the human lot in order to show the necessity of humility and submission to the will of God. In this religious form of the compliant solution, man *moves toward* God. It is God alone who is the source of happiness (though not in this life), and the way to win His favor is to be weak, humble, and miserable. He who esteems himself, he who is dissatisfied with man's fate, or he who feels that he has some rights and asserts his human dignity shall forfeit the favor of the inscrutable Deity, even if in purely human terms he is a good man. In this sick religion man offers up his guilt, suffering, and self-abasement to the glory of a tyrannical God. Man hopes to enslave God by his dependency; he seeks through his helplessness and self-loathing to master the universe. This is a final and desperate effort to solve the problems of life through a neurotic love relation in which the masochistic compliant type submits to and thereby binds to him the sadistic aggressive type. Because in its religious form this relation is wholly imaginary and promises no present rewards it is less subject to total failure than any other form of the compliant solution; it is the last hope.

VI

Psychological analysis not only accounts for the inconsistencies of the implied author; it also reveals remarkable similarities between Thackeray's characters and Karen Horney's aggressive and compliant types. This recognition leads both to a better understanding of the fiction and to a profound admiration of Thackeray's genius in the presentation of characters and relationships. Critics who regard Amelia and Dobbin as puppets have failed to appreciate the complexity of their characterization; and those who object to various aspects of the behavior of the major characters have not seen that their actions, though often abnormal, are invariably consistent with their neurotic motivational systems. It is not only the major characters, but also a whole host of minor characters who are basically either aggressive or compliant in their dealings with others. The central contrast in *Vanity Fair* is essentially between the character structures, the value systems, and the world views associated with the aggressive and the compliant solutions.

Most of the characters in *Vanity Fair* can readily be seen as either aggressive or compliant, and most of the relationships fall into one of three categories: one party is aggressive and one is compliant, both parties are aggressive, or both parties are compliant. The last category has only a few members, though the important relationships of Dobbin and Amelia and Rawdon and Lady Jane fall within it. To give some idea of the prevalence of the first two kinds of relationships, I list them here, more or less in the order in which they occur in the novel (see page 94).

The relationships between aggressive characters generate much of the fun and excitement in the novel. The seducer seduced, the tyrant bullied, the exploiter exploited, and the wit out-witted are among the classic situations of comedy. These situations are so structured that no moral issue intrudes, no sympathy need be felt; and we can enjoy the clever schemes, the hostile exchanges, the vindictive triumphs, and the discomfiture of victims. For the implied author, these situations permit the enactment of his aggressive impulses in ways that do not violate the taboos of his compliant solution. They serve a similar function, of course, for the reader.

The relationships between aggressive and compliant characters are the backbone of the novel. In the first half-dozen chapters seven such relationships, including three of major importance, are developed. These are most commonly master-slave relationships in which there are strong elements of exploitation and morbid dependency; but there are interesting variations, such as the attraction of Miss Crawley to both Amelia and Lady Jane. Some of these relationships are portrayed in great detail and with amazing insight; we must not make the mistake of thinking that we have understood them when we have put them into a category. We shall look closely at a few of them when we come to discuss the major characters.

These aggressive-compliant relationships give rise to one of the novel's most important patterns. This is the pattern of the worm turning, which produces a series of showdown scenes in

Character Relationships in *Vanity Fair*

Aggressive-Compliant

Miss Pinkerton—Miss Jemima
Miss Pinkerton—Amelia
Becky—Amelia
Becky—Miss Jemima
George—Amelia
Cuff—Dobbin
George—Dobbin
Becky—Rose Crawley
Miss Crawley—Briggs
Becky—Briggs
Sir Pitt—Rose
Mr. Osborne—Amelia
Miss Crawley—Amelia
Becky—Rawdon
Peggy O'Dowd—Michael
Lady Southdown—Mr. Pitt
Lady Southdown—Lady Jane
Miss Crawley—Lady Jane
Becky—Lady Jane
Georgy—Amelia
Sir Pitt—Lady Jane
Mr. Osborne—Jane Osborne
Becky—Dobbin
Becky—Jos

Aggressive-Aggressive

Miss Pinkerton—Becky
Becky—George
Becky—Sir Pitt
Becky—Mrs. Bute
Becky—Miss Crawley
Becky—Rawdon
Mrs. Bute—Miss Crawley
The Bute Crawleys—Sir Pitt
Rawdon—George
George—Mr. Osborne
Frederick Bullock—Mr.
   Osborne
Becky—General Tufto
Becky—Lady Bareacres
Lady Southdown—Miss
   Crawley
Georgy—Mr. Osborne
Miss Horrocks—Mrs. Bute
Becky—Lady Southdown
Maria—Mr. Osborne
Becky—Wagg, Lady
   Stunnington
Becky—Lord Steyne

which a compliant character finally defies, attacks, or tells off his oppressor. These scenes are the dramatic high points of the novel. They include Dobbin's fight with Cuff, Amelia's denunciation of Becky in Brussels, the new Sir Pitt's wresting of power from Lady Southdown, Rawdon's attack on Lord Steyne and his rejection of Becky, Lady Jane's ultimatum to Sir Pitt, and Dobbin's denunciation of Amelia in Pumpernickel. In the worm turning pattern a character who has suffered much abuse and who seems helpless in the hands of his tormentor finally explodes with righteous anger or shows unexpected determination and shifts the balance of power, or, at the least, gains a vindictive triumph. The protagonist is usually a gentle, humble, weak, or ineffectual person who has strong taboos against hostility, violence, or even healthy self-assertion. His outburst of aggression is justified because it is so long overdue, because he has suffered so much and is so much in the right.

For the reader the showdown scenes are intensely exciting; he has so long felt anger and frustration on behalf of the compliant protagonist that he experiences a delightful release of tension and enjoys the aggressive behavior without guilt or reservation. For the author, the worm turning pattern is another device, along with his satiric mission and his juxtaposition of aggressive characters, by which the expansive side of his personality can be expressed without violating the taboos of his self-effacing solution. It is interesting to note that the moral of the showdown scenes, that it pays to be self-assertive, is never explicitly drawn in the novel.

VII

The psychological approach to *Vanity Fair* is nowhere more valuable than in enhancing our understanding and appreciation of the major characters. Becky has from the first been hailed as one of the great creations in fiction; most studies, however, focus

not upon Becky herself but upon her role in the novel or Thackeray's attitude toward her. As Thackeray observes in his remarks
"Before the Curtain," Amelia and Dobbin have a smaller circle
of admirers but were created with no less care. We miss one of
the most important values of fiction if we dismiss these characters
as insipid or old-fashioned. Like many other self-effacing characters in Victorian fiction, they are devoid of personal charm and
brilliance; but they are quite fascinating if we study them as
mimetic portraits and attempt to understand their motivations.

Thackeray does not tell us much about Becky's childhood, but
just about all the information that he gives us is highly relevant
to a psychological understanding of her character. Her mother
was a French opera girl of low origins, who conceived, and perhaps delivered, Becky out of wedlock, and who died sometime
during Becky's childhood. Her maternal connection seems to
have filled Becky with shame and to have re-enforced her sense
of the lowness of her position. Her need to compensate for the
stigma attached to her birth is clearly revealed by her lies about
her mother's family. There is no evidence that Becky received any
tender loving care from her mother. The fact that she herself has
"no soft maternal heart" indicates the barrenness of her childhood and her failure to identify with the feminine role.

Becky's father "was an artist. . . . with a great propensity for
running into debt, and a partiality for the tavern. When he was
drunk, he used to beat his wife and daughter" (Ch. 2). Such a man
was incapable of giving Becky the economic and emotional
security of paternal care. Instead, he required care himself; and,
as a result, Becky developed "the dismal precocity of poverty":
"she had never been a girl, she said; she had been a woman since
she was eight years old." In the history of the arrogant-vindictive
person, writes Horney, we usually find that the child has been
forced to stifle his softer feelings and to undergo "a hardening
process in order to survive" (NHG, 202). There is obviously no

one in Becky's environment to give her sympathy or affection or to take an interest in her needs and feelings. She must suppress those parts of her nature which leave her vulnerable or which interfere with her compensatory strategies. The need for love does not entirely disappear, but it is perceived by Becky as a kind of weakness which threatens her life-style. Her contempt for those in whom it is uppermost indicates how strongly she must defend against such feelings in herself.

Becky's father is important in her life not only as a source of abuse and deprivation, but also, to some extent, as a model and a re-enforcer of certain of her tendencies. There is little doubt that Becky identifies with him when he rails "at the world for its neglect of his genius" and that this contributes to her own sense of unappreciated merit. Her project is to *make* the world recognize her worth, and the way in which she goes about this is also influenced by her father and the kind of environment that he provides. Just as Becky identifies with her father, so Sharp sees some of his own qualities in his daughter and fosters them through his appreciation. He is "very proud . . . of her wit" and is delighted by her mimicry (Ch. 2). His daughter is his favorite companion, presides over his evening entertainments, and is obviously his pride and joy.

In the society of loose and clever men with which Sharp surrounds his daughter, Becky establishes one of her most important patterns of gratification—namely, the conquest of men through her wit, vivacity, and sexual allure. Life at Miss Pinkerton's school is so horrible to Becky not only because she is made constantly aware of the inferiority of her position, but also because she is unable to compensate for this by sexual conquests. Throughout the novel Becky's greatest difficulties are in relation to women, who are impervious to (and often threatened by) her cleverness and charm. Her conquest of society is to be by the means discovered in her early conquests of her father and his

friends. If we were to make a list of the men whom Becky captivates in the course of the novel, it would be a long and varied one
indeed.

When Becky begins the world over again, upon leaving Chis-
wick Mall, she has a set of character traits, motives, and strategies
which have been firmly established in her childhood and which
undergo little change. Like Napoleon, whom she hails, and the
French nation, with which she identifies, Becky is out to conquer
the world. Life for her is a series of battles, and she is determined
to come out on top. She feels that all the world has used her ill,
and she is burning with a desire for revenge. Her first memorable
act, flinging back the dictionary, secures a vindictive triumph.
Her "countenance, which had before worn an almost livid look
of hatred, assumed a smile that perhaps was scarcely more agree-
able, and she sank back in the carriage in an easy frame of mind"
(Ch. 2). Becky carries with her a mortified pride which is in
constant need of assuagement. A successful retaliation always
puts her into a good humor; her later cheerfulness is often the
sign of an achieved revenge. Throughout much of the novel
Becky is such a poised and masterful figure that we are apt to
forget that she is motivated by the feelings of rage and vindictiveness which are so close to the surface in the early scenes.

In terms of the Maslovian hierarchy, Becky is frustrated in her
needs for safety, love and belonging, and self-esteem and is
therefore arrested at an early stage of psychological development. She represses the need for love and seeks to fulfill the
other needs, which have become distorted, in neurotic ways.
Having experienced insecurity and humiliation in childhood,
Becky wants power and status. She takes great pride in her skill
at manipulation (which is her form of power) and she has a deep
craving for respectability, which symbolizes the secure acceptance that she has never had. The healthy drive for self-esteem
is replaced by the self-idealization and neurotic pride which generate the search for glory. "Feeling like a pariah," says Horney,

the arrogant-vindictive person "must prove his worth to himself" (NHG, 204). For Becky, proving her worth means proving her superiority; and she seeks to do this by exploiting or making fools of others and by rising to the highest levels of society.

Some of Becky's neurotic character traits are of great help to her in her battle with the world. She has emerged from her impoverished childhood needing no one and caring for no one. This enables her to streamline her emotional life, to channel her energies into her ambitious schemes, and to use the softer feelings of others for her own purposes. Feeling that life is a battle of each against all and that she has been denied her rightful place in the world, she has no scruples about using any weapons that come to hand. As Lord Steyne testifies, "she is unsurpassable in lies" (Ch. 52). Her lack of a firm center of self and of authentic feelings makes it easier for her to maintain her facade and to play whatever role the situation requires. Like her father, Becky is an artist; part of her appeal is in the pleasure she gives through her brilliant performances. Thackeray heightens this pleasure by keeping us aware of Becky's real attitudes and motives, so that when she is acting, we know it.

Her early experience teaches Becky that she can succeed with men through wit, charm, and seductiveness. It also teaches her that there are times when she must conceal her talents and play the compliant role. Though she probably got her earliest practice in this part when she had to coax and wheedle tradesmen and to play upon their sympathy, she comes to see that this strategy is especially successful with women, and it becomes her chief means of manipulating members of her own sex.

Seeming meek, helpless, and humble, and professing the values of the self-effacing solution endears Becky to aggressive women, who see her as manageable, and to compliant women, who think that she is a kindred spirit. Before she took her in, Miss Pinkerton "believed Rebecca to be the meekest creature in the world" (Ch. 2). Mrs. Sedley concludes that "the little, humble, grateful, gentle governess" would never dream of marrying Jos (Ch. 4); and after Becky's rejection of Sir Pitt, Miss Crawley blesses and admires her "little protégée . . . as a dear, artless, tender-hearted creature" (Ch. 15). With Lady Jane and Amelia, Becky plays the role of the tender or bereft mother who is frequently seen "hemming a shirt for her dear little boy" (Ch. 44) or who laments how cruelly her darling has been torn away from her.

It frequently happens that Becky abandons her pose or is revealed as deceitful, and then her victims turn upon her with great anger. Miss Pinkerton feels that she has nourished "a viper" in her bosom, and Miss Crawley never forgives Becky for marrying Rawdon. Several of the showdown scenes center upon the denunciation of Becky by a compliant character who has long been in her power. The anger which these people feel stems in part from the fact that Becky has made fools of them, and they know it. Much of Becky's behavior is a parody of compliant attitudes. The fact that this mockery of the compliant solution is never really counterbalanced in the novel is one indication of a powerful aggressive component in the implied author's personality.

Becky's mimicry of compliant attitudes is in part an expression of her scorn for weakness, softness, and sentimentality. She is amused by compliant people, and rather likes them because they are so easily manipulated; but at the same time she is disturbed by them and is full of a bitter contempt. The intensity of her revulsion against such people is most vividly rendered in her reactions to Lady Jane:

> Lady Jane's sweetness and kindness had inspired Rebecca with such a contempt for her ladyship as the little woman found no small difficulty in concealing. That sort of goodness and simplicity which Lady Jane possessed annoyed our friend Becky, and it was impossible for her at times not to show, or to let the other divine her scorn. . . . gentle thoughts and simple pleasures were odious

> to Mrs. Becky, they discorded with her; she hated people for liking
> them; she spurned children and children-lovers. (Ch. 45)

Becky hates her son because he represents the claims of affection,
which she has ruthlessly excluded from her life; and the "paternal
softness" of her husband only increases "her scorn for him" (Ch.
37).

Becky plays upon the sentimental attitudes of others partly
because she, like Iago, needs to show that people who trust their
fellows are fools and that believing in "Christian" values exposes
one to exploitation. She must prove to herself that her rejection
of sentiment is justified, that her values and life-style are called
for by the nature of the world. Her reaction to Lady Jane indicates
that Becky is beset by inner conflicts, that Lady Jane, and people
like her, rouse up her own compliant tendencies, which she must
then defend herself against. In effect, there is something in Becky
which responds positively to Lady Jane, but this is very threatening to her whole solution. If she were to allow such feelings, she
would be flooded with self-contempt; she would violate the
taboos of her expansive pride system and her compliant side
would pass a very negative judgment on her aggressive behavior.
The hatred which she feels for compliant people is in part a
defense against and in part an externalization of the self-hate
which is generated by any emergence of her repressed yearnings.

Becky's strong reaction against compliant attitudes is but one
evidence of a hidden side of her personality. On several occasions
we get glimpses behind her facade which make us aware of Becky
as a suffering human being who is beset by inner conflicts. When
Rawdon becomes suspicious of her relation with Lord Steyne, he
keeps her constant company; and Becky becomes again the
cheerful and attentive wife that she had been in the early days of
their marriage: "He fell asleep after dinner in his chair; he did not
see the face opposite to him, haggard, weary, and terrible; it
lighted up with fresh candid smiles when he woke. It kissed him

gaily" (Ch. 53). On the surface it seems as though Becky thoroughly enjoys her role playing—and, indeed, it does provide certain satisfactions; what we see here is the terrible strain involved in constant hypocrisy and the isolation and self-division that it imposes. After she sees Georgy in Pumpernickel, she remembers the Sedleys with fondness: "they were kind simple people" (Ch. 64). When she meets Amelia, it jars "upon her, to be obliged to commence instantly to tell lies in reply to so much confidence and simplicity" (Ch. 66). She is touched by Amelia's "frankness and kindness" and she admires Dobbin's nobility of heart (Ch. 66).

It is in Chapter 41, in which Becky returns to Queen's Crawley for the funeral of Sir Pitt, that we have the fullest revelation of her hidden side. The exchange of salutations and recognitions with the local inhabitants is "inexpressibly pleasant" to Becky: "It seemed as if she were not an impostor any more, and was coming to the home of her ancestors." Becky feels that she has risen above her original station because she has "brains . . . and almost all the rest of the world are fools"; but she has also, it seems, been feeling like an impostor and has had the sense of hollowness and vulnerability which accompanies such a feeling.

Queen's Crawley, under the guiding influence of Lady Jane, rouses up feelings which Becky normally keeps well buried. The experience can only be a passing one. Becky cannot permit herself seriously to entertain thoughts of being honest and humble and doing her duty and marching straightforward on her way: "She eluded them, and despised them—or at least she was committed to the other path from which retreat was now impossible."

The other path is, of course, the path of aggressive strivings; and Becky is committed to it not only because she is ensnared by her own intrigues, but also because it offers her the excitements and triumphs which are the very meaning of her life. Becky's career is not without its high points, as she gains entrée into the most elite society; and the glamor of her achievement is re-enforced by the implied author's obvious delight in the pomp and splendor by which Becky finds herself surrounded. After the English victory at Waterloo, Becky has a "period of elation" in Paris, where she is "received with much distinction" amid "the splendours of the new Court" (Ch. 36). Upon her return to England, she must fight hard for acceptance into the upper world; but she succeeds at last. On her way to see the King, "Becky felt as if she could bless the people out of the carriage window, so elated was she in spirit, and so strong a sense had she of the dignified position which she had at last attained in life" (Ch. 48).

At Gaunt House, just before her downfall, Becky reaches the peak of her career. With her success in the charades,

> she had reached her culmination: her voice rose trilling and bright over the storm of applause: and soared as high and joyful as her triumph. . . . The greatest triumph of all was at supper time. She was placed at the grand exclusive table with his Royal Highness the exalted personage before mentioned, and the rest of the great guests. She was served on gold plate. She might have had pearls melted into her champagne if she liked—another Cleopatra; and the potentate of Peterwardin would have given half the brilliants off his jacket for a kind glance from those dazzling eyes. (Ch. 51)

Becky's "soul swelled with pride and delight at these honours; she saw fortune, fame, fashion before her" (Ch. 51).

This is, of course, the pride which goeth before a fall. What is actually before her, only a day or two away, is the utter collapse of her position and the destruction of her hopes. Becky has overreached herself. The deceit upon which her career is founded is finally revealed; and Becky is left in despair, with thoughts of suicide. Becky's fall is called for by the novel's moral pattern, in which the attempt to master one's fate through aggressiveness must be punished; and it is interesting to note that she is brought down by two of the compliant characters whom she most despises —Rawdon and Lady Jane. But her fall is also the natural conse-

quence of her life style and demonstrates, without authorial forcing, the inadequacy of her neurotic solution.

   Becky's worldly failure is not the only evidence of the inadequacy of her solution. Even when she is successful, she does not
experience happiness, except in brief periods of elation. As Horney observes, when aggressive people "do attain more money,
more distinction, more power, they . . . come to feel the whole
impact of the futility of their chase. They do not secure any more
peace of mind, inner security, or joy of living" (NHG, 26). Having
gotten what she has always longed for, Becky begins to wish for
other modes of existence, in which she imagines that there is joy:

> Becky's former acquaintances hated and envied her: the poor
> woman herself was yawning in spirit. "I wish I were out of it," she
> said to herself. "I would rather be a parson's wife, and teach a
> Sunday School than this; or a serjeant's lady and ride in a regimen-
> tal waggon; or, O how much gayer it would be to wear spangles
> and trowsers, and dance before a booth at a fair." (Ch. 51)

We know, of course, that none of these roles would satisfy Becky,
though each of them appeals to a part of her nature.

   Becky survives her downfall as well as she does because for her
it is not an unmitigated disaster. She is close to achieving her
dream of pre-eminence and respectability, but she has already
had premonitions that success brings boredom rather than contentment. Her fall releases her from a life in which she was beginning to feel trapped, a life in which there were no more worlds
to conquer. It puts her back into the situation (of having to make
it) to which she is so well adapted. She has her moments of
despair; but, on the whole, the Bohemian life into which she falls
is well suited to her temperament and offers many of the satisfactions which she had experienced in her climb to the top.

   In childhood when she has to coax and wheedle the tradesmen,
during her period of social climbing when she lives on nothing

a year, and after her fall when she plunges into a dissolute existence, Becky is leading essentially the same kind of life—one of
peril, dissimulation, and intrigue. She seems to need excitement
of this kind in order to feel alive. When there is no opportunity
for her to perform her tricks, when she cannot have the adventure, the risk, and the sense of triumph that she insatiably craves,
Becky becomes restless or bored and is ready to upset whatever
equilibrium she may have achieved. It is distinctly possible that
she took such a foolish risk with Rawdon because she needed the
excitement and unconsciously wished to be discovered.

We are left at the end with a sense that Becky is caught between
conflicting needs. The conflict between her aggressive and compliant sides is so far beneath the surface as to be scarcely visible.
What is obvious is that she both loaths and craves respectability,
that she can live neither with it nor without it. The same childhood conditions which have made it "Becky's aim in life" to "be,
and to be thought, a respectable woman" (Ch. 48) have also
produced a system of defenses, a set of values, and a character
structure which make the respectable life, as society defines it,
unbearable to her. In our last glimpse of her she is attempting
to re-establish her reputation and to secure acceptance by once
again playing a compliant role:

> She busies herself in works of piety. She goes to church, and never
> without a footman. Her name is in all the Charity Lists. The Desti-
> tute Orange-girl, the Neglected Washer-woman, the Distressed
> Muffin-man, find in her a fast and generous friend. She is always
> having stalls at Fancy Fairs for the benefit of these hapless beings.
> (Ch. 67)

When Becky is not chuckling to herself about what fools she is
making of her partisans, we can be sure that she is yawning in
spirit and longing for the excitements of her Bohemian days. It
seems unlikely that she can stand this life for very long.

VIII

Amelia Sedley is, of course, the opposite of Becky Sharp. Whereas Becky seeks safety and a sense of belonging through an aggressive pursuit of mastery, Amelia pursues these goals by the self-effacing strategies of weakness and amiability. Her "kindly, smiling, tender, gentle, generous heart [wins] the love of everybody who [comes] near her" (Ch. 1). She spoils "everybody . . . with kindness and compliments" (Ch. 65). She has a "soft and yielding nature" (Ch. 56) and is "so utterly gentle and humble as to be made by nature for a victim" (Ch. 59).

Though Amelia is presented through much of the novel as the victim of a "struggling, violent world" with which she is unfit to do battle (Ch. 50), her feebleness is actually a trait which gains her a considerable amount of safety, protection, and control. Her "weak and tremulous" sensibility (Ch. 38) forces others to treat her with special consideration: ". . . as for saying an unkind word to her, were any persons hard-hearted enough to do so—why, so much the worse for them. Even Miss Pinkerton, that austere and god-like woman, ceased scolding her after the first time, and . . . gave all masters and teachers particular orders to treat Miss Sedley with the utmost gentleness, as harsh treatment was injurious to her" (Ch. 1). It is Amelia's "weakness" which is the secret of her appeal to men: she displays "a kind of sweet submission and softness, which [seems] to appeal to each man she [meets] for his sympathy and protection" (Ch. 38). Amelia's chief means of dealing with the world is to force others to care for her by her infantile behavior.

If Becky Sharp has never been a girl, Amelia Sedley never becomes a grown-up woman. Enfeebling social attitudes toward upper-class women and an extremely sheltered childhood combine with "a disposition naturally simple and demanding protection" (Ch. 57) to produce a woman who, even in her thirties, is "no more fit to live in the world than a baby in arms" (Ch. 67). When confronted with frustration or stress, Amelia weeps, becomes hysterical, pines away, or goes out of her mind. Again and again Dobbin perceives her as an "infant in pain" (Ch. 30) and displays a parental anxiety and protectiveness. Near the end, after Dobbin has left in anger, we find Amelia being fathered by her son (who speaks "words to his timid companion, indicative of sympathy and protection") and mothered by, of all people, Becky Sharp: "She treated Emmy like a child and patted her head" (Ch. 67). Amelia is so helpless, so unhappy, so vulnerable, that it is unthinkable to treat her harshly or to leave her to fend for herself.

Amelia has many other traits which can be properly understood only if we relate them to her self-effacing character structure, value system, and life style. She has a strong taboo against pride and is most comfortable when she is in a submissive role. "It needs not to be said," observes Thackeray, "that this soft and gentle creature took her opinions from those people who surrounded her, such fidelity being much too humble-minded to think for itself" (Ch. 26). She experiences considerable anxiety when she must exercise authority. She begins "to blush most absurdly" after checking the carriage at Brighton (Ch. 22), presides at her own table "with exceeding shyness and timidity" (Ch. 26), and is "terrified at the idea of having a servant to wait upon herself" (Ch. 60). She seeks to place herself beneath whomever she encounters and speaks "to domestics with the most reverential politeness" (Ch. 60).

Amelia suffers greatly from the harshness of fate and of the world, but she does not rebel or complain. She places herself entirely in the hands of a higher power. She is most pious and "prays with an humble humble heart" (Ch. 50). She believes that "in his own might, no man shall be strong"; and she glorifies weakness, humility, and suffering as pleasing to God. She despises herself, feels that the world's neglect is justice, and strives to think that it is right that "her selfish, guilty love" should be punished by the loss of both husband and son. She "thought in her heart that she was a poor-spirited, despicable little creature, whose luck in life was only too good for her merits" (Ch. 57). Thackeray apostrophizes her over and over again as a saint-like victim and martyr; at some level, no doubt, Amelia perceives herself in the same way.

One of the reasons why Amelia feels so selfish and guilty is that she has strong taboos against wanting anything for herself. Her shoulds tell her to live for others, to do her duty, to sacrifice self:

> Directly she understood it to be her duty, it was this young woman's nature . . . to sacrifice herself and fling all that she had at the feet of the beloved object. During what long thankless nights had she worked out her fingers for little Georgy whilst at home with her; what buffets, scorns, privations, poverties had she endured for mother and father! (Ch. 57)

After the death of her husband, she retires to her own little room and her own little bed "for many long, silent, tearful, but happy years" (Ch. 38). Her "very joy," Thackeray tells us, "was a sort of grief"; and it may be that her grief was a sort of joy, that suffering and sacrifice put her most in harmony with her shoulds. When, on the continent, she experienced the "wonders of Mozart and Cimarosa" for the first time, she "would ask herself when she went to say her prayers of a night, whether it was not wicked to feel so much delight" (Ch. 62). It may be that one of her motives for resisting marriage to Dobbin is that it would generate guilt and deprive her of the role of martyr to duty in which she feels so comfortable. When Thackeray laments Amelia's victimization by the world, he fails to note that her fate is to a significant degree self-imposed.

Another reason Amelia feels her love for husband and son to be guilty and selfish is that she is seeking through these relationships a forbidden earthly glory. After the death of her husband, "all she hoped for was to live to see her son great, famous, and glorious, as he deserved to be" (Ch. 46). Georgy is "her heart and her treasure—her joy, hope, love, worship—her God almost!" (Ch. 50). Through him she hopes to experience vicariously a fulfillment of the repressed expansive drives which are so much at variance with her conscious values and which she cannot act out for herself. This is one cause of her subservience to the child; if he is to gratify her pride, he must be the master.

Amelia's relationship with her son is, in many ways, a re-enactment of her relationship with his father. George was her protector, her knight in armor: ". . . having George at her side [she] was not afraid . . . of any sort of danger" (Ch. 20). Amelia wants a man who will at once confirm her sense of her own insignificance by being far above her and at the same time feed her pride by allowing her to merge her identity with his. George fulfills her needs completely: "She had never seen a man so beautiful or so clever . . . Not amongst all the beaux at the opera . . . was there any one to equal him. He was only good enough to be a fairy prince; and, oh, what magnanimity to stoop to such a humble Cinderella!" (Ch. 12). She is vaguely disturbed by his selfishness and indifference, but if he had treated her better, she would have worshipped him less. With her deep feelings of inadequacy, she cannot take seriously a man who praises and cherishes her. Her sense of worth must derive not from any qualities of her own, but from the qualities of her lover, who can bestow them upon her only by possessing her completely. When George returns to renew the engagement, Amelia cries over his hand and kisses it "humbly, as if he were her supreme chief and master, and as if she were quite a guilty and unworthy person needing every favour and grace from him" (Ch. 20).

Before George returns Amelia longs for death. She does so partly out of despair, but partly also because she sees death as a way of retaining possession of her hero: "Then, she thought, I shall always be able to follow him" (Ch. 18). By giving herself completely to George, by becoming totally his possession, she gains a sense of possessing him. This is why, after George dies, she wishes to remain faithful to his memory. As she had before, Amelia glorifies George; only now there are no stubborn realities to disturb her worship: ". . . she only remembered the lover, who had married her at all sacrifices; the noble husband so brave and beautiful, in whose arms she had hung on the morning when he had gone away to fight, and die gloriously for his king" (Ch. 46). To remain identified with this hero in heaven and to possess his glory for herself, all that Amelia needs to do is to remain his. By living in her dream, Amelia sacrifices many of the gratifications that life could offer, but none of them can give her the sense of exaltation that she gains from her worship of George. Through her devotion to him, Amelia fulfills not only her expansive needs, but also her compliant shoulds. She is living out a romance of heroic fidelity and takes enormous pride in her own nobility.

If we examine Amelia's relationship with Dobbin in the context of her feelings about George, it is not difficult to understand why she is so unresponsive to Dobbin's love and so little inclined to marry him. She has initially "rather a mean opinion" of Dobbin because of his lack of all external grace and charm. Even after she comes to feel grateful for his "constant and kind heart" and to recognize his "beautiful and generous affection" (Ch. 61), Amelia cannot bring herself to think of Dobbin as a lover. His patience, devotion, admiration, and humility make him less rather than more appealing. Amelia needs a man who will dominate her, not another compliant person who reflects her own qualities and prostrates himself before her. Thackeray indicates that Dobbin could have had Amelia much sooner had he been able to act masterfully: "Why did he not take her in his arms, and swear that he would never leave her? She must have yielded: she could not but have obeyed him" (Ch. 58). Instead "she ordered him about, and patted him, and made him fetch and carry just as if he was a great Newfoundland dog" (Ch. 66). Dobbin fulfills Amelia's need for protection, but he exacts no price for this; she can refuse him and still have him. To marry Dobbin, Amelia must give up George; and it is evident that her imaginary relation with her dead husband fulfills her neurotic need for glory far more completely than would a living marriage with the Major.

Amelia becomes angry with Dobbin and determines to be free when she begins to pose too great a threat to her relation with George. The precipitating event is Dobbin's objection to having Becky in the house. His reminder that Becky was not always Amelia's friend evokes memories of George's flirtatiousness; and this, of course, threatens Amelia's illusion system at its weakest point: "The wound which years had scarcely cicatrised bled afresh, and oh, how bitterly!" (Ch. 66). Her anger with George is displaced onto Dobbin; and this at once allays her anxiety and restores her pride both in George and in her own devotion: ". . . you insulted his memory. . . . You know you did. And I will never forgive you. Never!" (Ch. 66) Amelia sees her denunciation of Dobbin as displaying a "proper feeling and veneration for the late Captain Osborne" (Ch. 66). There is more to Amelia's reaction than this, however. Thackeray observes that Amelia has "found a pretext" in this affair for a prior determination to be free. Though it is not spelled out in the novel, it seems evident that Amelia has been feeling under a growing pressure to marry Dobbin, that she has found it more and more difficult to maintain her resolution to remain faithful to George, and that she needs to break with Dobbin in this way in order to free herself from temptation and preserve her glory.

There are several factors which lead Amelia to call Dobbin back to her. For almost her whole adult life he has been her guardian and protector, her chief source of security. She feels now that she has "lost her power over him" and, with it, her place in the world. She feels keenly her inability to fend for herself and to care for her boy. Dobbin's care had permitted her to live in her romantic dreams; she must now confront the world and her need for a husband. In addition, Dobbin's changed behavior alters the psychodynamics of their relationship. His denunciation and departure are masterful acts which crush her pride and greatly enhance his attractiveness. Her unfairness, coming after his years of sacrifice and devotion, makes her feel guilty and puts her in a morally inferior position. When they meet again, Dobbin's face is "full of sadness and tender love and pity. She understood its reproach, and hung down her head" (Ch. 67). Amelia's need of Dobbin is so great that she calls him back even though it means violating her shoulds and giving up her pride in her fidelity. Becky's revelation about George releases Amelia from her inner conflict: " 'There is nothing to forbid me now. . . . I may love him with all my heart . . .' " (Ch. 67).

The novel closes with Amelia, the "tender little parasite," growing "green again . . . round the rugged old oak" to which she clings (Ch. 67); but the predominating note is one of disenchantment. George, "the idol of her life," has been "tumbled down and shivered at her feet" by Becky's revelation of his proposal in Brussels; and Dobbin, who had worshipped her for eighteen years, is "kind and gentle" but no longer ardent. Amelia has the guidance and protection which her childlike nature demands, and she no longer has occasion to cry; but her life is devoid of romantic intensity and she is mildly discontent.

Some critics feel that there are serious flaws in Thackeray's representation of Amelia, that he has ascribed to her qualities which we cannot believe in because we never see them in action.[8] It is true that part of our picture of Amelia is derived from description rather than from the dramatized portions of the novel but it is quite possible for description to be an effective means of characterization. Our psychological analysis has shown that Thackeray's descriptions of Amelia are often very subtle and that they add many important details to his portrait. What is objectionable is vague description, a reliance upon general epithets. When Thackeray describes Amelia as "amiable," "tender-

hearted," "gently constituted," "a simple yielding faithful creature," and a "pious simple heart," we do not know in any specific
way what qualities he is ascribing to her. Such descriptions are
on the borderline between representation and interpretation;
they are intended not only to portray Amelia, but also to present
her in a favorable light. As representation they are ineffective; as
rhetoric they leave us sceptical.

The chief problem in Thackeray's presentation of Amelia is not
that he leaves her character unrealized or that he praises her for
virtues which she does not have, but that he poeticizes her weaknesses and has such a predilection for self-effacing qualities that
he sees many of the objections to Amelia as "in truth prodi-
giously complimentary to the young lady whom they concern"
(Ch. 12). Thackeray sees clearly enough that Amelia is infantile,
has a "soft and foolish disposition" (Ch. 65), is a "simpleton" and
a "parasite." His aggressive side despises her for these qualities;
but for the most part he finds them endearing or sees them as a
result of the martyrdom imposed by a society of "Turks" upon
good women: "Tender slaves that they are, they must needs be
hypocrites and weak" (Ch. 56). Like Dobbin, the implied author
is extremely vulnerable to Amelia's kind of woman; he, too, hovers about her, full of admiration, pity, and paternal solicitude.
He, too, feels that "ever since her womanhood almost" she has
"been persecuted and undervalued" (Ch. 50). In one passage he
offers her as a model of true womanhood: "He [Georgy] had
been brought up by a kind, weak, and tender woman . . . whose
heart was so pure and whose bearing was so meek and humble,
that she could not but needs be a true lady" (Ch. 56).

Amelia's story has a different meaning, of course, for each
component of the implied author's personality. In the novel's
rhetoric the self-effacing view of her predominates. From this
point of view, Amelia's is the pathetic story of a "poor simple
lady, tender and weak" (Ch. 50) who is a "harmless lost wanderer
in the great struggling crowds of Vanity Fair" (Ch. 26). She is a

saintly fool whose lack of worldliness exposes her to exploitation
and contempt, but who is in reality far superior to those who use
and abuse her. In the end her sufferings are relieved as she finds
a haven in the arms of a Christian gentleman who has been one
of the few people to appreciate her good qualities. If twentieth
century readers cannot respond to Amelia's story as the rhetoric
intends, this is not simply because our tastes in women have
changed. It is also because Thackeray himself, in his mimetic
portrait of Amelia as a person, has given us good reason to be
sceptical of his interpretations.

IX

Like Amelia, William Dobbin is idealized by the implied author. If she is the true lady, he is the true gentlemen: ". . . his
thoughts were just, . . . his life was honest and pure, and his heart
warm and humble" (Ch. 62). Thackeray is aware of some of his
weaknesses, but he finds them, like Amelia's, to be amiable. If we
see Dobbin exclusively in terms of the novel's rhetoric, we find
him to be a simple character, almost too good to be true, whose
story is rather dull, and about whom there is little of interest to
say. If we approach him as a mimetic portrait and attempt to
understand him psychologically, we find him to be the most fascinating and complex character in the book.

Dobbin suffers, above all, from low self-esteem. When, under
the influence of George's ridicule, Amelia makes "light" of him,
he "very humbly" acquiesces in her opinion (Ch. 25). Many years
later, when he finally declares his love, he finds Amelia not ungrateful, but "indifferent": " 'I have nothing to make a woman to
be otherwise' " (Ch. 59). Dobbin's entire life-style is governed by
his feeling of worthlessness, a feeling which is quite understandable in the light of his unhappy childhood.

In school, Dobbin is subject to constant humiliation. He has a
good intelligence but is so demoralized that he cannot apply

himself to his studies. As a result, he is "compelled to remain among the very last of Dr. Swishtail's scholars," and is " 'taken down' continually by little fellows with pink faces and pinafores" when he marches up "with the lower form, a giant amongst them, with his downcast stupefied look . . . and his tight corduroys" (Ch. 5). He is at the bottom of the school also in terms of social and economic status. His father is a grocer who pays for his son's schooling "in goods, not money." When his father's cart is discovered at the Doctor's door, the jokes are "frightful and merciless against him": " 'If a pound of mutton-candles cost seven-pence-halfpenny, how much must Dobbin cost?' " Dobbin has no way of resisting the boys' equation of himself with his father's unprestigious merchandise.

Dobbin's low parentage, his incompetence, his clumsiness, his lisp, and his lack of self-respect and aggressiveness all combine to make him a constant target of contempt and derision:

> High and low, all made fun of him. They sewed up those corduroys, tight as they were. They cut his bed-strings. They upset buckets and benches, so that he might break his shins over them, which he never failed to do. They sent him parcels, which, when opened, were found to contain the paternal soap and candles. There was no little fellow but had his jeer and joke at Dobbin; and he bore everything quite patiently, and was entirely dumb and miserable. (Ch. 5)

Dobbin, no less than Amelia, seems to have been made by nature for a victim.

One of Dobbin's responses to this treatment is, understandably, to move away from his fellows. After the discovery of his father's cart, "Mr. William Dobbin retreated to a remote out-house in the playground, where he passed a half-holiday in the bitterest sadness and woe." Sometimes, by withdrawing into a world of books and fantasies, he manages to escape his pain. Just before he witnesses the brutal treatment of George by Cuff, he is "lying under a tree in the play-ground, spelling over a favourite copy of the Arabian nights which he had—apart from the rest of the school, who were pursuing their various sports—quite lonely, and almost happy." Compliance, however, rather than withdrawal, becomes Dobbin's chief defense.

There can be no doubt that the harsh treatment to which he is subjected engenders intense rage in Dobbin, and it is striking that he never fights back or stands up for himself. There are several possible reasons for this. He did not receive the kind of support at home which would have counterbalanced the derision of the boys and given him a sense of his own dignity: his father "respected him for the first time" when he won a French prize-book at the age of twelve or thirteen. It is likely that, with his already damaged self-esteem, he accepts the verdict implied by the boys' abuse and does not regard himself as worth fighting for. There may be a masochistic element in Dobbin's behavior. He seems to fall readily into his role and to cooperate with his tormentors. It appears that he has already developed a self-effacing defense system and that he clings to his lowness and has strong taboos against self-assertion.

Dobbin *is* able to be aggressive, but not on his own behalf. He defies Cuff when the latter shows disrespect for his mother ("old Mother Figs"), he fights Cuff in defense of little George Osborne, he frightens away the crowd at Vauxhall with his fierceness, he defends Amelia against George, his sisters, Mr. Sedley, and Mr. Osborne, and he very energetically promotes the marriage of Amelia and George. As Thackeray observes, Dobbin is "most active in anybody's concerns but his own" (Ch. 59):

> . . . it is certain that our friend William Dobbin, who was personally of so complying a disposition that if his parents had pressed him much, it is probable he would have stepped down into the kitchen and married the cook, and who, to further his own interests, would

have found the most insuperable difficulty in walking across the street, found himself as busy and eager in the conduct of George Osborne's affairs, as the most selfish tactician could be in the pursuit of his own. (Ch. 23)

Thackeray attributes the "timid" and "diffident" Dobbin's "active and resolute" pursuit of other people's interests to "the secret mesmerism which friendship possesses" (Ch. 23). It is more accurate to see it as an aspect of his "complying . . . disposition." As Horney observes, the basically compliant person scorns selfishness, and "to him selfishness includes doing anything that is just for himself" (NHG, 218). He "may display considerable energy and skill in attaining something for others . . . ; but he is tied hand and foot when it comes to doing the same thing for himself" (NHG, 219). According to "his inner dictates, [he] should be the ultimate of helpfulness, generosity, considerateness, understanding, sympathy, love, and sacrifice" (NHG, 220).

Dobbin's aggressiveness on behalf of others serves not only to fulfill his shoulds, but also to release some of his pent-up hostility. Most of his anger is turned upon himself, re-enforcing his sense of worthlessness. Occasionally, however, he is able to discharge his rage in a way that is acceptable to his compliant value system, just as the implied author can be aggressive in a good cause. In the Vauxhall episode, Dobbin is treated most cavalierly by the rest of the party: he carries the shawls, pays at the door, and then is left to visit the hermit while the rest are having dinner. Dobbin feels no resentment and makes no attempt to assert his claims; being "very little addicted to selfish calculation," he takes satisfaction in the enjoyment of his friend and accepts the fact that he would "only be *de trop*" (Ch. 6). When the drunken Jos brings embarrassment on the party, Dobbin comes to the rescue: " 'Be off, you fools!' said this gentleman—shouldering off a great number of the crowd, who vanished presently before his cocked-hat and fierce appearance—and he entered the box in a most agitated state." Dobbin's fierceness and agitation indicate the intensity of his angry feelings, some of which were, no doubt, generated that very evening.

The most notable instance of Dobbin's aggressiveness is, of course, his fight with Cuff. Cuff is "the unquestioned king of the school" and represents to Dobbin all that has oppressed him. Thackeray lists among Dobbin's possible motives "a hankering feeling of revenge"; perhaps he "longed to measure himself against that splendid bully and tyrant, who had all the glory, pride, pomp, circumstance, banners flying, drums beating, guards saluting, in the place" (Ch. 5). This confrontation belongs to the worm turning pattern, of course, in which a hankering for revenge is justified by a long course of oppression and abuse. Even so, Dobbin would never have fought Cuff directly on his own behalf. He is moved to intervene by the sight of "a big boy beating a little one without cause," and he enters the fray as the champion of another underdog, not himself.

Dobbin seems terribly overmatched; he is the clumsiest and most despised boy challenging the most accomplished and re-spected. He is David to Cuff's Goliath. His secret weapon is the sheer energy of his pent-up hostility. After he loses the first three rounds, his limbs are "in a quiver" and his nostrils are "breathing rage." In the fourth round he begins to attack, and by the twelfth Cuff has "lost all presence of mind and power of attack or de-fence." Dobbin, on the contrary, is "as calm as a quaker. His face being quite pale, his eyes shining open, and a great cut on his under lip bleeding profusely, gave this young fellow a fierce and ghastly air, which perhaps struck terror into many spectators." It is obvious that Thackeray takes great pleasure in Dobbin's ferocity and in his vindictive triumph, even if Dobbin himself does not.

Dobbin's victory radically alters his circumstances at school. He gains the respect of the boys, it is "voted low to sneer at

Dobbin about his accident of birth," and "Old Figs" becomes "a name of kindness and endearment" (Ch. 5). Dobbin's spirit rises, he makes "wonderful advances in scholastic learning," and his father respects him for the first time. Dobbin's reaction to all this is extremely interesting. He is "much too modest a young fellow" to take credit "for this happy change in all his circumstances." He chooses,

> from some perverseness, to attribute his good fortune to the sole agency and benevolence of little George Osborne, to whom henceforth he vowed such a love and affection as is only felt by children—such an affection as we read in the charming fairy-book uncouth Orson has for splendid young Valentine his conqueror. He flung himself down at little Osborne's feet, and loved him. Even before they were acquainted, he had admired Osborne in secret. Now he was his valet, his dog, his man Friday. He believed Osborne to be the possessor of every perfection, to be the handsomest, the bravest, the most active, the cleverest, the most generous of created boys.

All this is even more amazing when we realize that George is five years younger than Dobbin—seven or eight to Dobbin's twelve or thirteen.

Thackeray is probably being ironic when he speaks of Dobbin's "perverseness"—he really admires his humility—but he may have some sense, even so, of the abnormality of Dobbin's behavior. In attributing his "good fortune to the sole agency and benevolence of little George Osborne," Dobbin is, of course, altering reality to make it acceptable to his compliant defense system. As Horney observes, there is in the self-effacing person an "anxious shunning of pride, triumph, or superiority" (NHG, 216). He must "deny—to himself—his active share in his doings. Even if he has made a place for himself in the world, he does not feel that he has done it" (NHG, 166). By reversing the relationship between himself and George, Dobbin makes his success come about not through his own aggressiveness, which frightens him, but through the self-effacing virtues of admiration, affection, and devotion. He manages, even in his triumph, to remain passive and subservient, to get lower than the boy he has rescued. Dobbin's exaltation of George is partly for this purpose; he cannot tolerate the superior position.

It is not only his need to be on the bottom, however, which leads Dobbin to idealize George and to become "his valet, his dog, his man Friday." Even as a young boy George clearly displays expansive attitudes and seems destined for conquest. It is George, we must remember, who espied the cart of Dobbin & Rudge and who brought "down the storm" upon poor William. Not only does Dobbin bear no malice; but, we are told, he admires "Osborne in secret" long before the fight with Cuff brings them together. It seems likely that George's abusive act is a source of his attractiveness to Dobbin. Horney observes that a relationship of morbid dependency is often initiated by insulting behavior on the part of the aggressive person. The compliant person "craves to surrender himself body and soul, but can do so only if his pride is bent or broken. . . . The initial offense is . . . intriguing because . . . it opens the possibility for self-riddance and self-surrender" (NHG, 246). His conquest of Cuff heightens Dobbin's need for self-surrender. Surrendering himself to George becomes a way of life for Dobbin, one which, in his mind, protects him against isolation and the contempt of his fellows.

Dobbin, like Amelia, seeks to participate in the mastery of life vicariously and to gain glory through identification with George and service to him. George is later described as a "regular Don Giovanni" (Ch. 13), a kind of imitation Byron: he has "an air at once swaggering and melancholy, languid and fierce" and looks like a man who has "passions, secrets, and private harrowing griefs and adventures." He tramples "over all the young bucks of his father's circle" and is "the hero among those third-rate men" (Ch. 21). Dobbin's manners and values are the opposite of George's; yet he "fanatically" admires him (Ch. 21) and takes him to be "an Admirable Crichton" (Ch. 13). Years later he tells old Osborne that he has never seen George's "equal for pluck and daring, and all the qualities of a soldier": " 'I . . . was flattered beyond measure by his preference for me; and was more pleased to be seen in his company than in that of the Commander-in-Chief" (Ch. 61). It is difficult to reconcile Dobbin's worship of so shallow a person with Thackeray's celebration of him as the true gentleman. His behavior is quite consistent, however, with his character structure.

Just as it was necessary to examine Amelia's attitudes toward Dobbin in the context of her relationship with George, so we must see Dobbin's devotion to Amelia as in part determined by *his* relationship with their mutual hero. It is not difficult to understand Dobbin's admiration of Amelia. Amelia is what the compliant side of Dobbin (and of Thackeray) feels that a person—and especially a woman—ought to be; and, as such, she is a fitting object of worship. Dobbin's love for Amelia begins, however, before he has had an opportunity to observe her character. " 'I think I loved you,' " he tells her, " 'from the first minute that I saw you, when George brought me to your house, to show me the Amelia whom he was engaged to' " (Ch. 59). He may have sensed immediately what kind of a woman Amelia was; but it is the fact that she belonged to George, more than her appearance or personality, which accounts for his love at first sight.

It serves Dobbin's psychological needs to fall in love with and then to center his life upon a woman who belongs to someone else. His solution places the meaning of life in the love relation and demands that he be noble, giving, self-sacrificing; but he has such strong taboos against self-interest and is so convinced of his unlovableness that he cannot court a woman for himself. He tells George that he is "not a marrying man" (Ch. 25). Amelia is a safe woman for him to love; in serving her, he cannot possibly be serving himself; and, since he makes no claims, he cannot be rejected. The frustration which he is bound to experience in such a relationship fits in with his sense of worthlessness and satisfies his need for self-punishment. At the same time, it permits him the glory of heroic devotion and self-sacrifice. Dobbin's taboos prevent him from having a life of his own; but he can lead an intense vicarious existence by living for, in, and through others. By loving Amelia, he serves and honors George; through George, he engages in a love relation with Amelia. If he is possessed by George, and George possesses Amelia, then he, too, in a sense, possesses Amelia. One of his reasons for promoting the marriage may be that it is only by uniting her to George that he can continue to see Amelia and to participate in her life. Another is that playing a providential role gives him the feeling that his own existence is worth something. When Amelia and George are reunited, he is "content, so that he [sees] her happy; and thankful to have been the means of making her so" (Ch. 20).

Dobbin's chief motive for promoting the marriage is, of course, his conviction that if Amelia is "balked of her husband" she will "die of the disappointment" (Ch. 20). With the possible exception of the implied author, there is no one on whom Amelia's strategies work as effectively as they do on Dobbin. Amelia's suffering has such a powerful effect upon Dobbin because it is part of his character structure to feel responsible for whatever goes wrong and to have a compulsive need to set things straight.

One of the shoulds of the compliant person is that "he assume full responsibility" for his associates: "He should be able to solve everyone's problem to everyone's instant satisfaction. This implies that *anything* that goes wrong is his fault. . . . such a person is forced to be the helpless victim who must feel guilty and set everything right" (NHG, 119). These feelings arise largely as a defense against the anger which such a person is at first afraid and is later forbidden to feel. He has been abused, but the expression of anger threatens both his safety and his idealized image; so he directs his rage at himself and makes himself responsible for the abuse. This defense against anger, combined with his taboo against being critical or feeling superior, eventually leads him to feel guilty in the presence of any injustice, conflict, or suffering.

Thackeray does not depict many of the intra-psychic processes just described, and he certainly does not account for Dobbin's responses in this way. But the foregoing analysis is highly congruent with Dobbin's early experiences and with what we are given of his character structure; and it is the only way in which I can account for a number of passages in which Dobbin reacts with irrational guilt to the spectacle of suffering or defeat. When, before he induced George to return, Dobbin saw Amelia's "ghastly" appearance and look of "despair," "inexpressible grief, pity, and terror pursued him, and he came away as if he was a criminal after seeing her" (Ch. 18). His grief, pity, and terror are more or less appropriate responses—though he experiences them in a heightened way—but his feeling of criminality can only be understood in terms of his neurosis. Later, before the battle of Waterloo, Dobbin feels "a guilty shock" as he looks at Amelia's face of despair; and "the remembrance of it haunted him afterwards like a crime" (Ch. 30). Such reactions are not confined to Amelia. Dobbin feels guilty when he announces the marriage to Mr. Osborne (Ch. 24), and he has a particularly strong response to the sight of the fallen Mr. Sedley: "A feeling of shame and remorse took possession of William Dobbin as the broken old man so received and addressed him, as if he himself had been somehow guilty of the misfortunes which had brought Sedley so low" (Ch. 20). Dobbin's feelings are partly a reaction to Sedley's respectful behavior, which triggers his need to humble himself, to get lower than the ruined man.

After George's death, Amelia is more miserable and more vulnerable than ever, and it becomes the chief object of Dobbin's life to watch over her. Though he eventually professes his love and seeks a return, for a long time he seems content to have things remain as they are, with Amelia devoted to George, and Dobbin the loyal servant of both. Dobbin participates in Amelia's ro-

mance of heroic fidelity and self-sacrifice; her constancy only
exalts her in his eyes. After Mr. Osborne broke the engagement,
when his sisters teased him about the possibility of his marrying
Amelia, Dobbin heatedly rejected the idea: " 'I marry her!' Dobbin said, blushing very much and talking quick. 'If you are so
ready, young ladies, to chop and change, do you suppose that
she is?' " (Ch. 18) Years later, after his return from India, Dobbin
still cannot wish Amelia to be less faithful: " 'Ought I to be
. . . hurt that such a heart as Amelia's can love only once and
forever?' " (Ch. 58) When Amelia tells him explicitly that she is
George's " 'now as when you first saw me,' " Dobbin replies, " 'I
will not change, dear Amelia. . . . I ask for no more than your love.
I think I would not have it otherwise' " (Ch. 59).

An unconsummated relationship with Amelia suits Dobbin for
a number of reasons, many of which we have already discussed.
Just as Amelia needs a hero in whose identity to submerge her
own, so Dobbin can only love a heroine, a woman whom he feels
to be above him. The fact that Amelia continues to belong to
George, his hero, and that she displays an exemplary fidelity
serves to raise her above him and to keep his "love . . . as fresh,
as a man's recollections of boyhood are" (Ch. 43). Her exploitation, domination, and indifference help to keep him comfortably
subordinated to her, however much he plays the role of protector.

If they were to marry, not only would Amelia be a less exalted
being, but Dobbin would lose some of his own glory. For Dobbin,
too, is acting out a romance of self-sacrifice and fidelity. It is in
this light only that we can understand the intensity of his despair
when Amelia congratulates him on his supposed engagement to
Glorvina O'Dowd:

> "O Amelia, Amelia," he thought, "you to whom I have been so
> faithful—you reproach me! . . . And you reward me after years of
> devotion by giving me your blessings upon my marriage, forsooth,

> with this flaunting Irish girl!" Sick and sorry felt poor William:
> more than ever wretched and lonely. He would like to have done
> with life and its vanity altogether—so bootless and unsatisfactory
> the struggle, so cheerless and dreary the prospect seemed to him.
> . . . Amelia's letter had fallen as a blank upon him. No fidelity, no
> constant truth and passion, could move her into warmth. She
> would not see that he loved her. (Ch. 43)

Dobbin is so upset because Amelia seems blind to his nobility. He
exalts her devotion to George, which he sees as heroic, romantic,
beautiful. He needs his similar devotion to herself to be likewise
appreciated. Apart from his shoulds, Amelia is his chief audience.
She need not marry him, but she must recognize his moral grandeur if life is to have any meaning for him. Her letter indicates
that she sees him as the kind of being who would marry a Glorvina O'Dowd, and not as a romantic hero. Amelia does not reproach him in her letter; Dobbin is externalizing the self-
reproach he would feel if he were to be what Amelia evidently
takes him for.

Dobbin does not need to possess Amelia in marriage, but he
does want her to love him. When he returns to England, he is
content "to look and long" if Amelia will only show signs of
affection and allow him to stay near her. I do not mean to suggest
that Dobbin has no wish at all to marry Amelia; there is evidence
that he resents as well as admires her constancy to George and
that he cherishes a secret hope that Amelia will someday be his.
But his feelings are very ambivalent; he has strong motives for
maintaining the status quo; and it is quite possible that but for
the crisis in Pumpernickel the relationship would never have
been consummated.

The crisis is precipitated by Dobbin's anger at Amelia's decision to befriend Becky and by Amelia's use of the occasion to
carry out her determination to be free. Dobbin is "quite angry"
when Amelia ignores his warnings against Becky because this
violates the rules of their game, constitutes a rejection of his

claims, and jeopardizes his entire investment. He has professed himself to be content with a minimum of reciprocation, but it is evident that he has come to feel increasingly over-extended and to have a growing resentment of the one-sidedness of the relationship. Amelia's cavalier rejection of his established rights and authority cannot help but provoke his anger. Her turning upon him when he alludes to Becky's flirtation with George and her determination never to forgive him for his insult to George's memory produce reactions of despair and indignation. In a personality like Dobbin's there is a connection between these two responses. The compliant person normally represses all resentment; "only when he feels driven to despair," says Horney, "will the locked gates break open and a flood of violent accusations rush out" (NHG, 232). Dobbin perceives that his "fair palace of hope" has collapsed, is indignant that a few words "uttered in a hurried moment, are to weigh against a whole life's devotion," and tells Amelia that she is "not worthy of the love" which he has lavished upon her (Ch. 66). Though he tells Amelia that he finds no fault with her, his remarks constitute a devastating indictment —one which is not entirely fair in view of his complicity in her behavior.

After this scene, Dobbin's feelings toward Amelia change; he loves her no more "as he had loved her" (Ch. 67). Instead of seeing Amelia as a romantic heroine, he now sees her as unworthy of his noble devotion, as a "little heedless tyrant" who has destroyed his love. Having felt and expressed his resentment, he must justify it by continuing to accuse Amelia. Having prided himself on his constancy and having left, he must defend himself against self-hate by holding Amelia responsible for the destruction of his love. His own participation in their romantic game is excused as " 'a fond mistake. Isn't the whole course of life made up of such?' " Now that he has "declared his . . . superiority" (Ch. 66), Amelia has lost her magic for him; she can no longer satisfy his neurotic need for glory through self-surrender to an exalted being.

When Amelia declares her love, Dobbin returns. He "has got the prize he has been trying for all his life" (Ch. 67), but it no longer has much value to him. When the subordinate partner in a relationship of morbid dependency finally succeeds in gaining love, says Horney, "he does not reap the benefits. His need for triumph is fulfilled and dwindles, his pride has its due but he is no longer interested. He may be grateful, appreciative for love given, but he feels it is now too late. Actually he cannot love with his pride satisfied" (NHG, 254; I have changed the gender of the pronouns). Dobbin is "kind and gentle," and he never thinks of "a want" of Amelia's that he does "not try to gratify"; but it is evident that he is not much interested in the relationship. When he must go to Brussels to attend to Jos, he leaves home "with reluctance"; for he is "deeply immersed in his 'History of the Punjaub' . . . and much alarmed about his little daughter, whom he idolizes," and who is "just recovering from the chicken-pox." There is no mention whatever of a reluctance to leave Amelia.

X

What are the implications of the mode of analysis employed here for our judgment of *Vanity Fair*? I shall try to suggest some of the ways in which my psychological approach to the novel is (and is not) related to evaluation.

The Horneyan interpretation of *Vanity Fair* confirms our feeling that the novel lacks aesthetic coherence, but it adds nothing to the judgment that we reached on the basis of purely thematic analysis. It may affect our experience of the novel by making it more intelligible, and hence more enjoyable, but it does not affect the quality of the work itself. When it is combined with a study of culture, the Horneyan approach may help us to understand *Vanity Fair's* popular success by revealing the psychological basis of its appeal to readers of Thackeray's day and of our own; but it is difficult to say how much of this understanding would be relevant to our estimate of the novel as art.[9]

At an earlier stage of my work on Thackeray I felt the illuminative value of *Vanity Fair* to be seriously impaired because the novel provides no healthy perspective in terms of which the characters' solutions can be seen for what they are. I have moved away from this position, but I should like to present the arguments for it in order to clarify the critical problems involved.

Psychological analysis reveals *Vanity Fair's* vision of human values, human nature, and the human condition to be defective. All of the value systems and solutions in the novel are neurotic. The novel's conclusions about human nature are drawn exclusively from neurotic characters. Since many people are more or less neurotic, these conclusions have wide applicability, but they by no means do justice to the potentialities of the human species. The novel is highly successful in portraying the characters and fates of individual men, but it fails in its effort to depict the nature and condition of Man. Thackeray's compliant value system led him to place an excessive importance upon love; and since his characters are incapable of loving in a healthy way, his picture of the human situation is excessively dark. Failures and frustrations are an inescapable part of man's fate, but Thackeray often presents as fundamental characteristics of the human lot problems which are essentially social or neurotic.

In Karen Horney's *Neurosis and Human Growth* there is a penetrating discussion of the relation between art and neurosis which includes a value theory similar to that governing the foregoing criticism of *Vanity Fair*. Dreams resemble artistic creations, says Horney, and art may resemble dreams. In dreams "our unconscious imagination can create solutions for an inner conflict that is disquieting us for the time being," and art, too, is a search for solutions. The solutions arrived at in dreams and in art "may be constructive or neurotic ones, with a great range of possibilities in between." The quality of the solution it embodies has great relevance, Horney feels, "for the value of an artistic creation":

> We could say that, even if an artist presents only his particular neurotic solution well, he may still find a powerful resonance because there will be many others tending toward the same solution. But I wonder if the general validity of, for instance, what the paintings of Dali or the novels of Sartre have to say is not thereby —despite superb artistic facility and astute psychological understanding—diminished? To avoid misunderstandings: I do not mean that a play or a novel should not present neurotic problems. On the contrary, at a time when most people suffer from them, artistic presentation can help many to wake up to their existence and significance and to clarify them in their minds. . . . A work of art leaves us confused if we do not sense where the author stands, or if he presents or advocates a neurotic solution as the only one. (pp. 330–331)[10]

Presumably, a work of art can help people wake up to the existence of their problems and to clarify them in their minds only if there is within the work a moral norm, both consistent and healthy, which identifies neurotic solutions as destructive and suggests constructive alternatives.

There is a similar reasoning behind Wayne Booth's objection, in *The Rhetoric of Fiction,* to the absence of reliable norms in modern fiction. Fearful that the reader may be led astray by long inside views of vicious characters, Booth argues that the "author has an obligation to write well in the sense of making his moral orderings clear" (p. 386). As we have seen, Booth demands not only that the author's moral position be clear, but also that it be valid: "The author himself must achieve a kind of objectivity far more difficult and far more profound than the 'objectivity' of surface hailed in many discussions of technique. He must first plumb to universal values about which his readers can really care" (p. 395).

I believe my earlier conclusion that *Vanity Fair* offers neither fundamental insights into human nature and the human condition nor healthy values to be essentially correct. What I now question is my judgment that because of this deficiency the illuminative value of the novel is seriously impaired. I doubt very much not only that fiction often has the consequences for good and ill that Horney and Booth ascribe to it, but also that the communication of healthy norms and a balanced view of life is the kind of illumination that specially belongs to fiction. For this kind of illumination I am inclined to go to psychologists like Horney and Maslow, who are likely to know more about what is healthy and what is sick than do literary artists. When a novelist comments through his work on the human scene, as does Thackeray, we are tempted to judge him in terms of the adequacy of his thought and the soundness of his values. But Thackeray's fiction has a value and a validity that are in no way affected by his philosophic failures and his neurotic attitudes; and his ability to illuminate our world in a specifically artistic way is likely to escape us if we judge him primarily in terms of what he has to say thematically.

Compared to some novelists, Thackeray shows us very little of his characters' inner processes. Even so, one of the great achievements of *Vanity Fair* is its dramatization of complex patterns of feeling, behavior, and interaction. There is no awareness in the novel itself that its characters do not embody the full potentialities of human nature, but its fictional rendering of neurotic solutions and their inadequacy is brilliant. Becky, Amelia, and Dobbin are not rendered as fully as Julien Sorel, Maggie Tulliver, or the underground man; but, as psychological analysis has shown, they are complex characters who are portrayed with considerable subtlety.

The great illuminative power of realistic fiction, it seems to me, is not that it plumbs to universal values, but rather that it helps us to grasp in their concreteness and inner reality phenomena

that philosophy and social science treat objectively and categorically. Horney and Thackeray come at the same range of experience, but from quite different directions, and each gives us a
possession of the experience that cannot come from the other.
The psychologist may be able to understand Thackeray's characters in ways that Thackeray cannot; yet Thackeray understands
his characters perfectly on an intuitive level, and he gives us
artistic formulations of certain patterns of experience that can
never be replaced by abstract analysis.

The artist often gets into trouble, as Thackeray does, when he
tries to interpret the experience that it is his great gift to grasp
intuitively and to present mimetically. There is no reason why the
artist should be wise or have healthy values just because he is an
artist. To ask the novelist to provide universal values or insights
into the essential nature and condition of man is to ask him to go
beyond his gift. Unlike Wayne Booth, I do not regret the absence
of moral norms in modern fiction, for I no longer ask the novelist
to be an ethical guide, and I have no reason to trust his values
any more than I trust those of his characters.

The trouble with *Vanity Fair* is not that it contains no healthy
solutions; it is that the narrator's attitudes are not, as in *Henry
Esmond,* made part of the representation. The narrator of *Esmond*
has a psychic structure similar to that of the implied author of
Vanity Fair; but, because he is the central character, the novel
does not suffer aesthetically from his inner conflicts. Esmond's
inconsistencies are not necessarily those of the novel; like the
underground man's, they belong to the author's portrayal of
character. As Wayne Booth observes, the kind of first person
narration that we find in *Henry Esmond* or *Notes from Underground*
has the effect of eliminating or vastly reducing the element of
interpretation. Hence, it also eliminates or vastly reduces the
disparity between representation and interpretation which is so
common a product of omniscient narration. I at one time thought
that *Vanity Fair* is flawed because an inwardly divided author is

bound to produce an inorganic novel. I now believe that the problems of such novels as *Vanity Fair, The Red and the Black,* and *The Mill on the Floss,* are not so much psychological as technical.

We must not forget, however, that a novel's weaknesses and strengths are often complementary and that it may be impossible to realize all of the values of fiction simultaneously. *Henry Esmond* is a more integrated but less powerful novel. Omniscient narration, in *Vanity Fair,* results in thematic confusion and a troubling disparity between representation and interpretation. But no other technique could have produced the same brilliance in social satire and comedy.

Chapter IV

The Transformation of
Julien Sorel

The Red and the Black is a novel of both social and psychological realism. It contains brilliant mimetic treatments of certain aspects of post-Napoleonic France and of its protagonist, Julien Sorel. Julien is one of the most fully drawn characters in literature. Complex as Thackeray's characters are, they seem incompletely conceived, especially in their inner lives, when compared with Stendhal's hero.

In addition to its mimetic component, *The Red and the Black* has a strong interpretive element. It is a novel of education in which the protagonist errs, learns from his mistakes, but is destroyed by the consequences of his errors. Though in terms of his worldly fortunes he suffers a crushing defeat, he rises, through his fall, to a position of moral grandeur. He errs not because he is essentially bad, but because he is young and is ill-used; his mistakes are largely the fault of the society which punishes him for them. He dies, moreover, not only because he has sinned, but also because he has learned. The educated Julien can no more find a viable life for himself than could the ambitious peasant. Only by dying can he preserve his new values and his new happiness.

The novel's aesthetic pattern and its thematic structure coincide nicely. There is less harmony, however, between theme and form and the novel's mimetic component. When we understand Julien as a person, what Julien and his creator conceive as growth appears to be a shift from a failed neurotic solution to one which is well suited to his new situation. There is no doubt that Julien dies happy. There is considerable doubt, however, that he dies educated. The following pages will explore this disparity between representation and interpretation by examining first Stendhal's thematic handling and then his mimetic portrait of Julien.

In the first part of the novel Julien has happiness available to him in a life of simplicity, natural beauty, and the love of a spontaneous woman; but he is distracted by his "black ambition," the frustration of which leads to his attack on Madame de Rênal. His crime and the imminence of death lead him to see "everything in a fresh light."[1] His ambition fades. He becomes "a more honorable man at the approach of death than he had been during his life" and asks himself if he is "wicked," a question which "would have troubled him little when he was ambitious" (Ch. 69). He lives "from day to day" (Ch. 75) instead of in dreams of future glory. He never gives "a thought to his Parisian successes," which bore him, but finds a "strange happiness" when he abandons "himself entirely to the memory of the happy days which he had spent in the past at Verrières or at Vergy" (Ch. 69). Julien feels that he has "learned the art of enjoying life" at last (Ch. 70). The man who has been a consummate hypocrite and dissembler dies "simply, decorously, and without affectation" (Ch. 75).

This view of Julien's story is drawn largely from Julien's own interpretation, but there is considerable evidence that it is Stendhal's interpretation as well. The epigraphs to Chapters 65 and 70—"*Mon Dieu, donnez-moi la médiocrité!*" and "It is because I was foolish then that I am now wise"—precede Julien's utterance of similar sentiments and indicate the author's concurrence. Before Julien's transformation there is a distance between author and character and a readily discernible difference in their perspectives; afterward Julien comes to see himself much as Stendhal had seen him earlier and the distance between them virtually disappears. Finally, Julien's change puts him in harmony with the value system which has governed the novel's rhetoric throughout and gives it its most explicit expression.

In the first two chapters of the novel, Stendhal places great emphasis upon the natural beauty of Verrières and its surroundings, to which the inhabitants are insensitive, regarding the beauty only as a tourist attraction which will yield a return. Julien is equally incapable of a free aesthetic response. His head is full, not of "small financial interests," but of grand ambitions and hankerings for revenge. These make him a more poetic figure than the Rênals and Valenods, but they distract him no less from an appreciation of his natural surroundings. There is clearly a distance here between Julien's perspective and that of the author. The change in Julien is manifest in his retrospective cherishing of his past experiences of beauty, in his last thoughts, and in his choice of a final resting place.

Julien's last rites, arranged by Mathilde, seem quite out of keeping with his final values. The "savage grot" is "adorned with marbles sculptured at great cost, in Italy" (Ch. 75). We have here the culmination of a thematic contrast which has run through the novel—namely, the contrast between the natural and the artificial. Associated with artificiality, in the novel's thematic pattern, are vanity, hypocrisy, role playing, conformity, fear of ridicule, restraint of thought and feeling, boredom, ugliness, love as conquest, and the society of the day. Associated with naturalness are unpretentiousness, transparency, spontaneity, originality, free play of thought and feeling, happiness, appreciation of beauty, love as passion, and the simple, private life. Julien embraces first the one and then the other set of values, though he has early glimpses of the joys of the natural life and never wholly escapes from the influence of society. The author all along is committed to the values associated with naturalness. Through the conversation between Falcoz and Saint-Giraud and through Julien's fate, he raises a doubt, however, as to whether these values are realizable anywhere in post-Napoleonic France.

Madame de Rênal and Mathilde are the prime exemplars of naturalness and of artificiality, respectively. Julien himself is frequently conscious of the contrast between the two women. He finds "nothing artless, simple, tender" in Mathilde's attitude. Hers is a "love born in the brain" (Ch. 49). Stendhal seems to be wholly in love with Madame de Rênal. His attitude toward Mathilde is more complicated. She, like the early Julien, is meant to contrast unfavorably with Madame de Rênal; but, like Julien, she has a pride, a daring, and an intelligence which set her apart from the mediocre world and endear her to the author. With all of her absurdities, she is a woman of spirit. Her failings are those of an overcivilized but superior being; unlike Julien, she does not outgrow them.

Julien finds true bliss with Madame de Rênal only when he allows himself to be spontaneous. He gains control over Mathilde by means of the ludicrous stratagems provided by Prince Korosoff, and he recognizes that he can retain her love only by the most rigid self-control. The author treats much of this relationship as a comic spectacle. There is a mechanical, puppet-like quality in the absurd gyrations of these lovers.

Madame de Rênal's letter to the Marquis de La Mole accuses Julien of seducing the most influential woman of a house in order "to make a position for himself and to become somebody" (Ch. 65). This is close to the truth. Julien seduces Madame de Rênal in order to triumph over the Mayor and all that he represents, but in time his pride is assuaged and he comes to love his mistress for herself. In his relation with Mathilde, love and ambition are inseparable. When ambition dies in his heart, so does his love for Mathilde. His passion for Madame de Rênal, on the other hand, is reawakened and purified. There is, for Stendhal, no more vivid sign of Julien's maturation than his loss of interest in Mathilde, with her concern for "a public" (Ch. 69), and his discovery of true happiness in the love of Madame de Rênal.

Stendhal's interpretations of Julien, though often perceptive, sometimes leave us confused or sceptical. Stendhal has contradictory attitudes toward such values as pride, ambition, heroism, and glory. Again and again characteristics which both the narrator's commentary and the education pattern of the novel clearly identify as defects are the very things which mark Julien as a superior being and win him the author's interest and affection. The ambivalence of Stendhal's feelings toward the untransformed Julien (and towards Mathilde) cannot help but blur the novel's thematic pattern.

From the novel's point of view, Julien learns how to live by confronting death. The imminence of death enables him to sort out the things that really matter from the false values imposed upon him by the accident of his birth and the corruptness of society. His is a fortunate fall; it costs him his life, but it enables him to find happiness.

If Julien had truly learned the art of enjoying life, presumably he would want to live. It is difficult through a purely thematic analysis to account for the suicidal nature of Julien's death. If he has learned how to live, moreover, it should be possible to envision a life for him were he to be pardoned; but no satisfactory life is conceivable; and we, like Julien, are content to have his existence terminated.

One reason it is impossible to conceive of a life for Julien is that the kinds of happiness which he relishes in prison would either be unavailable to him in ordinary life or soon cease to satisfy him. His relationship with Madame de Rênal has an incestuous quality which makes it at once highly gratifying and criminal; and his speech to the jury suggests that he has a need to pay for this love with his life. Even if his love for Madame de Rênal were innocent, however, and he could secure it permanently, Julien would not long remain content to sacrifice all for love. Ambition dies in his heart when he faces death, but it would surely revive were he to have a future—indeed, it does revive on the day of his trial. Julien thinks that he would be happy if he had "two or three thousand livres a year to live quietly in a mountain village like Vergy" (Ch. 66). This is surely a delusion. He had toyed with such an idea much earlier (Ch. 23), but its appeal was temporary then and would be no more permanent now. In his youth, we are told, "perhaps not an hour of Julien's life had been passed without his reminding himself that Bonaparte, an obscure subaltern with no fortune, had made himself master of the world with his sword" (Ch. 5). Were he to be set free, a destiny like Napoleon's would still be the only fate, one suspects, that would satisfy his imagination.

We find it difficult to give Julien's story the meaning which Stendhal wants it to have because the author's rhetoric clashes with our sense of the character he has created. Stendhal presents Julien's transformation as a profound and permanent change of direction which leads him to a discovery of true values. If we look at Julien closely, we cannot help feeling that his change is not basic and that, though he dies happy, his solution is a destructive one. In order to substantiate this we require, of course, a psychological analysis of Julien's character. Such an analysis will provide us with a better understanding of Julien's experience and a greater appreciation of Stendhal's mimetic achievement than we can get in any other way.

II

It is customary to see Julien's problems as deriving mainly from his relation to society. The repressive atmosphere of post-Napoleonic France offers no suitable avenues of recognition and advancement to a poor but gifted young man whose aspirations have been excited by the glories of the Napoleonic era. This produces intense feelings of frustration and resentment and forces him into a life of hypocrisy. As a man of feeling and spirit, Julien would be an anomaly no matter what his birth; as a member of the dreaded lower class, he is doubly threatening to the establishment. There is no denying that Julien's problems are in large part historical and that Stendhal has given us a brilliant portrait of a pathogenic society. Psychological analysis shows, however, that historical circumstances are no more destructive to Julien's health and happiness than are his early experiences in the family.

Instead of fostering a basic trust which would enable him to grow and to be himself, Julien's family life produces a basic anxiety against which he must defend himself by rigid defensive measures. Julien is "an object of contempt to the rest of the household" because he is so unlike them. He feels like "a sort of foundling, hated by [his] father, [his] brothers, [his] whole family" (Ch. 7). There is no mention of his mother, who evidently died when he was quite young. His father treats him brutally, calling him "animal" and showering blows upon him at the least provocation. Julien trembles at the sound of his "terrible voice." His brothers also thrash him frequently; on at least one occasion they leave him "unconscious and bleeding freely" (Ch. 7).

Julien reacts to "his terrible father" (Ch. 5) with fear and hatred. It is his fear of his father, surely, which accounts for the anxiety attack which he has when he first enters the Seminary. Like his father, Pirard seems to him a "terrible man" with "a terrible eye," and his dread is so great that he falls "full length upon the floor" (Ch. 25). Later Pirard is transformed in his mind from a terrible into a good father.

The effects of Julien's anomalous position in his family are compounded, of course, by his anomalous position in society. His hypocrisy serves to ward off the punishment which he is sure awaits him if he reveals his true thoughts. He feels, as a child, surrounded by enemies against whom he must constantly be on guard. His experiences in the Seminary and in Paris tend to confirm his "mistrust of destiny and of mankind" (Ch. 6). Though Stendhal himself shares Julien's paranoia to a certain extent, and creates a world in which Julien's suspicions are often justified, the author perceives that Julien's fears and counter-measures are sometimes inappropriate or excessive; and he presents them, occasionally, in a comic light. Julien's precautions upon learning of M. de Rênal's offer or upon receiving Mathilde's declaration are quite understandable considering his anxiety; they are ludicrous, however, in view of the true situation. Stendhal predicts that Julien, had he lived, would have been cured of his "insane distrust" (Ch. 67). There is little reason to think so.

The rejection to which Julien is so constantly subjected severely damages his self-esteem. His social inferiority, the contempt with which he is treated by his father and brothers, and the fact that he is "universally despised as a feeble creature" (Ch. 4) all combine to produce a profound insecurity about his worth. His sense of inferiority is revealed in his readiness to feel scorned or insulted, in his spells of intense self-loathing, and in his frequent vindictive rages. His self-hate is both actively and passively externalized. He often despises others more intensely than their behavior warrants, and he sometimes feels more scorned than he actually is. Father Chélan and the Surgeon-Major are his only sources of support.

Julien suffers not only from the brutality and rejection which he encounters, but also from the isolation of his lot. He leads a "solitary life, compounded of imagination and suspicion" (Ch. 13). His isolation is partly due to the absence of kindred spirits, but it is also due to his fear of spontaneity and is to some extent self-imposed. His experience at home leads him to feel that there is something inherently dangerous in being himself, and society's antagonism toward his political and religious sentiments re-enforces his anxiety.

Julien defends himself against this anxiety by moving away from his fellows, by hiding himself in various ways. Only in his mountain cave can he "indulge in the pleasure of writing down his thoughts, so dangerous to him at other times" (Ch. 13). A retired life appeals to him, at times, quite strongly. It would require, however, the sacrifice of his ambition; and, "then, no career, no future for his imagination: it was a living death" (Ch. 27). Much as he loves freedom, Julien craves mastery more. When the imminence of death forces him to give up his ambition, he reverts quickly to this earlier dream of a retired life and imagines that he would be happy if he had enough money "to live quietly in a mountain village like Vergy" (Ch. 66).

Despite his hostility toward his kind, his suspicion, and his detachment, there are times when Julien experiences a powerful impulse to move toward his fellows. He has been deprived of both mothering and fathering; but he does not, like Becky Sharp, give up the child's role and try to become his own parent. Instead, he displays a pathetic eagerness to turn almost every male who is kind to him into a father surrogate. These include the Surgeon-Major, Father Chélan, the abbé Pirard, and, to a lesser extent, the Marquis de La Mole. He finds a mother substitute in Madame de Rênal and testifies to his "filial and unbounded adoration" for her in his fatal speech to the jury. The intensity of Julien's relationships with these characters can only be explained by the parental role which they play in his psychic life. Julien remains hungry for kindness and affection and is capable of being moved when they are offered.

"Hypocrisy and the absence of all fellow feeling" is Julien's "ordinary line of conduct" with others (Ch. 12); but toward those by whom he feels loved he often displays scruples and has impulses of self-sacrifice. He cannot "bear the thought of the slightest want of delicacy" towards Fouqué in the matter of the partnership (Ch. 12). When Mathilde's declaration offers him a triumph of which he has always dreamed, he is held back by his sense of gratitude to the Marquis de La Mole and grasps his opportunity only after severe inner conflict and furious rationalization. He is so moved by the fate of Pirard when he is forced out of the seminary that he cannot "think about himself"; in a strikingly uncharacteristic gesture, he offers the abbé his entire savings. It is Madame de Rênal, of course, who brings out Julien's self-effacing trends in the most powerful way. At the sight of her distress over her son's illness, he feels that he has "ceased to count here" and asks only what he "can . . . do for her"; he is ready here to undergo martyrdom for the woman he loves (Ch. 19).

Julien's self-effacing impulses are very much in conflict with his other trends; and, for the most part, they play a distinctly subordinate role in his psychic life. Julien feels "great confusion" at his affection for Pirard because such an emotion violates the taboos of both his aggressive and his detached solutions (Ch. 31). He has a similar experience earlier when Father Chélan gives him fatherly counsel (Ch. 8). In prison his self-effacing trends are no longer in conflict with the dictates of his ambition, and he experiences them much more powerfully than ever before.

For most of the novel, of course, Julien's primary strategy is neither self-effacement nor withdrawal, but aggression. He is outraged by the way he is treated and constantly craves vindictive triumphs to assuage his injured pride. His hostile, contemptuous demeanor is a protection against the rejection he expects to receive, a retaliation for past insults, and a way of asserting his superiority. He frequently displaces onto others the detestation which his father and brothers have heaped upon him.

Two of Julien's chief weapons in this battle with the world are his intellectual powers and his sexual attractiveness. His feats of memory and intelligence lead to a number of triumphs which create small peaks of excitement in the novel. Well before puberty, apparently, he begins to dream of sexual conquest as a path to glory and revenge. He dreams of being loved by one of the beautiful ladies of Paris "as Bonaparte, when still penniless, had been loved by the brilliant Madame de Beauharnais" (Ch. 5).

Julien pays court to Madame de Rênal in pursuance of this dream, but he cannot be satisfied with her until he has had a crack at the beautiful ladies of Paris. His initial feelings are far less amorous than vindictive: his chief interest is in "scoring off" the Mayor, who is so rich and powerful and who has shown him "such contempt" (Ch. 11). Later, the thought of triumphing over the Marquis de Croisenois makes Mathilde's advances irresistible to him and completes "the rout of [his] lingering trace of virtue" (Ch. 43).

By moving away from people, Julien seeks to protect himself from danger; by moving against them he seeks to discharge some of his anger, to assuage his feeling of inferiority, and to prove his worth. What he wants most of all is to show the people by whom he feels despised—his family, the people of Verrières, the rich and the noble—that he is their equal—indeed, their superior. Like Becky Sharp, Julien experiences humiliations in childhood and develops a need for glory and revenge: "He is and will be infinitely better than 'they' are. He will become great and put them to shame. He will show how they have misjudged and wronged him. He will become the great hero (in Julien's case, Napoleon). . . . Driving himself from victory to victory, in large and small matters, he lives for the 'day of reckoning' " (NHG, 203).

Julien's most powerful defense against his feeling of inferiority is, of course, self-idealization. As a child, he spends much of his energy building "cloud castles," and, upon entering the world, he endeavors to turn his dreams into reality. In his imagination Julien is a superior being, another Napoleon, whose true grandeur will someday be acknowledged by the world. His sense of this other and true identity is so vivid that he has trouble believing in his actual parentage; the story that he is the son of a nobleman feels quite right to him. The fact that he sees "no obstacle between himself and the most heroic actions, save want of opportunity" (Ch. 11) shows that in his own mind Julien is already a hero. Only a step-motherly providence threatens the fulfillment of his dreams. As we shall see, by his death he conquers fate and establishes his nobility forever.

Given Julien's expansive orientation, the recent history of France, and his friendship with the Surgeon-Major, it is not surprising that his idealized image is modeled upon Napoleon. Julien, like his author, seems to feel that the example of Napoleon has aroused unattainable aspirations in the young which will doom them to a life of frustration (Ch. 17).[2] Julien is not ambitious, however, because of Napoleon; he identifies with Napoleon because his damaged self-esteem leads him to develop a neurotic pride which can be satisfied by nothing less than some form of absolute triumph. For Julien, as for many other men of the nineteenth century (both fictional and real), Napoleon provides the most vivid embodiment of the expansive ideal.

Julien's self-idealization gives rise to the whole constellation of intra-psychic phenomena which Horney identifies as the pride system. Julien devotes himself to a search for glory; the meaning of his life lies in actualizing his idealized image. When his project seems to be succeeding, he experiences intense exaltation; when it seems to be failing, he is cast into despair. Nothing else matters. Julien's idealized image gives rise to neurotic claims which make him extremely vulnerable to frustration and to signs of disrespect. He has an "easily wounded vanity" (Ch. 37) and "cannot endure contempt" (Ch. 55). When he feels balked or insulted, he reacts with explosive rage and seeks to restore his pride through vindictive triumphs. Julien's shoulds (which he thinks of as his duties) are derived largely from his model, Napoleon, whose memoirs are "his sole rule of conduct," as well as "the sole object of his transports" (Ch. 8). Since his idealized image incorporates detached and self-effacing characteristics as well as aggressive ones, Julien's shoulds are sometimes in conflict. His aggressive trends are so powerful, however, that his personality is seldom in danger of disintegration. When he fails to live up to his shoulds, he experiences intense self-hate and tends to feel suicidal. Julien takes great pride in his triumphs and in his expansive characteristics and is usually ashamed of his softer feelings—though he also regards them as another proof of his superiority. He is extremely proud of his pride, and is unabashed in "defending [its] lawful rights" (Ch. 40).

It is his pride system, more than anything else, which determines the nature of Julien's inner life. It tosses him on "waves of passion" and makes "almost every day . . . one of storm" (Ch. 11). It raises him to the heights and plunges him to the depths. It tells him what to desire and what to fear. Julien is far more confined within the prison of his pride system than he is within the walls of the Seminary or the conventions of society. He is more afraid of his shoulds than he is of external punishments; he dreads his self-hate more than the contempt of others. The ideas and desires which he must hide from the people around him are not truly his own; they belong to his pride system, which speaks through him as a ventriloquist speaks through a puppet. The solitude of the mountains, the dark of night, the love of Madame de Rênal, and the imminence of death all seem to have a liberating effect upon Julien; but they can neither release him from his internal prison nor reverse the process of his self-alienation. The spontaneity which he achieves under these conditions is not a living from his true self, which he has abandoned long ago; it is simply the free expression of his actual self, which is largely neurotic. In the process of protecting himself from the tyranny of others, Julien has created an inner tyranny from which he can never escape.

By the time Julien encounters Madame de Rênal at the age of eighteen his character has been formed, his goals have been set, and his defenses have been established. What the various episodes of the novel show us is Julien reacting to a variety of situations in accordance with the laws of his neurosis. Julien learns little from them, but they teach us much about him. So far we have examined Julien's character structure and the early experiences which formed it. In the discussion which follows, we shall observe his character in action, first in his relation with Madame de Rênal, then in his affair with Mathilde, and finally in his behavior in prison.

III

Though the conquest of a beautiful woman figures in Julien's dreams from a very early age, "his solitary life . . . [has] kept him aloof from everything that could have enlightened him" about what actually takes place between the sexes (Ch. 13). Inspired by "certain things which Napoleon says of women," Julien decides that it is "his *duty* to secure" Madame de Rênal's hand (Ch. 8). He watches Madame de Rênal "like an enemy with whom he [will] presently be engaged," spends a whole day "fortifying himself by reading the inspired text," and determines to "go up to [his] room and blow [his] brains out" if he does not take Madame de Rênal's hand at the stroke of ten (Ch. 9). "After a final interval of tension and anxiety, during which the excess of his emotion [carries] Julien almost out of his senses," the clock strikes and Julien is victorious. His heart is "flooded with joy" because his "fearful torment" is over; and the next morning the thought that he has "done his *duty, and a heroic duty*" gives him "an entirely new pleasure" in "reading about the exploits of his hero."

In all of this Julien "barely" gives Madame de Rênal "a thought." His behavior has almost nothing to do with her; it is the result of an internal transaction between Julien and his pride system. Julien incorporates his new bits of sexual knowledge into his idealized image and then is driven by his shoulds into acting out the role of sexual aggressor. His anxiety is so great because so much is at stake. If he cannot live up to his shoulds he will not be the hero that he needs to be; he will have to forfeit his claims and will be flooded with feelings of worthlessness and self-hate.

After "the artless confidences" of Fouqué lead Julien to conclude that he owes it to himself to become Madame de Rênal's lover (Ch. 13), he once again undergoes fearful torments. He is so "extremely anxious" that he prepares "a plan of campaign in great detail" and even commits it "to writing" (Ch. 14). He is so intent upon living up to his shoulds that he once again is hardly aware of Madame de Rênal. Even "the transports" which he excites fail to overcome his rigidity: "the idea of *duty* was continually before his eyes. He feared a terrible remorse, and undying ridicule, should he depart from the ideal plan that he had set himself to follow" (Ch. 15). The ridicule which Julien fears is that which his idealized self would heap upon his actual self should he be derelict in his "duty."

Julien's pursuit of Madame de Rênal is motivated, of course, not only by the tyranny of his shoulds, but also by his desires for triumph and revenge. He sees becoming her lover as "a good opportunity to repay her all the contempt" she has shown him. It is not she who has shown him contempt, of course, but the world which she symbolizes; and his conquest of her is a triumph over the whole of society. Even when he becomes less compulsive in his behavior and almost completely loses "the idea of a part to be played," his love is "still founded in ambition: it [is] the joy of possessing—he, a poor creature so unfortunate and so despised—so noble and beautiful a woman" (Ch. 16). "His mistress's rank seemed to raise him above himself."

In order to explain the evolution of Julien's relationship with Madame de Rênal from these early stages in which he is so selfish and calculating to its later, more passionate phases, we must understand not only Julien's psychology, but Madame de Rênal's as well. As one of Stendhal's chapter titles ("Elective Affinities") suggests, Julien and Madame de Rênal are made for each other; their needs and character structures are highly complementary. In Stendhal's view, they are both sensitive organisms, sur-

rounded by a crass world, who find in each other a response to
their feelings and a home for their spirits. There is some truth in
this interpretation; but we will understand the dynamics of their
interaction far better, I think, if we see them as fulfilling each
other's neurotic needs in a peculiarly intense way.

Beneath her "extreme timidity" (Ch. 5) and her "unalterable
gentleness" (Ch. 16), there dwells in Madame de Rênal a "delicate and haughty nature" which leads her to "pay no attention
to the actions of the coarse creatures into whose midst chance
[has] flung her" (Ch. 7). This includes her husband, to whom she
submits only in order to be left alone. In effect, Madame de Rênal
protects herself from the "brutal insensitivity" of the "money-
grubbing creatures among whom she [has] to live" by detaching
herself almost completely from her surroundings. She has a
"peace-loving nature" (Ch. 6) and is content as long as she is left
free to raise her children and enjoy her gardens. She thinks
"about the passions, as we think about the lottery: a certain
disappointment and a happiness sought by fools alone" (Ch. 8).

Madame de Rênal is, like Julien, starved for human intimacy,
and she quickly finds "much pleasant enjoyment in the sympathy
of this proud and noble spirit . . . Generosity, nobility of soul,
humanity, seemed to her, after a time, to exist only in this young
cleric. She felt for him alone all the sympathy and even admiration which those virtues arouse in well-bred natures" (Ch. 7).
Sympathy and admiration are soon replaced by far more powerful emotions. Before meeting Julien "Madame de Rênal had
never . . . adored anyone save God, while she was at the Sacred
Heart in Besançon" (Ch. 7). " 'I feel for you,' " she tells Julien
in prison,

> "what I ought to feel only for God: a blend of respect, love,
> obedience. . . . In truth, I do not know what feeling you inspire in
> me. Were you to bid me thrust a knife into your gaoler, the crime
> would be committed before I had time to think. Explain this to me

in simple terms before I leave you, I wish to see clearly into my own heart. . . ." (Ch. 73)

The explanation is that, captivated by Julien's expansiveness, Madame de Rênal abandons her detachment and reverts to the self-effacement of her convent days. She enters into a relationship of morbid dependency in which the whole meaning of her life lies in being possessed by Julien. Julien becomes her God and she his slave; the worship of him is her religion.

The two characteristics which precipitate Madame de Rênal's morbid dependency are Julien's haughtiness, which breaks her pride, and his "genius" (Ch. 17), which gives promise of a "rise" to the "heights" (Ch. 20). In effect, she transfers her pride to Julien and realizes it, henceforth, through him. Julien's potential greatness sets him above her, making him a fit object of devotion, and offers her a safe outlet for her own expansive drives:

> His intelligence positively frightened her; she thought she could perceive more clearly every day the future great man in this young cleric. She saw him as Pope, she saw him as First Minister, like Richelieu.
> "Shall I live long enough to see you in your glory?" (Ch. 17)

The love of Madame de Rênal answers a number of Julien's needs in addition to those for triumph and revenge. She gives him the mothering for which he is starved. The feeling of safety and acceptance which she provides allows him to live more spontaneously and to experience the "exquisite . . . pleasure [of] being sincere" (Ch. 16). Above all, by sharing his dream of glory and worshipping him as a God, she confirms his idealized image, re-enforces his pride, and assuages his self-doubts.

Madame de Rênal's self-effacing trends rise to the fore when her pride is crushed; Julien's emerge when his pride is fed. The illness of Stanislas convinces Madame de Rênal that by loving Julien she is murdering her son and damning her soul to hell, but she cannot give up her lover. Julien is "deeply touched": his "distrust and suffering pride . . . could not stand out against the sight of so great, so indubitable a sacrifice. . . . He adored Madame de Rênal" (Ch. 19). Madame de Rênal's guilt and irrational fear are symptomatic of her self-effacing solution, which, re-enforced by her early religious training, leads her to feel responsible when things go wrong and to be terrified of retaliation. She seeks to relieve her anxiety by submission and self-punishment: " 'I must destroy and humble myself; it may be that such a sacrifice will appease the Lord.' " Julien, his own self-effacing trends now predominant, enters completely into her feelings, despite his conviction of their irrationality, and is ready to sacrifice himself for her: " 'Let me punish myself. I too am guilty. Would you have me retire to La Trappe? The austerity of the life there may appease your God. . . . Oh, heaven! Why can I not take upon myself Stanislas's illness?' " (Stendhal's ellipsis).

The guilt and anxiety which are activated by Stanislas' illness increase Madame de Rênal's dependence on Julien. She clings "to him like the ivy to the wall." When he leaves for Besançon she feels her "heart freezing" and hopes that she is "going to die" (Ch. 23). In Julien's absence she seeks to relieve her anxiety and to restore her self-esteem by clinging to God; she becomes devoutly religious. But when Julien visits her on his way to Paris, she can "refuse nothing to [the] idea of lifelong separation" (Ch. 30), and the conflict between her guilty love and her religious duty is reactivated.

Madame de Rênal is torn between two aspects of her self-effacing solution, her devotion to Julien and her fear of God. Her inner conflict can be resolved only by death, which will release her from torment and pay for her sin. While Julien is in Paris she "sincerely long[s] for death," and when he shoots her, she is in ecstasy: " '. . . to die by the hand of Julien is the acme of bliss' " (Ch. 66). Such a death is the acme of bliss because it means total possession by Julien, complete, oblivious submergence in him.

Madame de Rênal's death, three days after Julien's, is, in its way, as happy as his. It obliterates her pain, pays for her sin, and is her last testament of devotion.

That Julien's self-effacing devotion is but a passing phase we can see by his excitement at going to Besançon, by his behavior to Amanda Binet, and by his lack of concern for Madame de Rênal's feelings when he visits her on his way to Paris. When he is separated from Madame de Rênal, Julien's ambition quickly reasserts itself; and when he returns to her bedroom it is pride, not love, which is uppermost in his mind. The triumph of his "boldness" over her remorse means only that hers "is a heart in which it is glorious to reign!" An act which "destroys [Madame de Rênal's] self-esteem and dooms [her] to lifelong misery" puts Julien "in ecstasies" (Ch. 30). Fortified by his triumph, he is ready for Paris.

IV

Despite the vast difference in their social positions, Julien and Mathilde are much alike. They are both expansive persons who feel themselves to be vastly superior to the people around them and who are actively engaged in a search for glory. They have both formed idealized images of themselves which are modeled upon heroic figures living in heroic times. Both feel stifled by the oppressive society of post-Napoleonic France and are searching for a way to realize their heroic aspirations despite the cramping environment. Each finds in the other the means of living out his dream; hence the intensity of their relationship.

Mathilde's search for glory does not originate, like Julien's, in a feeling of inferiority and a need for compensations. Its source, rather, is a very privileged existence which makes her feel that she is an exceptional person who ought to have an exceptional destiny. Julien is an arrogant-vindictive person; Mathilde is narcissistic. By the age of twelve she has fallen in love with the period of

Henri III, which she feels is "the heroic age of France" (Ch. 40), and has identified profoundly with both her ancestor, Boniface de La Mole, and his mistress, Marguerite de Navarre. She feels "equal to everything that is most daring and great" (Ch. 41) and wants not "a moment of her life to pass that [is] not filled with some extraordinary action" (Ch. 69): " 'What should I not do with a king who was a man of feeling, like Louis XIII, sighing at my feet" (Ch. 41).

Mathilde wants to make history, but she lives at a time when the main goal of the established order is to prevent history from being made. She constantly measures her age against that of Henri III and the people around her against her heroes; and, as a result, she suffers from "the most profound boredom" and "a despair of finding any pleasure" (Ch. 38). The young men of her own circle seem "pale and lifeless copies" to Mathilde, "all made to the same pattern" (Ch. 49). Julien attracts her attention because he is "not exactly like all the rest" (Ch. 38). Julien's pride, his "astounding ambition" (Ch. 42), and his contempt for others stir Mathilde's imagination, and she quickly invests him with the grandeur of her heroes: " 'He has greatness, and they are shocked by it' " (Ch. 42). As Julien's partner, Mathilde will be rescued from the ordinariness and obscurity which she dreads: " 'I shall continue to attract attention, I shall by no means pass unperceived through life . . . for the man of my choice has character and unbounded ambition' " (Ch. 48). Her eager imagination soon exalts her passion for Julien into "the love of Marguerite de Valois for young La Mole, the most distinguished man of his time" (Ch. 42). Her love is a dream come true.

Julien's arrogance is an essential part of his appeal to Mathilde, not only because it enables her to glorify him as a superior being, but also because it crushes her pride. The Marquis de Croisenois has no chance with Mathilde because he can never challenge her superiority or disturb her self-possession. When Julien looks at her with contempt, she is "shocked . . . profoundly" and is unable to forget him: "She had been scorned by Julien, and was unable to scorn him" (Ch. 39). Her declaration of love is precipitated by "the sombre, frigid expression" which Julien assumes when he suspects that Mathilde and her friends are trying to make a fool of him (Ch. 43).

Mathilde's pride, however, is not easily crushed. Ever "since she [has] been aware of herself, [it] has reigned alone in her heart" (Ch. 44), and "the birth of a sentiment which [makes] all her happiness attendant upon another [is] attended by a sombre melancholy" (Ch. 43). When, at her invitation, Julien appears in her bedroom, Mathilde is "shocked by his air of triumph. 'He is my master, then!' . . . Already she was devoured by remorse" (Ch. 46).

Mathilde is suffering from severe inner conflict. If she is to realize her dream of glory through Julien, she must relinquish her dominance, surrender her will, and transfer her pride to him. When she places herself in his power, however, her pride rebels against this violation of all its taboos. She experiences intense feelings of mortification and is compelled to reassert her mastery. Her scorn for Julien is externalized self-hate. After her second submission, she implores Julien to keep her in subjection: " 'Punish me for my atrocious pride. . . . Yes, thou art my master . . . reign over me for ever, punish thy slave severely when she seeks to rebel' " (Ch. 49). Within a few days, however, she rejects Julien completely: "The delights of satisfied pride flooded Mathilde's bosom. . . . 'And so this little gentleman will understand, and once for all, that he has not and never will have any power over me' " (Ch. 50). When Julien's studied coldness and his courtship of Madame la Marechale de Fervaques provoke Mathilde into asserting her claims (" 'you are forgetting me entirely, me who am your wife' "), her inner conflict manifests itself in physical symptoms: "her pride, astonished by the fearful impropriety of her action, stifled her; she burst into tears, and a moment later appeared . . . to be unable to breathe" (Ch. 59). After she expresses her love and submission, she falls "to the ground in a dead faint."

Only if Julien maintains utter mastery can Mathilde transfer her pride to him and escape the pangs of humiliation. Fortunately, by the time of her third capitulation Julien has learned that he must treat her harshly and keep her uncertain of his love if he is to retain her devotion. Julien's growing absorption in his ambition, which makes him unresponsive to her "keen affection," heightens his appeal: "Never had he appeared so great, so adorable in the eyes of Mathilde" (Ch. 65). Instead of attacking Julien, she now accuses herself. In her demeanor toward him she is meek, humble, and submissive—though, since her "pride [must] find some outlet . . . she [shows] all the more arrogance towards anyone else who [comes] near her" (Ch. 62). When Julien is in prison, his abstraction and indifference keep Mathilde's pride in submission. After she discovers his love for Madame de Rênal, "her passion [knows] no bounds nor measure" (Ch. 69).

After his imprisonment, changes occur in Julien which make him lose interest in Mathilde. For Mathilde, however, Julien is more than ever the man of her dreams. Not only does his "noble revenge" prove him a hero; but, equally important, his imprisonment gives her an opportunity to prove her own greatness, to "astonish the public by the intensity of her love and the sublimity of her actions" (Ch. 69). After Julien's death, Mathilde *becomes* her idealized self, as she re-enacts the heroism of Marguerite de Navarre. As she carries Julien's head upon her knees, she successfully concludes her search for glory. She at once unites herself with the heroic past and becomes herself an historic figure. She conquers her own time, and, indeed, time itself. She has, however, no future.

When, in his mountain cave, Julien's soul wandered "in contemplation of what he imagined that he would one day find in Paris," this was "first and foremost a woman far more beautiful and of a far higher intelligence than any it had been his lot to see in the country. He loved with passion, he was loved in return" (Ch. 12). Mathilde is the woman of his dreams. He finds her more elegant, more beautiful, and far more of a grand lady than Madame de Rênal. "Ambition" distracts him "from the senti-ments that Madame de Rênal [inspires] in him. Mathilde [ab-sorbs] all; he [finds] her everywhere in his future" (Ch. 54).

Julien's initial hostility toward Mathilde is defensive; her supe-riority threatens his pride, so he protects himself by being aloof and critical. His defensiveness is soon overcome by her "meek, friendly air," which flatters his "self-esteem," and by her devo-tion to the memory of Boniface de La Mole, which makes him aware of her as a kindred spirit (Ch. 40). "His heart throbbing with ambition," he becomes obsessed with the thought that Mathilde might love him, and with plans of seduction (Ch. 40). When Mathilde declares her love, Julien is "mad with happi-ness"; his "joy" borders "on delirium": " 'And so I . . . I, a poor peasant, have received a declaration of love from a great lady!' " (Ch. 43). His vindictive triumph gives him "the bearing and pose of a hero." What he feels at the moment of possession is not love, but "the keenest gratification of his ambition": "he felt himself carried to an immense height. Everything that had been above him the day before was now on his level or far beneath him" (Ch. 46).

Mathilde's rejection of Julien shortly after her capitulation crushes his pride. This causes him to love her passionately; and, at the same time, it casts him into "the most violent despair" (Ch. 48). When Mathilde loves him, he is his glorified self; when she scorns him, he is his despised self. His "vivid imagination," which has hitherto been in the service of self-glorification, is now the servant of his self-hate. He wishes to "cover with ridicule that odious being whom I call *myself*" (Ch. 56); and finally, in a frenzy of self-detestation, he exclaims, " 'Great God! Why am I my-self?' " (Ch. 58)

Mathilde's rejection affects Julien so profoundly because it at once undermines his idealized image and activates the anxiety and self-contempt against which he has so elaborately defended himself. His pride in Mathilde's love constitutes an acknowledgement of her worth which leaves him completely vulnerable to her opinion of him. Though she despises him, he cannot despise her. Her scorn finds a ready ally in the self-hate which, with the defeat of his pride, has now risen to the surface. His self-contempt is increased by his shoulds, which punish him mercilessly for his failure. Since Julien has no way of coping with the world except through conquest, his defeat leaves him feeling anxious, vulnerable, and inadequate. Since life has no meaning for him without his dream of glory, the collapse of his hopes leaves him in despair. In his struggle to regain Mathilde's love, Julien is driven by both dread and desire. Only by reconquering Mathilde can he escape the hell of self-hate. If he fails, he literally does not know what will become of him; madness or self-destruction seem the most likely alternatives. If he succeeds, on the other hand, he will enter the heaven of a dream come true.

When he does succeed, he is at first completely absorbed in maintaining his mastery through a desperate self-control. As his pride is restored by Mathilde's slavish devotion and by his elevations in rank and fortune, Julien becomes more and more absorbed in his ambition and pays less and less attention to Mathilde. When he learns that Mathilde is pregnant, he begins to invest his pride in his child. His change of name fills him with astonishment: "he embraced the abbé, he saw himself recognized" (Ch. 65).

V

If we are to understand Julien's reaction to Madame de Rênal's letter, we must enter fully into his mental state at this time. Julien is euphoric; he is a conquering hero, a god. His expansive solution is working to perfection; his dream of glory is coming true. Providence is no longer stepmotherly; he is getting at last the station in life, the recognition, and even the ancestry that are his due. The despised peasant has become the noble being that he has always felt himself to be; he has vindicated himself both to himself and to the world. He has enormous pride in his achievement: " 'At last . . . the tale of my adventures is finished, and the credit is all mine' " (Ch. 64). At the moment when Mathilde's footman arrives with the message that "all is lost, " he is "in the midst of the transports of the most frenzied ambition": he can "think of nothing but glory and his son" (Ch. 65).

Madame de Rênal's letter plunges Julien into a state of "semi-insanity" (Ch. 66). Not only does it shatter his dream, but it outrages his pride by portraying him, not inaccurately, as a calculating seducer. Julien reacts with uncontrollable vindictive rage; all is lost, but he can at least restore his pride by avenging himself. In shooting Madame de Rênal, Julien is striking back not only at the woman who has brought him down, but also at all of his enemies and denigrators, whom she now symbolizes. At the sight of the "woman who had loved him so dearly," Julien cannot shoot; when she turns her head and becomes a representative of her class, Julien fires. Like Mathilde, Julien at first sees his act as "a noble revenge." He rejects the idea of remorse: " 'Why should I feel any. I have been outraged in a terrible manner; I have taken life, I deserve death, but that is all' " (Ch. 66).

Julien's transformation begins when he learns that Madame de Rênal is alive. His "state of irritation and semi-insanity" passes away, and he begins to repent of his crime. He does not wish to escape because he feels that he is guilty. Within a few days he sees "everything in a fresh light": he has "no ambition left" and he no longer thinks "of all that was occupying [his] mind" before the arrival of Madame de Rênal's letter (Ch. 66). When Mathilde arrives, he imagines "once again that he [is] in love with a queen," and abandons "himself with ecstasy to Mathilde's love"

(Ch. 68). But he soon becomes bored with Mathilde and feels wicked because of his ingratitude. Mathilde is permanently replaced in his heart by Madame de Rênal, with whom he is now "hopelessly in love" (Ch. 69). He is happiest when, "left absolutely alone," he can "abandon himself entirely to the memory of [his] happy days" at Verrières and Vergy. He withdraws more and more into "a heedless existence full of tender fantasies" and is irritated when Mathilde and Fouqué try to discuss his case: " 'Leave me to enjoy my ideal life. . . . your details of real life. . . . would bring me down from heaven' " (Ch. 70).

Julien's transformation is not the product of maturation or of a basic change in his character structure. It involves, rather, a shift from an expansive solution which has failed to self-effacing and detached attitudes which have hitherto played a subordinate role in his psychic life. With his imprisonment, it is no longer possible for Julien to actualize the expansive component of his idealized image. The emergence of his self-effacing trends, which is triggered by the discovery that Madame de Rênal is alive, that he can still live for love, saves Julien from despair and gives meaning to his life. His intense guilt, his "compunction at the thought" of M. de La Mole and Mathilde (Ch. 69), his self-reproach for being an "egoist," his loss of interest in ambition and heroism, and his passion for Madame de Rênal are all part of his self-effacing solution.

Julien still lives in a dream, but it is a dream now of love and beauty. His self-effacing trends lead him to exalt his relation with Madame de Rênal, and his detachment frees him to respond to the beauty of nature. The new dream is far less vulnerable than the old one, for, with one exception, it has already been realized in the past and can be relived in memory. The exception is his hope for his son. He continues to identify with his son, but what he wants for him now and enjoys vicariously through him is not power and glory, but the maternal love of Madame de Rênal.

By withdrawing into his "ideal life," Julien escapes the pain of defeat and the frustration of living. His detachment permits him to enter "heaven" through a purely intra-psychic process. It also, of course, commits him to an early death. He wants to be left in peace (not to be troubled with appeals and plans of escape) so that he may remain in his ideal world till the end. From the point of view of his detached solution, his death is a happy one. As his head is about to fall, "the most precious moments that he had known in the past in the woods of Vergy [come] crowding into his mind with an extreme vividness" (Ch. 75).

Julien's expansive attitudes are reawakened by the "tender pity" that his presence inspires in the crowd which has gathered for his trial. As long as he feels that everyone wishes for his conviction, he defends himself by detachment: "Julien had slept well, he was quite calm, and felt no other sentiment than one of philosophical piety towards this crowd of envious persons who . . . were ready to applaud his death." The "sereneness of [his] heart" gradually melts, however, "before the marks of interest of which he [is] plainly the object" (Ch. 71). At the height of his detachment he had expressed indifference to other people and was irritated by Mathilde's "longing to astonish the public" (Ch. 70). The sympathy of the spectators, particularly of the women, reawakens Julien's desire for heroism; and an "insolent glance from M. Valenod" arouses his need for self-vindication. Thus, "inflamed by the idea of duty," Julien abandons his determination to be silent and addresses the jury.

Julien's speech to the jury has many motivations and provides him with a variety of satisfactions. It serves his self-effacing needs for self-condemnation—perhaps, indeed, for self-destruction—and for the expression of his love, respect, and gratitude toward Madame de Rênal. It serves his expansive needs to attack his judges and to assert his pride and courage. He tells the jury, in effect, "I am guilty and deserve death, but you are bound to be unfair and to condemn me for the wrong reasons." By giving up all hope of acquittal, he frees himself to give full expression to his accumulated resentment: "he said everything that was in his heart" (Ch. 71). By declaring himself guilty, moreover, he takes his fate into his own hands and is no longer at the mercy of his enemies. He shows that he is not afraid of them, that his pride is unbroken: " 'They believed that I was begging for mercy: that is what I cannot endure' " (Ch. 72).

Julien is immensely proud of his speech to the jury: " 'The advantages of noble birth I lack, it is true. . . . Do you suppose that Boniface de La Mole cut a better figure before his judges?' " (Ch. 72). All of his life Julien has wanted to prove himself noble. What he realizes now is that he can prove his nobility once and for all by dying courageously. The upper classes, he feels, assign courage only to themselves: " 'One may become learned, clever, but courage! . . . Courage is not taught at school' " (Ch. 72). By exhibiting courage in the face of death, he becomes the equal of anyone.

Once Julien discovers that it *is* possible, after all, to possess his glory, he becomes very sensitive to the appearance he is making and very anxious about his own courage. Driven once again by his expansive shoulds, he is in dread of disgracing himself; and his desire to have his idealized image acknowledged by others makes him terribly concerned about public opinion. He wants to die while his courage is up and before "the patrician faction" has time to spread its "infamous and humiliating lies" about him (Ch. 72).

The appearance of Madame de Rênal in his cell induces Julien to appeal. His dream of love is no longer merely retrospective; time begins to have meaning for him. When Madame de Rênal can come no more, he is cast into a "profound dejection" (Ch. 74). If a "great," "good," and "indulgent" God existed, one who forgave those who had loved much, Julien would "fall at his feet," confess his guilt, and beg for Madame de Rênal to be restored to him.

Despite the intensity of his passion and the importance of

Madame de Rênal to him, Julien is far from living for love alone. A series of incidents indicates his continued preoccupation with pride and glory. When a priest besieges the prison, hoping to make a name for himself by hearing Julien's confession, Julien is horrified: "The thought of that mud-bespattered priest, drawing a crowd and creating a scandal, was torture to his soul. 'And, without a doubt, at every instant he is repeating my name!' This moment was more painful than death itself" (Ch. 73). This is more painful than death to Julien because it attacks his idealized image, which he is quite ready to die for.

Julien dreads seeing his father more than anything else. From an early age he has been in terror of his father, and he fears that in his father's presence he will lose his composure, as he did at the first sight of Pirard. When his father arrives, his "severe reproaches" begin as soon as they are alone, and Julien cannot "restrain his tears":

> ". . . what a triumph for Valenod and for all the dull hypocrites who reign at Verrières! . . . Until now I could at least say to myself: . . . all the honours are heaped upon them, but I have nobility at heart.
>
> "And here is a witness whom they will all believe, who will assure the whole of Verrières . . . that I have been weak in the face of death! . . ."
>
> Julien was almost in despair. (Ch. 74)

Rarely experiencing despair at the thought of death, he experiences it frequently at the prospect of dishonor.

Julien has similar reactions to the proposal of his confessor that he help his cause by undergoing "a sensational conversion" and to Madame de Rênal's desires to "throw herself at the feet of King Charles X" (Ch. 75). Julien asks for a confessor because of his desire to acquit "himself in a decent fashion of everything that is due to public opinion in the provinces," but he rejects peremptorily the suggestion that he try to save himself by becoming a celebrated convert: " 'And what shall I have left . . . if I despise myself? . . . I should be making myself extremely unhappy if I gave way to any cowardly temptation." He warns Madame de Rênal that he will kill himself unless she swears not to make them both a public spectacle: " 'Let us not give food for laughter to the Maslons, the Valenods, and a thousand people better than they.' "

In his moments of fear and anxiety, Julien consoles himself with the thought that at the final moment "the eye of the public" will be "the incentive to glory" (Ch. 74). Two days before his execution he tells Fouqué, " 'no one shall see me blench' " (Ch. 75). As he approaches the scaffold, he is content: " 'There, all is well . . . I am not lacking in courage' " (Ch. 75). From the point of view of his expansive solution, Julien's death is a happy one. He proves to himself and to the world that he is truly noble, and this time his victory cannot be snatched away from him by the caprice of fate or the enmity of men. The notion that a man's true rank is revealed by "his manner of facing death" (Ch. 39) is expressed, in one form or another, a number of times in the novel, making it clear that the implied author shares Julien's perspective, that from his point of view Julien has mastered fate and captured his glory.

Clearly, Julien is not as much changed as the novel's aesthetic pattern and thematic structure would lead us to believe. Our sense of a new Julien at the end is an illusion which is created by the novel's rhetoric, but which is dispelled by a close examination of Julien's character. Once his ambition is reawakened, his outlook is not terribly different from Mathilde's. He continues to be indifferent to her not because he is still bored by heroism, but because he no longer needs her in order to gain his glory. Though their styles have diverged, their goals remain much the same. His choice of the mountain cave as a final resting place is indicative of Julien's detachment ("it is situated in a spot that the philosopher's heart might envy"), but it is also an expression of his expansive attitudes. This is the place where, "casting [his] gaze afar over the richest provinces of France, [he has] felt [his] heart ablaze with ambition" (Ch. 75). His burial in this cave, like his courageous death, marks for Julien his attainment of the moral superiority for which he has always longed. The elaborate rites over which Mathilde presides would be distasteful to him because of his detachment; but, most of all, they would strike him as superfluous. They are necessary for the enactment of her dream, but his has already been realized.

Though Julien by no means undergoes the transformation which the novel's rhetoric suggests, he does change in important ways. During his early days in prison, his self-effacing and detached trends emerge in a most powerful way. From the day of his trial, his expansive attitudes resume their predominance, but the other two trends remain very active. The imminence of death makes it unnecessary for Julien to repress his subordinate trends in order to avoid inner conflict. As a result, his personality at the end seems richer, more complex, more promising, perhaps, than it had earlier. Julien experiences, and the author celebrates, the values and fulfillments associated with all three of his solutions. Stendhal's poetic handling of Julien's satisfactions should not make us forget, however, that all three of his trends conspire to make him opt for death. Through death he expiates his guilt, proves his nobility, and is liberated from the uncertainty, frustration, and stress of real life.

Our psychological analysis of Julien leads us to see the novel's rhetoric in a new light. The implied author's sympathetic treatment of Julien at the end indicates that his value system is one in which expansive, self-effacing, and detached attitudes are all powerfully present. His poetic handling of such values as pride, ambition, heroism, and glory is a reflection of his expansive attitudes. His criticism of Julien's ambition, his celebration of Madame de Rênal, and his satirical treatment of Mathilde indicate, however, a considerable sympathy for self-effacing and detached attitudes and strong taboos against expansive trends. The values associated with naturalness in the novel's thematic structure tend to be those generated by the self-effacing and detached solutions, while those associated with artificiality are largely aggressive in origin. The fact that Julien's expansiveness at the end is obscured by the novel's rhetoric, while the emergence of his self-effacing and detached attitudes is emphasized, suggests that the implied author consciously repudiates aggressiveness and needs to disguise his enjoyment of it. The reader receives conflicting signals from the novel: much of its rhetoric is on the side of self-effacing and detached values, whereas the unconscious value system which is embodied in the action and characterization seems to be predominantly expansive.

Chapter V

The Inner Conflicts of
Maggie Tulliver

In *The Great Tradition* F. R. Leavis argues that Maggie Tulliver's "emotional and spiritual stresses, her exaltations and renunciations, exhibit . . . all the marks of immaturity," but that George Eliot, because her own needs or hungers lead her to over-identify with Maggie, has little awareness of the inadequacy of her heroine's solutions:

> There is nothing against George Eliot's presenting this immaturity with tender sympathy; but we ask, and ought to ask, of a great novelist something more. 'Sympathy and understanding' is the common formula of praise, but understanding, in any strict sense, is just what she doesn't show. To understand immaturity would be to 'place' it, with however subtle an implication, by relating it to mature experience.[1]

In two previous discussions of *The Mill on the Floss* I have quarrelled with Leavis's response, arguing, in both, that Maggie's is a story of moral education and that by the end she has resolved her inner conflicts and achieved an adequate philosophy.[2] I still have reservations about Leavis's critical position, but I now agree with many of his judgments. Maggie's "hunger for ideal exaltations" *is* immature; her "lack of self-knowledge" *is* "shared by

George Eliot"; and the ending *is* "a kind of daydream indulgence" (Leavis, pp. 41, 43, 45).

George Eliot's characterization of Maggie is brilliant; and, given brilliant characterization, we must say that, in one sense, the author has understood the character perfectly. But, while George Eliot's intuitive grasp and mimetic presentation of Maggie's psychology are flawless, her attitudes, values, and analyses are considerably less trustworthy. My previous interpretations are not wrong; they give Maggie's story the significance that the novel means it to have, and they account for Maggie's behavior in terms of the novel's own analysis of motives. They are so intent upon showing Maggie's function in the novel's overall thematic structure, however, that they fail to see how much of Maggie escapes such analysis, how little she can be understood as a person in this way. In order to understand the character that George Eliot has actually presented (rather than the one she *thinks* she has presented) it is necessary to employ not thematic, but psychological analysis.[3] A psychological approach will help us not only to understand Maggie, but also to see "what the weaknesses of *The Mill on the Floss* really are" (Leavis, p. 40) and to appreciate its excellence, the nature of its achievement.

II

Leavis speaks of Maggie as immature; I prefer to speak of her problems in other terms. Her trouble is not simply that she is young and has not yet completed her development. From childhood on, she develops in an unhealthy way; and there is little likelihood that she could, had she lived, have grown into a self-actualizing adult.

It is not difficult to identify the destructive forces at work in Maggie's environment. There is a disparity from the outset between her given nature and the rigid ideas held by her society and her family of what she ought to be. Not only are Maggie's aesthetic and intellectual faculties starved in the oppressively narrow medium of St. Ogg's, they are regarded as inappropriate for a girl and hence contribute to Maggie's uncertainty about her worth. Not only is she a girl, and therefore an inferior being; she is an inferior girl. In talents, manners, and appearance, she is the opposite of what the Dodsons value in a female (Lucy embodies their ideal), and Mrs. Tulliver is engaged in a constant battle to transform her into an acceptable child. Mrs. Tulliver gets her sense of worth and of orientation in the world through her conformity to the ways and values of the Dodson clan. Maggie's deviations from the Dodson ideal fill her with anxiety, and she is deeply ashamed of her daughter. Her displeasure manifests itself in an "habitual deprecation" (III, ii) of Maggie, and her daughter's self-esteem wilts under her ceaseless criticism.[4]

Her mother's attitudes are echoed, of course, by the whole Dodson side of the family. Many times Maggie seems "to be listening to a chorus of reproach and derision" (I, vii); and on one occasion she runs away to the gypsies, seeking "a refuge from all the blighting obloquy that had pursued her in civilized life" (I, xi). Maggie's vulnerability to criticism is not simply a sign of her sensitive nature; it is also a manifestation of her profound insecurity. Since she has never been able to develop a healthy self-esteem, she is "as dependent on kind or cold words as a daisy on the sunshine or the cloud" (VI, iv). Her sense of worth soars or plunges in accordance with the treatment she receives. Maggie is so easily elated and deflated because at bottom she thinks very little of herself.

There are a number of ways in which Maggie tries to compensate for her feelings of inferiority. Even though he says that "a woman's no business wi' being so clever," Mr. Tulliver takes great pride in his daughter's intelligence; and Maggie, quite naturally, seizes upon intellectual pre-eminence as the readiest means to self-esteem. Her sense of worth is dependent upon the recognition by others of her cleverness, and she welcomes opportunities to demonstrate her superiority. After her father's failure, she turns to masculine learning in her search for an explanation of life and has fantasies of being "honoured for her surprising attainments" (IV, iii). Her quickness being the only thing for which Maggie has received praise, it is no wonder that she fastens on to it as the means to vindication and mastery.

Her need for compensations being strong, and her triumphs in life being few, it is no wonder, also, that Maggie creates a fantasy world in which she receives the love, admiration, and glory for which she hungers. The fantasy that most vividly reveals the co-existence in Maggie of self-rejection and a search for glory is the one in which she dreams of being a queen: "She was fond of fancying a world where the people never got any larger than children of their own age, and she made the queen of it just like Lucy, with a little crown on her head, and a little sceptre in her hand. . . . only the queen was Maggie herself in Lucy's form" (I, vii). As she grows up, Maggie gives up her childish fantasies, but the desire for pre-eminence that they express, the need to be somebody very special, remains with her to the end.

Maggie employs all three of Horney's defensive strategies in her relations with other people. Her withdrawal into a world of books and day-dreams is an attempt to escape her dependence upon the real, unsatisfactory people around her. Her desire to be a queen and her displays of cleverness reveal expansive drives; she seeks safety and a sense of worth through mastery and recognition. Her aggressive trends are most clearly seen in her relations with her mother and her aunts. She deeply resents these stifling, rejecting women, and her anger manifests itself in frequent outbursts of hostility and vindictiveness, as well as in behavior of a more subtly thwarting kind. She is full of rage, and of powerful cravings to get revenge—to thwart, hurt, and humiliate her tormentors. This is most vividly manifested in her use of "a Fetish which she punished for all her misfortunes":

> The last nail had been driven in with a fiercer stroke than usual,
> for the Fetish on that occasion represented aunt Glegg. But im-
> mediately afterwards Maggie had reflected that if she drove many
> nails in, she would not be so well able to fancy that the head was
> hurt when she knocked it against the wall, nor to comfort it, and
> make believe to poultice it, when her fury was abated; for even
> aunt Glegg would be pitiable when she had been hurt very much,
> and thoroughly humiliated, so as to beg her niece's pardon. (I, iv)

Maggie's triumphs of vengeance, like her triumphs of recognition, are most completely realized in her fantasy life.

Although Maggie has strong tendencies in all three directions,
her predominant solution is not to move away from or against,
but to move toward people.[5] She tries to gain affection, approval,
and care by being good and loving. When Tom behaves vindic-
tively toward her, Maggie's first reaction is often anger and a
desire to make him sorry, but it is always she who ends up pleading for forgiveness:

> . . . her need of love had triumphed over her pride, and she was
> going down with her swollen eyes and dishevelled hair to beg for
> pity. . . . she rushed to him and clung round his neck, sobbing, "O
> Tom, please forgive me—I can't bear it—I will always be good—
> always remember things—do love me—please, dear Tom!" (I, v)

Whenever there is a conflict between her desires for glory or
revenge and her need of being loved, her need for love always
subdues her.

The meaning of life for Maggie lies in being loved by her father
and by Tom. The most important person in her life is Tom—
"What was the use of anything, if Tom didn't love her?" (I, v)—
and her life goal is to secure his favor.[6] Her mother's approval
seems inaccessible, and, besides, Mrs. Tulliver's weakness makes
her support of little value. The love of her father and brother is
of such value mainly because they are arrogant-vindictive types
and, as such, powerful figures who can fight her battles for her:

"O how brave you are, Tom! I think you're like Samson. If there
came a lion roaring at me, I think you'd fight him—wouldn't you,
Tom? . . .

"But the lion *isn't* coming. What's the use of talking?"

"But I like to fancy how it would be," said Maggie, following
him. "Just think what you would do, Tom."

Maggie strongly identifies with her father and brother, partly
because she wants them to identify with her in return, and partly
because through them she can vicariously experience her aggressive drives.

Maggie's relation with Tom, so much at the center both of her
life and of the novel, is one to which Horney's analysis of morbid
dependency is perfectly applicable. Tom thinks Maggie a silly
thing, but Maggie glorifies his boyish accomplishments: "Maggie
thought this sort of knowledge was very wonderful—much more
difficult than remembering what was in the books; and she was
rather in awe of Tom's superiority, for he was the only person
who called her knowledge 'stuff,' and did not feel surprised at her
cleverness." Though with part of her being Maggie wants recognition for her cleverness, another part of her needs to see Tom
as far stronger and wiser than she. Tom's scorn of her, even
though it is undermining, is part of his appeal for Maggie. The
self-effacing person is drawn to the arrogant-vindictive person
not only because he needs to be protected by and to live vicariously through someone who can master life aggressively, but also
because he can only love someone who can "knock his own pride
out from under him" (NHG, 245). Her father, Philip, and Stephen are all important to Maggie; but they feed rather than break
her pride; and they cannot, therefore, master her as does Tom.

In childhood, then, Maggie's predominant solution is to attach
herself to Tom; and it is because she compulsively needs his
approval and protection that her feelings toward him of love,
awe, admiration, and fear are all so exaggerated. Maggie's character structure and value system are the opposite of Tom's, and

she often feels herself his moral superior; but she has "an awe of him, against which . . . it [is] useless to struggle" (V, ii). She dreads "Tom's anger of all things" (I, v):

> Her brother was the human being of whom she had been most afraid, from her childhood upwards: afraid with that fear which springs in us when we love one who is inexorable, unbending, unmodifiable—with a mind that we can never mould ourselves upon, and yet that we cannot endure to alienate from us. (VII, i)

When Tom is cruel or unloving, Maggie is torn by feelings of fright and rage. Because she needs to love Tom so that he will love her, she suppresses awareness of her vindictive drives and acts them out only in indirect or disguised ways.

Except toward her mother, Maggie rarely expresses anger directly and on her own behalf. When she denounces the Dodson aunts for criticizing her father, and Tom for his cruelty to Philip, she is able to give vent to her rage only because she is defending someone else. Maggie's handling of resentments follows the typical compliant pattern: her taboos against feeling and expressing anger are lifted only when she is fighting another person's battle, when she is angry in a good cause.

If Maggie had developed in a healthy way, she could have endured an alienation from Tom; indeed, she would have chosen it rather than have Tom thwart her growth. But, as it is, she can do nothing that will disrupt her relation with her brother; and Tom, knowing this, is able to impose his will upon her. Maggie fears Tom's rejection so because it leaves her feeling alone and helpless in a hostile world: submission to Tom is the chief means by which she fends off her basic anxiety. Her dread of Tom is a dread of her own anxiety, and the intensity of her fear is a direct revelation of the weakness of her real self. With her self-esteem resting upon Tom's love and approval, she compulsively sacrifices her own legitimate claims in order to appease him.

III

Now that we have some idea of Maggie's character, we need to examine her history. "Her history," as George Eliot says, "is a thing hardly to be predicted even from the completest knowledge of characteristics. For the tragedy of our lives is not created entirely from within" (VI, vi). Much of Maggie's fate *is*, of course, created from within. Her solutions can never work very well. Her compliance, even when it brings approval from without, weakens her real self and hence heightens her anxiety and self-rejection. The idealization of her self-effacing qualities (which we shall soon examine) increases rather than allays her self-hate, for she can never become the saint that she needs to be. But the tragedy of her life does not follow inevitably from her neurosis. If circumstances had permitted her to devote herself to a partner whose character structure complemented her own, her inner conflicts and her suffering would have been much less severe. As it is, Maggie has the misfortune of finding not only her real self, but also her defensive strategies frustrated by particularly unfavorable environmental conditions.

The first big change in Maggie's life comes with her father's failure and subsequent illness. At first Maggie derives an intense satisfaction from the new opportunity for devotedness. But the privation of all aesthetic and intellectual satisfactions and the fact that now she gets "no answer to her little caresses, either from her father or from Tom—the two idols of her life" (IV, ii) eventually makes her more unhappy than she has ever been. She turns to masculine learning for the secret that will enable her to understand "and, in understanding, endure"; and she dreams, as we have seen, of being "honoured for her surprising attainments" (IV, iii). She entertains "wild romances of a flight from home in search of something less sordid and dreary." She rebels against her lot: ". . . fits even of anger . . .—would flow out over her affections and conscience like a lava stream, and frighten her with a sense that it was not difficult for her to become a demon."

George Eliot attributes Maggie's sufferings, as she had earlier attributed Mr. Tulliver's compulsive vindictiveness (IV, ii), to inadequate culture. Maggie came "out of her school-life . . . with no other part of her inherited share in the hard-won treasures of thought, which generations of painful toil have laid up for the race of men, than shreds and patches of feeble literature and false history" (IV, iii). She is put in touch with the moral tradition of the race through Bob Jakin's gift of a copy of *The Imitation of Christ*. The impact of Thomas à Kempis upon Maggie is, indeed, great; but this is not, as George Eliot would have it, because he provides a moral wisdom that is new to Maggie. *The Imitation of Christ* is a classic statement of the self-effacing solution, and it comes to Maggie "as an unquestioned message" because it articulates attitudes that exist in her already. Given her compliant trends, the activation of her inner conflicts, and the fact that submission to Tom and her father has proven to be an inadequate solution, it is not surprising that Maggie is profoundly receptive to à Kempis's assurances that the total subduing of self-love will bring "great peace and tranquility." The search for calm that is so central to Maggie's history is in reality a search for freedom from her inner conflicts, and in this quest the philosophy of Thomas à Kempis henceforth occupies a central position.[7]

À Kempis proposes a solution that is far more rigorous and far less vulnerable than any which Maggie has been able to devise by herself. His strategy is to suppress all expansive drives, to resign himself to suffering in this life, and to give up the fight for self-realization. Earthly joys and frustrations are unimportant, for one's true dwelling is in heaven. Instead of depending on other people, one submits oneself to God, who completely loves and rewards his self-effacing subjects. In God, moreover, one finds the perfect being—all-powerful, all-wise, all-loving—with whom to merge oneself. God takes the place of Tom for Maggie.

Through her submission and feeling of helplessness Maggie gains a sense of being taken care of. Her solution is to remain a child, to refuse to take over the direction of her own existence: " 'I think,' " she tells Philip, " 'we are only like children, that some one who is wiser is taking care of. Is it not right to resign ourselves entirely, whatever may be denied us? I have found great peace in that for the last two or three years—even joy in subduing my own will' " (V, iii).

Maggie does, indeed, find joy in self-renunciation. Thomas à Kempis offers his followers not only "inward peace" but also "an everlasting crown" (IV, iii). Before she reads à Kempis, Maggie feels that it is part of the hardness of her life "that there was laid upon her the burthen of larger wants than others seemed to feel —that she had to endure this wide hopeless yearning for that something, whatever it was, that was greatest and best on this earth." George Eliot seems to regard Maggie's spiritual cravings as part of her essential nobility of nature, but they are much more satisfactorily explained as manifestations of her search for glory. The "strange thrill of awe" that passes through Maggie when she reads *The Imitation* comes, in part at least, from the book's revelation that the path to glory is through self-effacing goodness. Her yearning for the greatest and best is no longer hopeless. By renunciation Maggie at once escapes frustration (" 'I was never satisfied with a *little* of anything' "—V, iii) and fulfills her ambition for pre-eminence.

Under the influence of à Kempis, Maggie's idealized image becomes fully articulated and her shoulds are firmly established. She forms plans of "self-humiliation and entire devotedness" and is "in ecstasy" because she thinks she has found the key to happiness (IV, iii). She denies herself even the most innocent pleasures and spends nights lying "on the hard floor for a penance" (V, i) when she fails to live up to her perfectionistic standards. Her behavior changes so much that her mother feels "a sort of puzzled wonder that Maggie should be 'growing up so good';

it was amazing that this once 'contrairy' child was become so submissive, so backward to assert her own will" (IV, iii).

IV

The serenity that Maggie achieves through total self-effacement is lost when the return of Philip Wakem stirs up her desires for love and a fuller life. She is so vulnerable to Philip's temptations because she has only repressed and not really resolved her inner conflicts. In response to Philip's attentions there rises again "her innate delight in admiration and love," but she feels that she must renounce friendship with him because of her family's enmity toward lawyer Wakem. When Philip argues that it is not "right to sacrifice everything to other people's unreasonable feelings," Maggie replies:

> "I don't know. . . . Often, when I have been angry and discontented, it has seemed to me that I was not bound to give up anything; and I have gone on thinking till it has seemed to me that I could think away all my duty. But no good has ever come of that —it was an evil state of mind. I'm quite sure that whatever I might do, I should wish in the end that I had gone without anything for myself, rather than have made my father's life harder to him." (V, i)

Maggie sees rebellion and callousness, the whole system of aggressive attitudes, as the only alternative to self-effacement. She cannot conceive of a healthy self-assertion, a self-assertion that respects the rights of others but insists upon one's own rights as well. The alternative to seeing Philip secretly is giving him up. It occurs neither to Maggie nor to the author that Maggie might assert her right to a relationship with Philip. Philip's position is a sounder one than Maggie's, and it is treated with some sympathy, but the narrator tells us that we "can hardly help blaming him severely" for tempting Maggie into a secret relation. Though Maggie's decision is presented as an extremely difficult one, with much to be said on both sides, the novel clearly leaves the impression that by continuing to see Philip, Maggie makes the wrong choice. She does, of course: she should have fought for her self-realization. As her dilemma is structured by the author, and by her own character structure, Maggie has a choice only of neurotic solutions. She can callously rebel against her family, she can sacrifice her legitimate claims to other people's unreasonable feelings, or she can at once take what she wants and avoid conflict by engaging in a morally destructive act of deception. There is no escape from pain, for even a healthy solution would involve great friction between Maggie and her family, but a person in Maggie's position need not behave self-destructively. Maggie, of course, behaves as she must.

There are a number of reasons why Maggie cannot fight for her growth and autonomy, the chief of which is that she is afraid to jeopardize the precarious peace she has achieved by suppressing both her self-realizing and her expansive drives. She feels that her impoverished existence is "like death" (V, i), but she is fearful of anything that might rouse her to life. Because she is afraid of being rejected, and, even more, of being bad, Maggie is terrified of hurting others. Self-assertion would mean violating her taboos against egoism and giving up her image of herself as a saint and martyr. It would mean giving up her suffering. Maggie displays the masochistic tendencies typical of the self-effacing person for whom suffering is both a way of life and a claim to virtue and superiority. Finally, as Maggie's spontaneous feelings have been replaced by a system of neurotic motivations, her legitimate desires have been transformed into "illimitable wants" (V, iii). When Philip argues against her "narrow asceticism" and proclaims that "poetry and art and knowledge are sacred and pure," Maggie replies: " 'But not for me—not for me . . . Because I should want too much. I must wait—this life will not last long.' "

When Maggie found that she could not have love, she turned to renunciation and goodness for her sense of safety and worth.

With the reappearance of Philip, she is once again drawn by the appeal of love. On her way to tell Philip that they must part, Maggie looks forward eagerly "to the affectionate admiring looks that would meet her" (V, iii); and her face, under Philip's gaze, is "like that of a divinity well pleased to be worshipped." Because of the feud between Tulliver and Wakem, her need for goodness and her need for love are in conflict with each other. She cannot see Philip without feeling very sinful. If her family did not disapprove, marriage to Philip would be one of the best courses open to Maggie; for Philip's love has a neurotic intensity that satisfies her need for indulgence and importance; and, at the same time, her devotion to such a weak and sexually unappealing man gives her a sense of virtue.

Indeed, it is because seeing Philip can be interpreted as an act of goodness that Maggie is able to rationalize away many of her guilt feelings and to bring her acts into mental accord with her self-effacing value system. She seizes upon Philip's unhappiness and his need of her to justify her seeing him as an act of charity. She can serve the cause of truth by helping Philip "to find contentment as she had found it" (V, i). Moreover, she needs the mental cultivation that Philip offers if she is to lead a life of the highest devotion.

The weakness and dependency that make Philip so appealing to Maggie are also responsible for the absence in Maggie's feelings for him of the intensity that characterizes her relations to Tom and Stephen. The self-effacing person, says Horney, does not want another self-effacing person as a sexual partner:

> He may like him as a friend because he finds in him more sympathy, understanding, or devotion than in others. But when starting a more intimate relationship with him, he may feel even repelled. . . . He sees in him, as in a mirror, his own weakness. . . . He is . . . afraid of the clinging-vine attitude of such a partner because the mere idea that he himself must be the stronger one terrifies him. (NHG, 244)

Maggie does not reciprocate Philip's feeling and is never quite easy about regarding him as a lover. When Tom forbids them to see each other, Maggie is enraged at his cruelty and is full of a "just indignation," but she is also "conscious of a certain dim background of relief in the forced separation from Philip" (V, v). Maggie feels relief partly because she has been rescued from evil and partly because she has been punished, but mostly, I suspect, because she has been delivered by a harshness not her own from an oppressive relationship.

V

Maggie is drawn to Stephen Guest by many of the same hungers that made her consent to a clandestine relation with Philip. Her life as a teacher in a third-rate boarding school has been lonely, barren, and oppressive. With no one to appreciate her sacrifices, and with a future that seems "likely to be worse than her past," Maggie, "after her years of contented renunciation," has "slipped back into desire and longing." Stephen offers her the things for which she is most starved—admiration, devotion, opportunities for culture and enjoyment—and in "poor Maggie's highly-strung, hungry nature" (VI, iii) there is, initially at least, little power of resistance.

But we have not yet explained the overwhelming force of Maggie's attraction to Stephen. Philip, too, offers adoration and escape from a dreary existence; but we cannot imagine Maggie, at this point in her life, being seduced by *him* into a violation of all of her feelings of duty. Philip loves her "devotedly, as she had always longed to be loved" (VI, ii); but he can never satisfy, as Stephen can, her need to submit and her desires for protection and conquest. When she trips and Stephen holds her up "with a firm grasp," Maggie finds it "very charming to be taken care of in that kind graceful manner by some one taller and stronger than one's self." She is always looking *down* into Philip's pale, pleading, feminine face. Stephen's easy arrogance, so annoying to the critics, at once offends Maggie and fascinates her. On the disastrous boating expedition, Maggie submits herself with exquisite pleasure to the "stronger presence that seemed to bear her along without any act of her own will" (VI, xiii). "Maggie obeyed: there was an unspeakable charm in being told what to do, and having everything decided for her."

Stephen is an expansive person of the narcissistic type who is drawn to Maggie partly because "to see such a creature subdued by love for one would be a lot worth having" (VI, vi). One of the reasons Stephen's love is so precious to Maggie is that through it she can satisfy her own expansive drives. Her "passionate sensibility," George Eliot tells us, "prevented her vanity from taking the form of mere feminine coquetry and device, and gave it the poetry of ambition." Maggie has always been helpless, odd, deprived. All this can be changed by the love of St. Ogg's richest and handsomest young man. By becoming the beloved of Stephen Guest, Maggie can achieve the position of pre-eminence, of "acknowledged supremacy" (VI, ix), for which she has always longed. She cannot resist Stephen's professions of devotion: " . . . to satisfy her lightest wish was dearer to him than all other bliss . . .; he would belong to her for ever, and all that was his was hers—had no value for him except as it was hers. Such things uttered in low broken tones . . . were like nectar held close to thirsty lips . . ." (VI, xiii).

Even though there is little direct evidence in the text, it is tempting to believe that Maggie's drifting away with Stephen is partly motivated by an unconscious desire for revenge on Tom. Nothing Maggie could do would hurt Tom more, and the disgrace comes just as Tom has, with great effort, redeemed the family's losses and re-established its traditions by returning to the mill. There is ample evidence, however, that her conquest of Stephen satisfies Maggie's deep, though suppressed, desire for a vindictive triumph over Lucy, in whose shadow she has always

been. Several years before she meets Stephen, Maggie returns
Corinne to Philip unfinished, telling him that she is " 'determined
to read no more books where the blond-haired women carry away
all the happiness' ":

> "If you could give me some story, now, where the dark woman
> triumphs, it would restore the balance. I want to avenge Rebecca
> and Flora McIvor, and Minna and all the rest of the dark unhappy
> ones . . ."
>
> "Well, perhaps you will avenge the dark women in your own
> person and carry away all the love from your cousin Lucy. She is
> sure to have some handsome young man of St. Ogg's at her feet
> now: and you have only to shine upon him—your fair little cousin
> will be quite quenched in your beams."
>
> "Philip, that is not pretty of you, to apply my nonsense to any-
> thing real," said Maggie, looking hurt. "As if I, with my old gowns
> and want of all accomplishments, could be a rival of dear little
> Lucy, who knows and does all sorts of charming things, and is ten
> times prettier than I am—even if I were odious and base enough
> to wish to be her rival. . . ."
>
> "Maggie," said Philip, with surprise, "it is not like you to take
> playfulness literally." (V, iv)

Maggie's defensive reaction is a clear sign that Philip has brought
to light a fantasy that attracts Maggie strongly, but against which
she has powerful taboos. This interpretation is confirmed by an
episode after her flirtation with Stephen has begun in which
Maggie is afraid that Philip remembers the conversation just
quoted:

> Had his mind flown back to something that *she* now remembered?
> —something about a lover of Lucy's? It was a thought that made
> her shudder: it gave new definiteness to her present position.
> . . . Philip must not have that odious thought in his mind: she
> would banish it from her own. (VI, vii)

Maggie suffers "horrible tumult within" because, strong as are
the drives which compel her into a relation with Stephen, the

drives which forbid such a relation are even stronger. For one thing, Maggie's own sufferings, combined with her highly developed powers of sympathy, make her shrink from inflicting pain upon others. This, of course, is the novel's explanation of Maggie's behavior, and it has its truth; but it does not, I think, account for the intensity of Maggie's inner conflict or for her persistent refusal, after she has already compromised all the affected relationships, to consider marriage with Stephen. Maggie tells Stephen at Basset that she would "rather die than fall into" the "temptation" of marrying him (VI, xi) because, whatever her cravings might be for triumph and fulfillment, her self-esteem depends upon her being good and doing her duty. What George Eliot interprets as "the gathered spiritual force of painful years coming" to Maggie's "aid in this extremity" I would explain as the persistence of Maggie's powerful self-effacing trends and a resurgence of the philosophy of renunciation articulated by Thomas à Kempis.

Given her feelings before she succumbs to Stephen's temptation, it is inevitable that Maggie should be appalled when she awakens to the discovery that she has acted out her secret wishes. Her first awareness of what she has done comes in the dream in which she is in a boat with Stephen and she sees Tom row past without looking at her: ". . . she rose to stretch out her arms and call to him, and their own boat turned over with the movement, and they began to sink, till with one spasm of dread she seemed to awake, and find she was a child again in the parlor at evening twilight, and Tom was not really angry" (VI, xiv). Earlier we are told that "to have no cloud between herself and Tom was still a perpetual yearning in her, that had its root deeper than all change" (VI, xii). Despite his charm, eminence, and conceit, Stephen cannot replace Tom for Maggie. As a suffering lover he can appeal to her sympathies, but he lacks Tom's power to chasten her pride and to master her will and conscience. By marrying Stephen, Maggie will cut herself off forever from Tom's approval;

by returning to accept judgment and punishment at his hands, she maintains the possibility of an eventual rapprochement.

In addition to cutting herself off from others whose approval she needs, Maggie has violated the strictest taboos of the self-effacing solution and has thereby roused up her profoundest feelings of anxiety and of self-contempt. I have no wish to deny the moral nobility of some of Maggie's feelings: she has a vividly imaginative sympathy with those whom she has injured, and she profoundly regrets having brought them so much pain. But her subsequent behavior, which is compulsive in nature, has much more to do with re-establishing her relation to herself, with repairing her defenses, than with minimizing or repairing the damage she has done to others. Maggie fears that she will "for ever sink and wander vaguely" and seeks to recapture "the clue of life —that clue which once in the far-off years her young need had clutched so strongly" (VI, xiv).

Maggie once again gives up all thought of earthly happiness and turns to renunciation as a refuge from her own nature and from the conflicts and imperfections of the human condition. This time the author unreservedly approves of her renunciation, for Maggie has learned that resignation is not joy but sorrow borne willingly. Maggie has not given up her search for glory and accepted the pain of being human; rather, she has learned the high price of perfect goodness and is compelled to pay it.

I cannot agree with those who argue that George Eliot at the end is aware of Maggie's limitations.[8] Though there are differences in the perspectives of Maggie and of the novel as a whole through most of the story, at the end these points of view seem to coalesce: Maggie's self-abnegation is presented as the "clue of life." In terms of the novel's thematic structure, Maggie's fall is in many ways a fortunate one; for it brings her firmly back to the philosophy of Thomas à Kempis, which she now properly understands. Her struggles of conscience mark her as a morally superior person, a being far above those who condemn her (see

VII, ii). One detects a kind of pride in Maggie and, even more, in the narrator at how "good" Maggie was to have returned, even though this is impractical and makes no sense to the world. Maggie is so noble that she does not even claim a right to be indignant at the terribly unjust treatment that she receives in St. Ogg's. Maggie suffers horribly from mistreatment and from her own errors, which are presented as the result, in part, of her superior endowment. But her suffering, instead of embittering her, is transformed by her nobility of nature into a powerful force for goodness: "Surely there was something taught her by this experience of great need; and she must be learning a secret of human tenderness and long-suffering, that the less erring could hardly know?" (VII, v). I see no distinction here between Maggie's view of herself and the author's view of her.

Maggie is presented so sympathetically because the perspective of the novel as a whole is that of the self-effacing solution at which she arrives by the end. The clue of life is total renunciation. There is nothing in the novel to suggest that Maggie's solution is not a good one, but only one to which she has unfortunately been driven by her nature and by the unfavorable circumstances of her life. Maggie's suffering is pitied, but it is presented as ennobling rather than as destructive. Maggie's earlier renunciation was defective because she had hoped through goodness to achieve happiness. At the end Maggie resigns herself to a suffering from which there is no relief and devotes herself to a goodness for which there is no reward. The novel's conclusion, which is a fantasy of the compliant solution working to perfection, releases Maggie from her suffering and rewards her goodness. It has often been noted that the goodness of George Eliot's heroines is magically followed by plot occurrences in their favor.

Maggie's solution has its rewards, of course, even before the ending. There is the reward of feeling perfectly good and completely misunderstood. George Eliot's emphasis upon true resignation as pain borne willingly without hope of gratification is but a refinement of Maggie's earlier religious ardor. The most glorious thing of all is to do without glory. All satisfactions are given up, but there remains the pride in being *really* perfectly good, a pride which is attended, of course, by intense satisfaction. There is no awareness in the novel that Maggie at the end is still engaged in a neurotic search for glory. Indeed, the novel itself invests her final sufferings and renunciations with an exalted glamour. Maggie, with her crown of thorns, is another Christist: "'I have received the Cross,'" she exclaims, "'I have received it from Thy hand; I will bear it, and bear it till death, as Thou hast laid it upon me'" (VII, v).

The ending vindicates Maggie to the world. With the coming of the flood Maggie feels as though she has entered upon a new life, for she senses that this is her opportunity to redeem herself in the eyes of others, to have her goodness recognized. Her torpor passes away, and she is filled with a glorious energy. She feels herself to be divinely protected, an agent of God, who has always seen in her the nobility to which men have been blind. Her moment of ecstatic triumph comes when Tom, "pale with a certain awe and humiliation," realizes how wrong he has been about her and gives Maggie the love and homage she has always wanted: "Maggie could make no answer but a long deep sob of that mysterious happiness that is one with pain." The novel's epigraph—"In their death they were not divided"—indicates that the author gives as much importance as does Maggie herself to the climactic reunion with Tom. Maggie's death preserves forever the glorious victory that she has wrested from defeat.

At the moment of her death Maggie has that which she has most wanted from life. Had she lived on, there would have been renewed turmoil and failure to mar her victory. For Maggie has not resolved her inner conflicts; she has only repressed them by totally inhibiting both her self-realizing and her expansive drives. After their quarrel over Philip releases her anger toward Tom, Maggie moves for a while toward autonomy. She refuses the stifling protection both of her brother and her aunts, and she goes off to teach, to earn her own way in the world. When, later, Tom complains that she won't be guided by his better judgment, Maggie replies: " 'I am grateful to you. But, indeed, you can't quite judge for me—our natures are very different' " (VI, iv). She tells Lucy: " 'I must not stay here long. It would unfit me for the life I must begin again at last. I can't live in dependence—I can't live with my brother . . . that would be intolerable to me' " (VI, vii). But Maggie has not the strength to become her own person. At school she is starved for the warmth and approval that she needs so much, and this makes her particularly vulnerable to Stephen's attentions. After she compromises herself with Stephen, she becomes totally incapable of self-assertion and is entirely at the mercy of her "dread." She reverts to a childish dependence and returns to Tom for punishment and for protection from herself.

Maggie is terribly afraid of herself, and with good reason; for her compulsive acts have wrought great harm. When Tom rejects her, she clings desperately to St. Ogg's and to her family, symbols of restraint and of security, and refuses all opportunities to make a new life for herself elsewhere. "All she craved," we are told, "was something to guarantee her from more falling: her own weakness haunted her like a vision of hideous possibilities, that made no peace conceivable except such as lay in the sense of a sure refuge" (VI, ii). Maggie sees no prospect of happiness (she is afraid, of course, of wanting anything for herself); her only recourse is to live out the self-effacing solution for the rest of her days. But she knows that there are powerful forces in her working against this solution, and she is oppressed by the fear that she will succumb to them. She has promised to bear the Cross till death: " 'But how long it will be before death comes! . . . How shall I have patience and strength? Am I to struggle and fall and repent again?—has life other trials as hard for me still?' " (VII, v). There is in Maggie a profound wish for death, for only in death is there the peace of a sure refuge. Not only is her wish for death granted, and not only does she die before she falls again, but her death comes, as we have seen, in her moment of highest glory.

My thesis, then, is that Maggie at the end has adopted an extreme form of the self-effacing solution. She wishes to die so that she might remain good. She senses, quite correctly, that if she lives she will be torn by endless conflicts. She will violate her inner dictates again and again, and every time she will be confronted by her profound dread and self-loathing. The novel succeeds brilliantly in its characterization of Maggie, but it fails to interpret her correctly and to see the destructiveness of her solution—though it dramatizes that destructiveness with great penetration. The ending is artistically weak because, though the action of the novel has everywhere else been realistic, it seems here to be controlled by the wishes and fantasies of the heroine. In her over-identification with Maggie, George Eliot loses sight of that disparity between inward and outward, wish and reality, which is usually a controlling principle in her fictional universe. The novel prepares us for catastrophe—or, at least, for the frustration of the heroine—but it gives us instead, as Leavis says, "the dreamed-of perfect accident that gives us the opportunity for the dreamed-of heroic act—the act that shall vindicate us against a harshly misjudging world, bring emotional fulfillment and . . . provide a gloriously tragic curtain" (pp. 45–46).

VI

F. R. Leavis is right in saying that George Eliot does not "understand" Maggie Tulliver's immaturity; but he is wrong, I think, in feeling that we "ought to ask" this kind of understanding "of a great novelist." We must regret George Eliot's over-identification with Maggie because it results in artistic failings—such as the inconsistent handling of distance, the disparities between representation and interpretation, and the mixing of realism and fantasy; but this is not Leavis's point. He wants George Eliot to understand Maggie from without as well as from within, to have a set of mature values against which Maggie's immaturity can be seen.

I would argue that this is not a legitimate demand to make upon a novelist, even if the novelist makes the mistake of thinking that it is and offers himself to us as moral guide or sage. George Eliot, of course, made this mistake; and she invited, therefore, the kind of criticism in which Leavis and other moral critics engage.[9] In a letter to Dr. Joseph Frank Payne, George Eliot described her novels as "simply a set of experiments in life—an endeavor to see what our thought and emotion may be capable of—what stores of motive, actual or hinted as possible, give promise of a better after which we may strive—what gains from past discipline we must strive to keep hold of as something more sure than shifting theory."[10] Caught, like ourselves, in a time of social and intellectual fragmentation, George Eliot despaired of arriving at theoretical formulations which would be widely accepted. She hoped, however, to discover through her fiction truths of feeling in which men would perceive unquestioned values and by which they would recognize themselves as brothers. If a moral posture could be shown to derive from life as felt rather than from life as thought, it would have an impressive claim to validity and would flash conviction upon the world.

I do not deny that if the configuration of experience presented in fiction corresponds in some significant way to our own sense of the world, the moral affirmations of the work may come, as did the philosophy of Thomas à Kempis to Maggie Tulliver, as an unquestioned message. But experiences of the world differ greatly, and we in fact respond strongly to only a small percentage of the works that we read. We are, to a large degree, predisposed by our strategies of defense to certain attitudes, values, and beliefs. When we encounter works of fiction in which our feelings about life are more fully and subtly articulated, we have a sense of being profoundly influenced and of our lives being made more meaningful. But the attitudes and values which are thus re-enforced are, from an ethical standpoint, not necessarily good ones.

The novelist may feel, as did George Eliot, that the ability of a formula to get itself "clothed" for him "in some human figure and individual experience"[11] attests to its validity, but this is not necessarily the case. It may show that the formula corresponds to a real human experience, but it does not provide him with a means for judging the desirability of that experience. Indeed, the author may be blind to the implications of his own portrayal of experience and end up celebrating a life style which he has shown to be destructive. The author, in the act of writing, and the audience, in the act of reading, may have a sense of discovering moral truths; but it is more likely that what they are discovering is themselves, the potentialities for ramification and rationalization of their own position.

If, as Maslow claims, we make continual discoveries of the good by observing the lives of healthy people, then fiction that was written from a healthy perspective or that depicted healthy characters could, indeed, fulfill the objectives that George Eliot defined for her own novels. George Eliot, however, for all her genius as an artist, did not possess the qualifications necessary for conducting such experiments in life.

I do not discover in *The Mill on the Floss,* therefore, either healthy solutions for problems such as Maggie's or a vision of "a better after which we may strive." I discover how it is to be a Maggie Tulliver and what values such a person must have. I discover what the experience of a Maggie Tulliver means, intellectually and emotionally, to a consciousness like that of the implied author. But this is a great deal; and there is, of course, more in the same kind. Even though I no longer go to George

Eliot as a great sage, I still value her highly and go to her as a great artist who gives me a kind of knowledge that I find nowhere else of certain patterns of experience. George Eliot's experiments in life do present enduring truths, but they are not the truths for which she was searching.

Chapter VI

The Withdrawn Man:
Notes from Underground

The most difficult task confronting the reader of *Notes from Underground* is to make sense of the vacillating, inconsistent, and often bizarre behavior of the underground man. How are we to account for his conflicting attitudes, for the disparity between his ideals and his deeds, for his spite and self-destructiveness? What is the relationship between the ideas he expresses in Part I and the events he portrays in Part II? Or, to put the question another way, what is the connection, if any, between his philosophy and his way of living? Finally, to what extent is his account of himself an accurate one? If he distorts, if he rationalizes, if he blocks awareness, how can we know it?

In their efforts to answer such questions, critics have employed two distinct modes of analysis, thematic and psychological. Thematic analysis tries to account for the underground man by showing what he meant to Dostoevsky, what Dostoevsky was trying to say, through him, about his time and about the nature and condition of man.[1] Ingenious as much of it has been, thematic analysis has not been very satisfactory, partly because the mimetic portrait of the underground man continually escapes its categories, but mainly because *Notes from Underground* does not interpret the experience it portrays. It is possible to infer from our knowledge of Dostoevsky's life and writings what significance his character might have had if he had chosen to give his story a thematic structure; but the fact is that there are few really reliable guides in the work itself to the implied author's attitudes and beliefs. The most reliable thematic device is parody; to appreciate it, the modern reader must reconstruct the philosophic and literary milieu within which the work was produced. Even when, like Professor Frank, he does this, he illuminates only a small portion of the work and touches upon nothing that constitutes its greatness. The underground man functions, of course, as an interpreter of his own experience, but we have no reason to believe that his interpretations are trustworthy or that they are affirmed by the work.[2]

The psychological approach seems decidedly more appropriate.[3] The novel is essentially a portrait of a character. It is *about* the underground man; what the implied author is saying is, Here is this man. When we have understood the man, we have understood the work. Every aspect of the novel, including the philosophical speculations of Part I and the way in which the material is ordered, is an expression of the underground man's psyche. When we have understood the peculiar inner logic of that psyche, we will have understood why the work is as it is and what each part is doing there. So far, however, no psychological analysis has been able to make very much sense of our extremely complex and spectacularly inconsistent protagonist.[4] There are several possible explanations of this. The underground man may be right in contending that human nature is ultimately inexplicable, and hence free. Dostoevsky, deliberately or through inadequacy, may have created a character whose behavior is reducible to no psychological laws. Or, critics may not yet have approached the work with a psychological theory which is congruent with it and adequate to its complexities. I incline toward the last explanation;

and I shall try in this essay to show that the underground man can be readily understood in terms of Karen Horney's analysis of neurotic processes.

II

It is not difficult to see that, in Horneyan terms, the underground man's predominant solution is detachment. His values, character structure, and life style all display the characteristics of this solution. He prizes freedom, will, caprice, individuality, peace, and intellectual superiority above all else, and has a profound aversion toward anything suggesting coercion, conformity to law, ordinariness, or stupidity. When his privacy is invaded or emotional demands are made of him (as in the episode with Liza), he becomes hysterical. He defends himself against his feelings of shame and failure by protestations of indifference—"I don't care"; "it doesn't matter"—and by escaping into dreams of glory: "I was a terrible dreamer, I would dream for three months on end, tucked away in my corner. . . . I suddenly became a hero."[5] He has the same "onlooker" attitude toward himself that he has toward life and is, as a result, an excellent observer of his own inner processes. His *explanations* of these processes are often rationalizations, however, and are not to be trusted.

At almost every stage of his life the underground man leads an extremely solitary existence. By the age of twenty-four, he tells us, his life was already "gloomy, ill-regulated, and as solitary as that of a savage. I made friends with no one and positively avoided talking, and buried myself more and more in my hole" (II, i). As soon as he receives a small inheritance, he retires from service and withdraws almost entirely into his underground world: " . . . my lodging was my private solitude, my shell, my cave, in which I concealed myself from all mankind" (II, viii). Some of the intra-psychic forces behind this behavior are suggested by Horney's description of withdrawal as a way of protecting pride:

> He [the person employing this defense] does not embark on any serious pursuits commensurate with his gifts lest he fail to be a brilliant success. . . . So, according to his economic status, he either does nothing worth while or sticks to a mediocre job and restricts his expenses rigidly. In more than one way he lives beneath his means. In the long run this makes it necessary for him to withdraw farther from others, because he cannot face the fact of lagging behind his age group and therefore shuns comparisons or questions from anybody about his work. In order to endure life he must now entrench himself more firmly in his fantasy world. But, since all these measures are more a camouflage than a remedy for his pride, he may start to cultivate his neurosis because the neurosis with a capital N then becomes a precious alibi for the lack of accomplishment. (NHG, 107)

It seems evident that the underground man was driven to an extreme form of the detached solution by a singularly bleak and loveless childhood. He was completely deprived of the warmth, re-enforcement, and protection of family life; and his resulting oddness (defensiveness) made him an object of scorn and derision to his peers. He was sent to school, he tells us, "by distant relatives upon whom I was dependent and of whom I have heard nothing since—they sent me there a forlorn, silent boy, already crushed by their reproaches, already troubled by doubt, and looking with savage distrust at every one" (II, iii). His schoolfellows met him "with spiteful and merciless jibes" because he "was not like any of them"; and he "hated them from the first" and shut himself "away from every one in timid, wounded and disproportionate pride" (II, iii). Feeling alone and helpless in a hostile world, he tried to cope with his anxiety by withdrawing from others and nourishing a belief in his own superiority.

By the time of his encounter with Liza, the underground man

is himself aware of the connection between his homelessness and his detachment. "If I had had a home from childhood," he tells Liza, "I shouldn't be what I am now. I often think that. However bad it may be at home, anyway they are your father and mother, and not enemies, strangers. Once a year at least, they'll show their love of you. Anyway, you are at home. I grew up without a home; and perhaps that's why I've turned so . . . unfeeling" (II, vi). These remarks, which introduce a glowing description of the joys (even in suffering) of family life, show a profound yearning in the underground man for the human warmth and intimacy of which he has been deprived. But since he has never been loved, he cannot help sensing the world as composed of enemies and strangers; and it is understandable that, despite a strong desire to do so, he cannot open himself to others and entrust himself to them.

In his school years, the underground man moved not only away from, but also against and toward his fellows. He tried to insulate himself from his schoolfellows' contempt and from his own feelings of inadequacy by keeping aloof and by scorning their stupidity and their respect for success. But he could not detach himself sufficiently to become indifferent to their mockery, and he was consumed by hatred and a desire for vindictive triumph: ". . . by then I did not desire their affection: on the contrary I continually longed for their humiliation. To escape from their derision I purposely began to make all the progress I could with my studies and forced my way to the very top. This impressed them. . . . The mockery ceased, but the hostility remained, and cold and strained relations became permanent between us" (II, iii). In the end, however, he could not bear this estrangement, and he began to move towards his fellows, but with little success: ". . . with years a craving for society, for friends developed in me. I attempted to get on friendly terms with some of my schoolfellows; but somehow or other my intimacy with them was always strained and soon ended of itself" (II, iii). When his relationships were not "strained" because of his aloofness and distrust, they were marred by his desire to "exercise unbounded sway" over the partner, and by his contempt for the weakness of anyone who would allow himself to be dominated.

We begin to see here the way in which the underground man's contradictory trends result in inconsistencies. His detachment leads him to scorn success, but his aggressive needs make him force his way to the top. When he leaves school, he gives up the special job for which he had been destined "so as to break all ties, to curse [his] past and shake the dust from off [his] feet" (II, iii); but he is deeply humiliated by his poverty and the insignificance of his position, and he feels terribly inferior to his more prosperous schoolmates. He craves intimacy so much that he frightens his friend with his "passionate affection"; but his fear of closeness makes him aloof and distrustful. When he succeeds in establishing a relationship, he is driven by his need for mastery into becoming a tyrant; and his aggressive values lead him to despise devoted souls.

By the time of the Zverkov-Liza episode, the underground man's basic character structure has been formed; it changes little from then on. He is a detached person whose aggressive and compliant trends are very close to awareness and rather evenly balanced.[6] They exist mainly as attitudes (his life style is determined by detachment), but they sometimes drive him into behavior from which he almost immediately recoils. He oscillates between identifying with his proud and with his despised selves, between feeling like a god and like a piece of dung. He experiences severe and almost continuous conflict between all three of his trends, and he is caught in a devastating crossfire of conflicting shoulds. As an analysis of several key passages and episodes will show, a great many of the underground man's vacillations and contradictions become intelligible when we see him as beset by inner conflicts in which tendencies toward detachment, compliance, and aggression, with their inter-personal and intrapsychic ramifications, are all powerfully at work.

III

In the opening pages of his "notes," when he is describing his life in the government service, the underground man tells us that he was a spiteful official. "I was rude and took pleasure in being so. . . . When petitioners used to come for information to the table at which I sat, I used to grind my teeth at them, and felt intense enjoyment when I succeeded in making anybody unhappy. I almost always did succeed. For the most part they were all timid people—of course, they were petitioners" (I, i). This sadistic behavior releases some of the underground man's pent up hostility and gives him a feeling of power that is deeply satisfying. But his compliant trends, which are quite close to the surface, prevent him from whole-heartedly enjoying his triumphs and lead him, indeed, to a denial of his spitefulness.

> But do you know, gentlemen, what was the chief point about my spite? Why, the whole point, the real sting of it lay in the fact that continually, even in the moment of the acutest spleen, I was inwardly conscious with shame that I was not only not a spiteful but not even an embittered man, that I was simply scaring sparrows at random and amusing myself by it. I might foam at the mouth, but bring me a doll to play with, give me a cup of tea with sugar in it, and maybe I should be appeased. I might even be genuinely touched, though probably I should grind my teeth at myself afterwards and lie awake at night with shame for months after. That was my way.
> I was lying when I said just now that I was a spiteful official. I was lying from spite. I was simply amusing myself with the petitioners and with the officer, and in reality I never could become spiteful. I was conscious every moment in myself of many, very many elements absolutely opposite to that. I felt them positively swarming in me, these opposite elements. I knew that they had

been swarming in me all my life and craving some outlet from me, but I would not let them, would not let them, purposely, would not let them come out. They tormented me till I was ashamed: they drove me to convulsions and—sickened me, at last, how they sickened me! Now, are not you fancying, gentlemen, that I am expressing remorse for something now, that I am asking your forgiveness for something? I am sure you are fancying that. . . . However, I assure you I do not care if you are. . . . (I, i; Dostoevsky's ellipsis)

In the first paragraph of this passage the underground man denies for two reasons that he was a spiteful or an embittered man. His awareness of his compliant tendencies makes him feel that his aggressive behavior does not reflect what he really is, and the shoulds created by his compliant trends make it impossible for him to admit his anger and his cruelty to himself. At the same time, however, the shoulds dictated by his aggressive trends are in operation, and he is ashamed of his softness, of the ease with which he can be touched and appeased. The aggressive part of him wants to be unabashedly sadistic and is full of contempt for his sentimentality; hence, when he is touched or appeased he grinds his teeth at himself and lies awake "with shame for months after." His compliant side is by no means the weaker in this conflict, however, for it forces him to deny the reality of his anger and cruelty. His conclusion that he was "simply scaring sparrows at random" and amusing himself by it testifies to his sense of his aggressive self as an empty facade, but it is hardly an adequate explanation of his behavior. It does accord, however, with the dictates of his detachment, which demand that his behavior be undetermined and that he have no strong feelings.

The violence of his inner conflict is evident in the second paragraph, when he speaks of the absolutely "opposite elements" (impulses toward compliance) which have been "swarming" in him all his life and which he "purposely" will not let come out. They "torment" him because they force him to hate himself for both his aggressiveness and his detachment; they must be suppressed because they threaten the other two moves in the most profound way. His aggressive self must repel trends which would judge it to be evil, and his detached self is deeply frightened of impulses which would drive him into unbearable intimacy and dependency. His aggressive values make him ashamed of being tormented by the thrust of his softer nature. Part of the underground man's difficulty, of course, is that his conflicting trends are not only all very powerful, but they are also all very close to the surface, so that he is driven to "convulsions" and "sickened" by the warfare between them. His detachment, which becomes more and more profound as he grows older, is in part an effort at resolving his conflicts by moving away from them. He attempts to substitute an intellectual awareness of his conflicting trends for the direct and painful experiencing of them; and, in a manner typical of the detached person, he takes great pride in his self-knowledge and intelligence.

His denial, at the end of the second paragraph, that he has been expressing remorse and asking for forgiveness, and his expression of indifference as to what his readers may think, both seem motivated by a combination of aggressive and detached values. His aggressive side cannot admit to feelings of remorse and defensiveness, especially when such feelings are generated by compliant drives; and it urges him to get back at the readers, who have been feeling superior, by denying the importance of their thoughts and judgments. The denial that he is experiencing uncomfortable feelings and that he cares about the readers' opinions is also generated by his need not to care, not to be vulnerable, either to himself or to others. It is no more to be taken at face value than is his declaration that he is not a spiteful man.

The underground man really is spiteful; he really is remorseful; and he really is indifferent. Like the romantic he describes, he has "great breadth." His problem is that since he contains everything, he feels that he is nothing; none of his attributes really defines his nature. "It was not only that I could not become spiteful," he tells us, "I did not know how to become anything: neither spiteful nor kind, neither a rascal nor an honest man, neither a hero nor an insect" (I, i). He cannot become anything because he is almost totally self-alienated, and the neurotic character structure which has replaced his real self has not achieved even a spurious integration. None of his acts, impulses, or values is an authentic expression of his real self; every one is subject to almost immediate repudiation by the conflicting components of his defense system. It is no wonder that he feels self-less, without definition or substantial reality. He is, in fact, a hollow man, a puppet pulled about by his contradictory compulsions, who, ironically, takes his slavery as an evidence of freedom.

In his relations with Liza the underground man displays again the many-sidedness of his character. His initial impulse is, of course, aggressive; he restores his pride, after the humiliations of the dinner, through sexual mastery and by successfully playing upon Liza's feelings. He is motivated not only by a need for vindictive triumph, however, but also by a feeling of rapport with Liza, a desire for human contact, and a long frustrated craving for self-expression.

His impassioned speeches to Liza are to a certain extent made up for the occasion and carefully calculated to produce their effect, but much of their content is drawn from his own long-harbored fantasies and fears. When we examine his speeches we find that they are largely an expression of his self-effacing and detached attitudes: they celebrate love and family life and depict with horror the slavery of the harlot's life (II, vi-vii). His glorification of married love and of parenthood and his assertion that love is "everything" (II, vii) reveal more vividly than anything else in the novel his yearning for human warmth and intimacy. If his praise of love is an expression of his own dreams, his picture of the horrors of enslavement is an expression of his own fears. In Liza he is speaking to a woman whose character structure has certain similarities to his own; she, too, displays marked tendencies toward detachment and, when this is broken down, toward self-effacement. She is profoundly moved when he brings forth what must have been one of his own most haunting fears, that of a lonely death followed by complete disappearance (II, vii).

The underground man hammers at Liza until she responds; but when she does respond, with despair and "an impulsive movement towards" him, he becomes "panic-stricken," is filled with "terror," and makes haste "to get away—to disappear" (II, vii). He gives her his address partly as a response to her need and partly to facilitate a quick escape. He is overwhelmed by the sight of her feelings and dreads the intimacy which they imply.

When he gets home he is beset by feelings of fear, rage, remorse, and desire. His predominant feeling is anxiety at the thought of Liza's invading his "private solitude" and finding him out. Yesterday he "seemed such a hero to her" (II, viii), but if she discovers his poverty and abjectness his triumph will be lost; he will once again be humiliated. Liza's arrival will bring reality into his retreat, his "cave," his "shell," the realm of his dreams, and confront him with his actual self, which he despises. She will bring with her, moreover, emotional demands which threaten his basic defense and to which he cannot possibly respond. He knows, therefore, that he will "be panic-stricken as usual" (II, viii).

When Liza does arrive the underground man is paralyzed, wishes to run away, is angry with himself, is angry with her, blames her for everything, wishes to kill her, does not care what happens, assaults her verbally, reveals his baseness, calls himself a scoundrel, wishes for peace, tells her he does not care about her, and urges her to go. When Liza understands his unhappiness and reacts with compassion, their roles are completely changed: she is "now the heroine," while he is "just such a crushed and humiliated creature as she had been before me that night" (II, ix). A "feeling of mastery and possession" flames up in his heart, and he makes love to her as "an act of vengeance" (II, ix). His pride restored, he becomes terribly impatient for her to leave. As she leaves he degrades her yet further by thrusting a five rouble note into her hand; but as soon as she is gone he rushes after her "in shame and despair" (II, ix).

The affair with Liza leaves the underground man overwhelmed by remorse and tortured by self-hate. He hates himself for his treatment of her. He hates himself because he longs desperately for love, and he realizes that he will always be cut off from it by his own nature. He has withdrawn from reality in order to protect his pride, to preserve his idealized image; the experience with Liza confronts him with his own warped and destructive nature, and he is flooded with self-contempt: "Had I not recognized that day, for the hundredth time, what I was worth?" (II, x).

His need to tell the story of his relations with Liza indicates that the underground man has never been able to resolve the feelings of remorse and despair which they engendered in him. As he narrates the events of long ago, he is once again overcome by self-loathing; and he not only reports his earlier self-accusations, but adds new ones: he is incredibly "spiteful and stupid," "incapable of love," corrupted by being "so out of touch with 'real life' " (II, x). It is no wonder that he has no wish to go on with his "Notes." He had begun Part II with the hope of obtaining "actual relief from writing" (I, xi); but he has only succeeded in administering to himself "a corrective punishment" (II, x). The only thing that he can do with such experiences is to run away from them; and so, for the time at least, he gives up writing from "underground."

IV

The preceding analysis of the underground man presupposes the reliability of the passages upon which it is based. It is evident, however, that the underground man is engaged from the begin-

ning both with himself and with his "readers" in a series of
maneuvers which are designed to protect his pride, and that these
involve evasion, denial, distortion, exaggeration, and rationalization. He is sometimes aware of these maneuvers himself and calls
our attention to them, but much of the time he is struggling to
live with himself and cannot afford to recognize his defensive
strategies.

We must be careful about taking any of his statements at face
value; but, in general, some parts of his narration seem more
trustworthy than others. He is an astute observer of his own
subjective states and he seems generally reliable when he is de-
picting these states and the patterns of behavior to which they
give rise. As we have seen, he provides a vivid and self-consistent
picture of his inner conflicts and their results. He is least to be
trusted when he offers interpretations of himself, though his
faulty interpretations also contribute to his self-portrait. There is
enough reliable descriptive material to permit us to understand
the underground man's character structure; and, equipped with
this understanding, we can identify his distortions and rationalizations and comprehend their function in his psychic economy.
We can perform this operation, of course, only with the aid of
psychological analysis; without it we are likely to be bewildered
by first person narrations, like this one, in which we are totally
dependent upon an untrustworthy narrator.

The underground man is sick, and knows that he is sick, and
hates his sickness; but he is trapped by it and must live with it;
hence he glorifies it. "People do pride themselves on their dis-
eases," he tells us, "and I do, may be, more than any one" (I, ii).
His withdrawal, his inertia and indecision, his vacillations and
contradictions all become marks of superiority, sources of pride.
He is diseased, to be sure; but his disease is that of being "too
conscious" (I, ii), too intelligent; and it places him far above the
stupid normal men of action whom he so envies and so despises.

As the underground man sees it, one of the primary differences

between the stupid normal man and the man of acute consciousness is the inability of the conscious man to make up his "mind
to do anything" (I, ii), and particularly his inability to take revenge. He cannot believe in his right to vengeance because he
can discover no basic principles upon which to act and judge. All
that science can tell him is that everything is determined and no
one is responsible. If he ignores questions of justice and virtue,
however, and acts simply out of spite, he finds that he has "not
even spite. . . . In consequence again of those accursed laws of
consciousness, anger in me is subject to chemical disintegration"
(I, iii).

The underground man has given us here an accurate picture
of his conscious mental processes; but he has not correctly identified the source of his difficulties. He is incapable of whole-
hearted feelings of anger not because he is so acutely conscious
or philosophically at sea, but because, though he is full of rage,
he has powerful taboos against both feeling and acting out his
anger. His "doubts and questions" derive not so much from his
intelligence as from the conflicting impulses of his own nature,
which find a sophisticated conscious expression in his relativistic
and deterministic attitudes. It is the laws of neurosis, not the
"laws of consciousness" which make his anger subject to "chemical disintegration." His vengeful feelings violate the taboos of his
self-effacing trends and imperil his detachment by threatening to
embroil him in conflict; he handles them on the conscious level
by rationalizing them away and unconsciously by converting
them into self-hate and self-destructiveness.

The underground man cannot act, he says, because he is
forever plagued by doubt, because he can find no "primary
causes" or "foundations" upon which to build. Intellect alone
can never provide the foundation for which he is looking; that can
be found only in the authentic values and strivings of the real self.
Since the underground man is almost totally alienated from his
real self, his intellect is an instrument not of self-actualization,

but almost wholly of rationalization. It is driven by three almost equally powerful neurotic trends, and it oscillates endlessly, settling nowhere. In one of his tirades of self-accusation, the underground man reveals that he knows this: "You boast of consciousness, but you are not sure of your ground, for though your mind works, yet your heart is darkened and corrupt, and you cannot have a full, genuine consciousness without a pure heart" (I, xi).

The underground man's inaction is a product not only of his self-alienation and inner division, but also of his pride system. By doing nothing he can preserve the possibility of being everything, a god, a hero. "A man of character, an active man, is pre-eminently a limited creature" (I, i). For the underground man nothing "but the foremost place" will do; and "for that very reason," he explains, he "quite contentedly" occupies "the lowest in reality. Either to be a hero or to grovel in the mud—there was nothing between" (II, ii). Any real activity is bound to fall short of his goals, to threaten his pride, to confront him with self-hate; this is why his experiences with Zverkov and Liza are so devastating to him. Hence, in the manner typical of the detached person, he gives up active strivings and seeks to actualize his idealized image almost wholly in imagination. The compliant and aggressive trends which he inhibits in daily life have a full flowering in his fantasies (see II, ii).

The underground man is not completely divorced from himself. He concludes that "it is better to do nothing! Better conscious inertia! And so hurrah for underground!" But he immediately confesses that "it is not underground that is better, but something different, quite different, for which I am thirsting, but which I cannot find! Damn underground!" (I, xi). I suggest that the something better for which he is thirsting but which he can neither find nor define is authentic, self-realizing existence. He expresses this longing only once, though we may assume that it contributes to his despair and to his efforts at honesty. Most of the time he cannot afford to recognize how truly lost he is.

V

Perhaps the most striking indication of the severity of the underground man's neurosis is the intensity of his self-hate. From beginning to end his notes are filled with incidences of extreme self-contempt, self-accusation, self-frustration, self-torture, and self-destructiveness. The underground man feels hated, despised, spat upon. Alternating with his claim of superiority is a sense of utter insignificance; he describes himself as a fly, a mouse, an insect, a worm, an eel. He accuses himself of being corrupted, out of touch with life, incapable of love. His liver is diseased, but he won't consult a doctor; Petersburg is too expensive and the climate is bad for him, but he won't leave. He lives in horrid lodgings with servants he cannot stand. At a certain period he repeatedly took strolls along the Nevsky which were not strolls "so much as a series of innumerable miseries, humiliations and resentments." "Why I inflicted this torture upon myself, why I went to the Nevsky, I don't know. I felt simply drawn there at every possible opportunity" (II, i).[7]

The underground man's self-hate originated, of course, in his early experiences of rejection and of self-betrayal. He develops his pride system in order to compensate for his feelings of worthlessness and inadequacy; but the pride system itself and the devices which he employs to protect his pride weaken him further and intensify his self-hate. As his claims become more grandiose, his vulnerability is heightened; as his shoulds become more stringent, his self-hate is intensified. He himself recognizes that his self-idealization and the demands which he makes upon himself cause him both to loathe himself and to feel despised by others: "It is clear to me now that, owing to my unbounded vanity and to the higher standard I set for myself, I often looked at myself with furious discontent, which verged on loathing, and so I inwardly attributed the same feeling to every one" (II, i). Characteristically, he manages to take pride in his self-hate by seeing it as a sign of his intellectual and moral superiority: "A cultivated and decent man cannot be vain without setting a fearfully high standard for himself, and without despising and almost hating himself at certain moments" (II, i).

Though the underground man has some understanding of his self-hate, there are aspects of it which puzzle him. He is puzzled, for example, by the disparity between his ideals and his actions. He not only fails to live up to his ideals, but he seems compelled to violate them. His spells of dissipation often begin "at the very moments" when he is "most capable of feeling every refinement of all that is 'good and beautiful'." He feels that this is "not accidental" in him, "but as though it were bound to be so." At first he struggles in agony against his depravity, then he comes to feel that it is his normal condition, and finally he takes pleasure in it.

There are several reasons why an intense consciousness of the good and the beautiful compels the underground man to degrade himself. We have already seen that he grovels in the mud because of his need to be a hero; he occupies the lowest place in reality because nothing but the foremost place will do. The more conscious he is of the good and the beautiful, the more anxious he becomes; for he cannot fulfill the demands of his shoulds and his pride system threatens to collapse. He protects his idealized image by not trying to live up to it; his dissipation is a defense against failure. It is, at the same time, a punishment for failure. He cannot be aware of his ideals without also being aware of his failure to live up to them, and this is bound to generate intense self-hate and a need for relief through self-flagellation. Yet another motive for the underground man's dissipation is his need to rebel against his shoulds. Being predominantly a detached person, he cannot stand any form of coercion, and nothing is more coercive than the tyrannical shoulds. Such people, says Horney, "may go through alternating phases of self-castigating 'goodness' and a wild protest against any standards . . . there may be a constant shuttling between an 'I should' and 'no, I won't.' . . . Often these people give the impression of spontaneity and mistake their contradictory attitudes toward their shoulds for 'freedom' " (NHG, 77–78).

The underground man finds an "enjoyment in the very feeling of his own degradation" (I, v), which "sometimes reaches the highest degree of voluptuousness" (I, iv). He has "taken up [his] pen" in order to understand this "strange enjoyment"; but he finds it "so subtle, so difficult of analysis," that it is impossible to fathom "all the intricacies of this pleasure." The underground man's pleasure in his self-degradation is, indeed, intricate. For one thing, he is seeking to escape pain through pain. "The specific masochistic way of lulling psychic pains," says Horney, "is to intensify them and wholly surrender to them. By the person's wallowing in humiliation his pain of self-contempt is narcotized and may then be turned into a gratifying experience" (NW, 272). As we have seen, the underground man's consciousness of his ideals fills him with a sense of failure and activates his self-hate. His reaction is to plunge into dissipation, to sink more deeply into his mire, and to be more and more inclined "to sink into it altogether." By intensifying his misery "and wallowing in self-accusations and feelings of unworthiness," Horney observes, "the masochistic person may derive satisfaction from an orgy of self-degradation" (NW, 272–73). The pain of self-reproach gives way to the pleasure of self-pity.

It is not only feelings of degradation that the underground man enjoys wallowing in, but also feelings of hopelessness, feelings that he has "reached the last barrier," that it is horrible, but that he can never change. He is one of those "who, despairing of ever being able to measure up to [their] standards, have consciously or unconsciously resolved to be as 'bad' as possible." Such a person wallows in his badness "with a kind of desperate delight" (OIC, 204). By losing everything, he protects himself against future blows to his pride and the pain of future defeat.

The underground man feels hopeless about resolving his problems and hopeless about living up to his shoulds. To escape the pain of his futile struggles and endless self-reproaches, he longs to have his pride crushed, to feel that he is foredoomed, that he might as well sink "in silent impotence . . . into luxurious inertia" (I, iii). His debauchery is a way of crushing his own pride, of proving to himself that he is irremediably lost. With at least part of his being, the underground man longs to be crushed, to be swallowed up, to have his identity obliterated and his impotence confirmed. This is why he wants to be thrown out of the tavern window and can imagine being glad of a slap in the face: "why then the consciousness of being rubbed into a pulp would positively overwhelm one" (I, ii). He wishes to escape from his inner torments by losing his selfhood, by being overwhelmed, by having his struggles and agonies subsumed into some larger, implacable phenomenon. This is why he likes to see himself as a helpless victim of the laws of nature.

Just as the underground man derives an enjoyment from being in "complete slavery" to his teeth, so he also takes a certain satisfaction in recognizing his slavery to his compulsions and to his inner paralysis, which he sees as a product of "the normal fundamental laws of over-acute consciousness, and . . . the inertia that [is] the direct result of those laws" (I, ii). By seeing himself as a victim of the laws of nature he tries to disclaim responsibility for his weaknesses and to defend himself against his self-hate and guilt: "a decent man is bound to be a coward and a slave. It is the law of nature for all decent people all over the earth" (II, i). This defense does not work, however; and he turns the fact that he continues to feel guilt into one more reason for feeling trapped, abused, full of self-pity.

The underground man feels that there is no rational solution to the problem of responsibility, and he sees himself as a victim of existential uncertainty: "it is simply a mess, no knowing what and no knowing who, but in spite of all these uncertainties and jugglings, still there is an ache in you, and the more you do not know, the worse the ache" (I, iii). It is quite natural for him to see his problem as a product of the human condition, but it should be clear to us by now that it is part of his sickness. His ache can never be stilled because his personality can never be integrated. His feelings of enslavement and his feelings of responsibility are both products of his defense system; they can never be reconciled because they serve contradictory needs.

VI

The underground man is so famous for his defense of free will and his defiance of necessity that it is somewhat surprising to realize that he also sees himself as a helpless victim of nature's laws and that he has a number of motives for doing so. His motives for denying necessity are, of course, equally strong, if not stronger, and issue in the philosophic passages which have attracted so much attention.

Replying to the rationalistic and utilitarian thinkers of his day, the underground man attacks the philosophy of enlightened self-interest. He cannot accept the idea that man "only does nasty things because he does not know his own interest" (I, ix). Man's destructiveness is not simply the product of his ignorance; it derives in part from nonrational forces in his nature which can never be eradicated by "common sense and science" (I, vii). Since man's will is governed only in small part by reason, a rational demonstration of his true normal interests will never compel him to will only the good. The rationalists have left out of their calculations, moreover, man's "most advantageous advantage," which is not "honour, peace, prosperity," or any of the goals which reason dictates, but the exercise of his caprice, the expression of his "own sweet foolish will." What man wants "is simply *independent* choice, whatever that independence may cost and wherever it may lead."

The rationalists dream of a scientific utopia in which all human behavior will have been subsumed under the laws of nature and in which our rational self-interest will have been thoroughly calculated. Human nature will be "completely re-educated," and man will be "compelled not to want to set his will against his normal interests." As the underground man sees it, men would never consent to this state of affairs, even if it were attainable; for the price of happiness would be freedom, the most advantageous advantage. They would "kick over the whole show and scatter rationalism to the winds" simply so they could "live once more at [their] own sweet foolish will."

The strongest part of the underground man's argument is his insistence upon the influence of nonrational forces on human behavior. His own experience is living proof that knowing the good by no means compels one to do the good. Indeed, as we have seen, consciousness of "the good and the beautiful" produces in him dissipation and depravity. It is no wonder that he sees "theories for explaining to mankind their real normal interests, in order that . . . they may at once become good and noble" as "mere logical exercises" (I, vii). His inner conflicts, the disparity between his ideals and his behavior, and his experience of powerful self-destructive forces gives the underground man a penetrating insight into the inadequacy of rationalist psychology, which simply leaves out of account the existence of unconscious motivations and neurotic compulsions.

The fact that the underground man makes some valid objections to the rationalist psychology does not necessarily mean that his own version of human nature is a balanced or accurate one. As we might expect, he sees his own traits as characteristic of the species and his own highest value as "the most precious thing for mankind" (I, viii). He does this not only because he is given to generalizing from his own experience, but also because he needs the reassurance of believing that in reality everyone is like him. It is important for him to affirm that it is not simply he, but all men who love suffering, chaos, and destruction. Human history provides powerful evidence for his contention; but this means that neurosis is widespread and not necessarily that man is essentially a self-destructive being.

The underground man is threatened not only by the utilitarian philosophers' belief in man's rationality, but also by their contention that human behavior is lawful and that it can therefore be explained, predicted, and controlled. His arguments on this subject have far less cogency than his attack on the overestimation of reason. Their vehemence and near hysteria indicate a high level of anxiety against which he must defend himself by a process of compulsive rationalization. The underground man's attack on the utilitarians is but a single episode in his lifelong battle against necessity. "The laws of nature," he tells us, "have continually all my life offended me more than anything" (I,v). He has "always been afraid of . . . mathematical certainty," and he is "afraid of it now" (I, ix). "Mathematical certainty" is, to him, "something insufferable": "Twice two makes four seems to me simply a piece of insolence. Twice two makes four is a pert coxcomb who stands with arms akimbo barring your path and spitting."

The underground man dislikes the laws of nature and the fact that twice two makes four for a number of reasons. "The more a person is alienated from himself," observes Horney, "the more his mind becomes supreme reality. . . . This is why the pride in . . . the supremacy of the mind . . . is a regular occurence in all neurosis" (NHG, 91–92). The laws of nature and of arithmetic limit the power of mind, of will, to determine reality. They insufferably frustrate our neurotic claims, insolently deny our personal grandeur, and bar the path to the actualization of our idealized image, which they force us to recognize as an imaginary

construction. Many neurotics, says Horney, "have an intense
. . . aversion to the realization that they [are] subject to *any*
necessity. The mere words 'rules,' 'necessities,' or 'restrictions'
may make them shudder. . . . In their private world everything is
possible—to them. The recognition of any necessity applying to
themselves, therefore, would actually pull them down from their
lofty world into actuality, where they would be subject to the
same natural laws as anybody else" (NHG, 45). In order to sustain his pride system, it is necessary for the underground man to
deny reality, to ignore or defy the actual conditions of life.

The underground man's intense aversion to the laws of nature
and of arithmetic is a product not only of his self-alienation and
self-glorification, but also of his particular neurotic solution,
which is detachment. As we have seen, the detached person
loaths all forms of restraint or coercion and has a compulsive
need for freedom and independence.[8] The underground man's
hatred of the laws of nature and fear of mathematical certainty
is, in effect, a phobic reaction. He is unusually disturbed by twice
two makes four.

He is unusually disturbed, also, by the possibility that human
behavior may some day be explicable, that "a formula" will be
discovered "for all our desires and caprices" (I, viii). If this happens, he contends, "then, most likely, man will at once cease to
feel desire, indeed, he will be certain to. For who would want to
choose by rule? Besides, he will at once be transformed into an
organ stop or something of the sort . . ." (I, viii). Here, as elsewhere, the underground man confuses descriptive with prescriptive law. But his confusion could never be cleared up by a logical
explanation; because of his hypersensitivity to constraint he *feels*
descriptive laws to be prescriptive. If he must feel and choose by
rule, then the only way he can maintain his freedom is to feel
nothing and to choose nothing. One of the reasons why the
doctrine of enlightened self-interest is so abhorrent to him is
that, as he perceives it, it contains an element of compulsion; man

will be "compelled" by reason "not to want to set his will against his normal interests" (I, vii). If reason compels him to do good, he will, of course, rebel and choose chaos and destruction. He will, if need be, "purposely go mad in order to be rid of reason and gain his point!" (I, viii).

The underground man's affirmation of freedom as the most advantageous advantage is, like his hypersensitivity to constraint, symptomatic of his detachment. The compliant person finds the meaning of life in love; the aggressive person finds it in mastery. For the detached person the highest value of all is freedom, independence. This can be a healthy value, and any appeal to it tends to be stirring; but, as Horney points out, "the fallacy here is that he looks upon independence as an end in itself and ignores the fact that its value depends ultimately upon what he does with it. His independence, like the whole phenomenon of detachment of which it is a part, has a negative orientation; it is aimed at *not* being influenced, coerced, tied, obligated" (OIC, 77). The underground man does not wish to be free so that he can fulfill his human potentialities. For him freedom is the goal of life, the highest fulfillment, and he is ready to embrace suffering, chaos, and destruction in order to have it.

One reason why the underground man wants freedom so much is that he possesses so little of it. His behavior is extremely compulsive; and, as we have seen, he is aware of the inevitability of his reactions and feels them to be expressions of natural law. His hatred of the laws of nature is in part a hatred of his own compulsiveness, which he longs to escape. There are times when he mistakes his contradictory attitudes toward his shoulds for freedom; but his vacillations and his rebellions are themselves compulsive. He glorifies his self-destructiveness as an evidence of free will and the futility of reason; but he is nowhere more driven than in this behavior, which, far from being capricious or incomprehensible, is thoroughly explicable in terms of his neurosis. He prizes caprice because "it preserves for us what is most precious

. . . our individuality" (I, viii); but he is incapable of spontaneity and feels like an automaton which is manipulated by forces beyond its control. That is why, to him, "the whole work of man seems to consist in nothing but proving to himself every minute that he is a man and not a piano-key!" (I, viii). There is a germ of health in his craving for autonomy, but a man who is truly in possession of himself does not feel a need to fight every minute against the threat of obliteration. It is the underground man's self-alienation and not the laws of nature, the certitude of mathematics, or the philosophy of the rationalists which threatens to transform him "from a human being into an organ-stop."

It is my contention that, whatever Dostoevsky's thematic or parodic intentions may have been, the philosophic arguments which take up sections vii–ix of Part I are quite consonant with the underground man's character structure and are both better understood and more permanently interesting as expressions of his neurosis than as thematic affirmations of the implied author. It is possible to see them as Dostoevsky's reply to utilitarian ethics and rationalist psychology, as a clue to Dostoevsky's conception of human nature and human values, or as an early expression of some of the central motifs of existentialism. Whatever their historical, biographical, or philosophical import, however, they are first and foremost an integral part of Dostoevsky's incredibly complex and subtle portrait of his character. As such they have an enduring aesthetic and mimetic truth which will make them fascinating even when their ideological content seems antiquated.

Chapter VII

The Dramatization of
Interpretation: *Lord Jim*

Though *Lord Jim* is not usually discussed as a realistic novel, its mimetic portrayal of Marlow and of Jim makes it similar to the works we have been examining. A full appreciation of these characters requires a psychological analysis. Thematically, *Lord Jim* is an unusually interesting book. In *Notes from Underground,* Dostoevsky avoided conflict between the classical moralistic and the problematic existential ways of presenting reality by virtually eliminating interpretation. Conrad, on the other hand, invites our closest attention to the meaning of Jim's character and fate. He avoids many of the pitfalls of nineteenth century realism by making the problematic nature of experience into the novel's central theme.

He does this by means of a narrative technique which dramatizes interpretation. He surrounds the issues to be explored with a variety of perspectives, each of which belongs to a character in the book and is in keeping with his psychology. The novel as a whole entertains all of these perspectives, but affirms none of them as adequate or final. It shows each of them to be valid, but limited. There are many truths, but there is no Truth. In their pursuit of an absolute, of the last word, both Marlow and the reader are confronted by existential uncertainty.

The novel falls short of complete thematic coherence because it contains one perspective which is not dramatized, that of the omniscient narrator of the first four chapters. The novel is written from two perspectives: from the absolute perspective of the first four chapters and the relativistic perspective which dominates once Marlow becomes narrator. I find it impossible to reconcile them.

The opening chapters establish the implied author's moral perspective and his conception of Jim's character. Since Marlow's views are parallel to those of the omniscient narrator, we have a strong sense of Marlow's reliability from the very beginning of his narration. The omniscient narrator presents Jim as a romantic dreamer who is innately unsound, and this is precisely the way in which Marlow sees him. This creates a problem, for Marlow comes to doubt the interpretation of Jim which has thus been endorsed by the implied author. When Jim's behavior in Patusan makes Marlow uncertain of his defectiveness, it is not only his version of Jim, but the omniscient narrator's as well which is being called into question. Marlow's doubts are also endorsed by the novel's rhetoric. They seem to be the product of existential uncertainty and to mark him as a superior person. For Marlow to become uncertain or to change his mind creates no difficulty as long as the changes are adequately motivated. Such shifts in the implied author, however, are confusing inconsistencies, artistic flaws. If interpretation had been consistently dramatized, these problems would not exist.

Conrad may have intended the omniscient narration of the first four chapters to be a beacon of light, a standard of truth, in the world of doubts, confusions, and multiple perspectives which Marlow comes to inhabit. It seems more likely, however, that Marlow's narration is intended to evoke the ineradicable uncertainties of the human condition, that the implied author came either consciously to doubt or unconsciously to shift his own position, and that the first four chapters are a mistake which was not corrected.

Despite its flaws, *Lord Jim* achieves greatness in its rendering of the uncertainty of human knowledge and the relativity of human judgments. Before I explore the judgments and uncertainties of which Jim is the occasion, I shall try to reconstruct the implied author's conception of his problematic hero. In doing so, I shall rely heavily upon the first four chapters, but I shall also draw upon passages from Marlow's narration which seem to have the stamp of reliability and upon whatever outside information is necessary for an understanding of the text. My thematic analysis of the novel will be followed by psychological studies of Jim and Marlow.

II

In Conrad's terms, Jim is a combination of the hollow man and the romantic. The meaning of his life lies in the ideal identity he has conceived for himself, in his dreams of personal glory. He sees himself as "a man destined to shine in the midst of dangers," "always an example of devotion to duty, and as unflinching as a hero in a book" (Ch. 1). His dreams are "the best parts of life, its secret truth, its hidden reality" (Ch. 2). For Conrad, too, there is a hidden reality which constitutes our true moral identity. It is not our dreams, however, but our capacity for faithfulness and resistance in the face of the dark powers that reveals our "inner worth," the "fibre of [our] stuff," the "secret truth of [our] pretences" (Ch. 2).

We are given glimpses of the secret truth of Jim's pretenses in the training ship and storm episodes. Instead of shining in the midst of danger, Jim is subject to paralysis and fear. He reverses the meaning of the training ship incident. At first he looks at the captain "with the pain of conscious defeat in his eyes"; but he persuades himself, finally, that when all men flinch, "he alone [will] know how to deal with the spurious menace of wind and seas" (Ch. 1). As he lies injured in his cabin during the storm, he is gripped by "an uncontrollable rush of anguish" and has a "despairing desire to escape at any cost" (Ch. 2). When the fine weather returns, he thinks no more about it; but the glimpse he has had of his own vulnerability is undoubtedly responsible for his decision to sail upon Eastern seas, with their "suggestions of infinite repose, the gift of endless dreams." As chief mate of the *Patna* there is, seemingly, nothing to challenge his claims of superiority, nothing to prevent him from feeling that his dreams *are* the secret truth, the hidden reality. When the ship strikes a submerged object, Jim has an opportunity to live out his dreams; for here, indeed, all men flinch (and the menace turns out to be spurious). But he jumps.

The first half of the novel clearly suggests that, for man, essence precedes existence. Our moral nature is predetermined. We can discover it through our deeds, but we can neither create it nor change it, even though we are defined by and responsible for it. Jim succumbs to the dark powers because he lacks the "power of resistance," the "instinct of courage" which ought to belong to a man of his parentage and appearance. He lacks the "inborn ability to look temptations straight in the face . . . an unthinking and blessed stiffness before the outward and inward terrors, before the might of nature and the seductive corruption of men—backed by a faith invulnerable to the strength of facts, to the contagion of example, to the solicitation of ideas" (Ch. 5).[1] To understand the implications of this important passage, we must examine it in the light of Conrad's beliefs about human nature and the human condition.[2]

The cosmic order is unconscious, amoral; man's existence in it is radically insecure. However benign or beautiful it may appear, there lurk within it "elemental furies" which have "a strength beyond control" and which threaten "to smash, to destroy, to annihilate" man and all that he holds dear (Ch. 2). Organic nature is the scene of a struggle for survival in which the instincts of aggression, lust, and self-preservation all play essential roles. Insofar as man is a product of this struggle, these instincts remain powerful within him, however much they may have been denied, repressed, fought against, or brought under control by the forces of civilization. The powers of darkness exist, then, both within and without—in the unconscious, instinctual component of the human psyche which links us to our savage and animal ancestors, and in the blind processes of inorganic nature which threaten our safety and, ultimately, claim our lives.

The cosmic process is alien, inimical; our salvation lies in the human community. Like Huxley, Spencer, G. H. Lewes, George Eliot, and many other nineteenth century evolutionists, Conrad sees the human order as an ethical process the goal of which is to combat the cosmic process out of which it has evolved. Through steadfastness, fidelity, and discipline, men can often overcome the elemental furies. In the training ship episode, the cutter is, like Jim, "under the spell" of the storm, which holds her "bound, and tossing abreast of the ship. A yelling voice in her reached him faintly: 'Keep stroke, you young whelps, if you want to save anybody! Keep stroke!' And suddenly she lifted high her bow, and, leaping with raised oars over a wave, broke the spell cast upon her by the wind and tide" (Ch. 1).

One of the chief agencies of the ethical process is the social medium which binds men together and mediates between the individual and the alien cosmos. We are not born into the cosmos, but into a community of values, traditions, and institutions. Conrad envisages this community as essentially national in identity: "Each blade of grass has its spot on earth whence it draws its life, its strength; and so is man rooted to the land from which he draws his faith together with his life" (Ch. 21). The national consciousness organizes and transmits the accumulated experience of the race; it embodies the ideals which have been found essential for the preservation and enrichment of human life.

Courage, loyalty, faithfulness to duty—the virtues which sustain the human community in its fight against the dark powers—require a resistance to the selfish instincts which are our inheritance from distant ages. As long as we are surrounded by our culture, we are sustained by the fear of censure, the power of example, and the force of tradition, by inspiring sights and sounds, by the eyes of others. If Jim had been in the home service, or had had a McWhirr as captain, he would have performed with honor, though not without fear. But, as Marlow observes, he " 'had none of these inducements—at least at that moment.' " What Jim lacks is an "inborn ability" to resist "the outward and inward terrors" when he must confront them alone, as on the *Patna.* What is this ability? Where does it come from?

It is an evolved racial unconscious, a biological inheritance of cultural ideals which renders men "organically moral."[3] The trustworthiness and restraint which are man's most precious traits cannot be adequately accounted for by ideals or beliefs or even by early conditioning. They are possessed only by civilized men—with a few rare exceptions—and in a higher degree by some nationalities than by others (race and nationality are virtually identical here). Why, Marlow asks in "Youth," did the crew of Liverpool scalliwags dutifully climb the masts and furl the sails of a burning ship doomed to arrive nowhere? It wasn't a drilled-in habit of obedience, it wasn't a professional sense of duty, it wasn't the pay: "No; it was something in them, something inborn and subtle and everlasting. I don't say positively that the crew of a French or German merchantman wouldn't have done it, but I doubt whether it would have been done in the same way. There was a completeness in it, something solid like a principle, and masterful like an instinct—a disclosure of something secret—of that hidden something, that gift of good or evil that makes racial difference, that shapes the fate of nations."[4]

Like many nineteenth century evolutionists, Conrad believed

in the inheritance of acquired characteristics. According to this theory, experience modifies organic structure, and the acquired structural modifications are biologically transmitted. Spencer and Lewes invoked the inheritance of acquired characteristics to explain the presence of *a priori* forms of thought, attempting in this way to reconcile the empiricism of Locke and Hume with the idealism of Kant. Conrad's belief in this theory is made evident by a passage in "Heart of Darkness" in which Marlow speaks of the savages' lack of a sense of time: "I don't think a single one of them had any clear idea of time, as we at the end of countless ages have. They still belonged to the beginnings of time—had no inherited experience to teach them as it were."[5] Conscience also is a product of inherited experience, of "the hereditary transmission of organized tendencies."[6] Man's innate moral sense does not bring with it definite conceptions of right and wrong, but "organized predispositions" which respond unconsciously to the social code and issue "spontaneously . . . in the beneficent forms of action which the experience of society has classed as right."[7]

Man is the product of a dual evolutionary process. His unconscious contains not only the instincts of the savage, but also the moral predispositions which have grown out of racial experience. In their cosmic unconscious all men are brutal, cowardly, corrupt; but some men have in their racial unconscious an "innate strength,"[8] an "instinct of courage," which provides them with "an unthinking and blessed stiffness before the outward and inward terrors" (Ch. 5). As long as an individual remains untested by the moral isolation or the elemental furies which "show in the light of day . . . the fibre of his stuff" (Ch. 2), he can identify himself with his principles. But in the face of a real test, "principles won't do." They are "acquisitions, clothes, pretty rags . . . that would fly off at the first good shake." He "must meet that truth with his own true stuff—with his own inborn strength."[9] This strength is derived, of course, from principles, but principles which have become unconscious predispositions. Behavior which is thus motivated has "a completeness in it, something solid like a principle, and masterful like an instinct." Jim knows his duty; he has imbibed the racial ideals as they are codified in British naval tradition. But he lacks the inborn strength which ought to belong to a man of his parentage; and, as a result, he betrays the dictates of his racial conscience.

Jim's fate is determined not only by his inner weakness and the omnipresence of the dark powers, but also by the fact that he is a romantic, that he wants more glamor than he can carry. In his dreams he is "always an example of devotion to duty," but he is not really interested in keeping stroke, in being faithful to his place in the ranks. He sees himself "saving people from sinking ships, cutting away masts in a hurricane, swimming through a surf with a line" (Ch. 1); what he wants is personal glory, to be like "a hero in a book."

Jim's need to be a hero drives him away from the sheltering community, from the external sanctions and examples which could have sustained him. When the accident occurs, Jim has before him the example not of steadfast fellow officers who un-thinkingly do their duty, but of a corrupt captain, an "odious and fleshly figure" who is "the incarnation of everything vile and base that lurks in the world we love" (Ch. 3). Jim knows his duty, but his rectitude is undermined by imagination and fear, both of which would have been controlled in the presence of other sights and sounds. The same imaginative faculty which makes him a romantic gives him the swift forestalling vision of disaster that paralyzes him when his glorious opportunity arrives. He jumps because he lacks the "instinct of courage" which would have given him "an unthinking and blessed stiffness . . . before the might of nature and the seductive corruption of men" (Ch. 5).

The secret truth of Jim's pretenses is now in the open, for all to see. Marlow sees it clearly. Jim sees it briefly, in the open boat, and thinks of suicide; but he soon mobilizes his defenses and begins to disown the act. Jim cannot live with the truth revealed by his jump from the *Patna;* and, in order to protect his exalted conception of himself, he embarks upon a series of artful dodges. Before he joins the *Patna,* Jim's plight is that he is at once a hollow man and a romantic, and he reacts to this plight by removing himself from danger and confining himself to imaginary realizations of his dream of glory. After his jump from the *Patna,* Jim confronts a new problem: how is he to live after his dream has been shattered? His situation is diagnosed brilliantly by Stein, and his behavior through the rest of the novel seems a perfect illustration of Stein's conception of how to be.

" 'A man that is born,' " says Stein, " 'falls into a dream' " (Ch. 20). Instead of being content to live in "this concrete and perplexed world" (Marlow's terms), he craves some absolute: " 'He wants to be a saint, and he wants to be a devil—and every time he shuts his eyes he sees himself as a very fine fellow—so fine as he can never be. . . . In a dream' " (Conrad's ellipsis). The "heart pain," the "world pain," comes because we cannot always keep our eyes shut: " '. . . it is not good for you to find you cannot make your dream come true, for the reason that you not strong enough are, or not clever enough.' " This, of course, is precisely Jim's case. When Marlow asks, " 'What's good for it?' " Stein indicates that the only thing that " 'can us from being ourselves cure' " is death; and Jim's case becomes "altogether hopeless." " 'The question,' " then, says Marlow, " 'is not how to get cured, but how to live.' " Stein replies with his famous advice on how to be, how to live without being cured. We must " 'in the destructive element immerse. . . . That was the way. To follow the dream, and again to follow the dream—and so—*ewig—usque ad finem.* . . .' " (Conrad's ellipses). If we try to live outside of the dream, we perish; our only choice is to follow the dream, to live destructively. To follow the dream is to live with our eyes closed; the dream is "the destructive element" because it blinds us to reality, a reality which is full of dark powers.

Jim's refusal to accept defeat, his determination to follow his dream, leads him to his great success in Patusan, where he proves his fidelity and triumphantly confronts every test of his courage. The destructiveness of Jim's dream becomes evident with the arrival of Gentleman Brown, that blind accomplice of the dark powers. The safety of the community requires that Jim be able to recognize the evil in Brown; but to do so would confront him with his own past weakness, which he still must deny. So he rationalizes on Brown's behalf. Brown's attack on Dain Waris destroys the community which Jim has built; and with its collapse, his dream is threatened once again. He determines to prove his courage and fidelity once and for all. By accepting death at Doramin's hands, he proves himself true—to his word, to his exalted conception of himself. His immersion in his dream has brought destruction to the community; now it claims his life.

By keeping his eyes shut and resolutely following his dream on to the end, Jim manages once again to wrest a kind of victory from defeat. In his final moment he becomes the hero of his fantasies; he sends right and left "a proud and unflinching glance." He is no longer the plaything of time and chance. Nothing can touch him. He is invulnerable at last.

As I have suggested, there are certain disparities between the first and second halves of the novel. Once Stein enters the picture, diagnoses Jim's case, and gives him an opportunity to realize his dream in Patusan, Jim seems to become more and more the romantic whose dream is bound to outstrip reality and less and less the romantic who is destined to betray his ideals because he is a hollow man. The first half of the novel raises the issue of Jim's (or of any man's) true moral identity and concludes that it lies in the qualities which are revealed by his acts rather than in the aspirations of his idealized self. The second half of the novel more or less abandons this issue and focuses on the question of how good and how bad it is to be a romantic. Jim's struggle after the *Patna* affair is to create his essence; but, whereas the first half of the novel indicates that this is impossible, the second half

shows him meeting emergencies and behaving with the intrepid-
ity of an unflinching hero. It is true that Gentleman Brown finds
his weakness and that, once again, he fails his community. He
fails, however, not because he lacks the instinct of courage, but
because he is romantic. He excuses Brown because he must excuse himself, because he must follow his dream on to the end. In
a sense this is moral cowardice; but it is hardly comparable to the
paralysis on the training ship, the funk during the storm, or the
jump from the *Patna*.

In terms of Conrad's conception, then, we seem to have two
somewhat different Jims. Both Jims are romantic; both have an
illusion of omnipotence which heightens their vulnerability to the
dark powers. But the first Jim is a hollow man who succumbs to
the outer and inner terrors, whereas the second Jim is an heroic
adventurer who reverses his previous behavior and can face anything but the truth about his human limitations.

It might be argued that these shifting conceptions of Jim are
not flaws or inconsistencies, but are essential to Conrad's thematic intention. In the early stages of his relationship with Jim,
Marlow believes that moral qualities are biologically determined,
that Jim is a hollow man, and that his moral identity is clearly
revealed by his jump from the *Patna*. But human beings are too
complex, too mysterious, too unpredictable, to be understood so
readily and so definitively. This is one of the things which Marlow, and through him, the reader, must learn. The difficulty is
that Marlow's initial beliefs about Jim and about human nature
are clearly supported by the omniscient narration of the first four
chapters. If this were not so, we could attribute the shifting conceptions of Jim exclusively to Marlow and see them as part of the
implied author's exploration of the problematic nature of experience. As it is, the first four chapters lead us to believe that Jim
is an intelligible character and that both the implied author and
Marlow understand him quite well. When Marlow shifts his position and the novel's rhetoric makes no effort to reconcile this shift

with the omniscient narrator's prespective, the reader becomes confused.

To put this problem another way, the opening chapters arouse in the reader generic expectations which are different from those aroused by the body of the novel. In the first four chapters we have a classical moralistic presentation of reality; in the remainder of the book reality is presented from a problematic existential point of view. Jim's final inscrutability is highly appropriate to the perspective and the thematic concerns generated by Marlow's narration; it clashes, however, with the feeling demands aroused by the omniscient narrator.

III

The central thematic affirmation of *Lord Jim* is that we crave certitude but live in a "world of doubts," a world in which "all assertion is a defiance . . . an insolence" (Ch. 23). The finality we long for is to be found only in death, which "exorcises from the house of life the haunting shadow of fate" (Ch. 16). In life, there is no escape from uncertainty and fear. The appearances of nature are deceptive, and so are those of men. We can know and trust neither ourselves nor others. Our beliefs, values, and judgments are subjective, perspective bound, partial truths at best, perhaps illusions. The cosmos presents a "vast and dismal aspect of disorder" which compels us to withdraw, tortoise-like, into our sheltering "conception of existence" (Ch. 33). We employ artful dodges to escape the grim shadow of self-knowledge. We require some dream, some illusion, some idealization of ourselves, our community, or our common nature to give value to life. The only truth we have is that we have no Truth, no Absolute; but this is abhorrent.

It is through Marlow's narration, of course, that the world of doubts is evoked. The omniscient narrator makes insolent assertions; Marlow's account becomes more and more tentative as the

novel progresses. As a result of his experiences with Jim, Marlow
gains a heightened awareness of the limitations of human knowledge and the relativity of human judgments. He comes to doubt
himself, his fellows, and the saving power of his racial heritage.
His judgment of Jim becomes increasingly complex and uncertain as he discusses Jim's "case" with a variety of people and
witnesses Jim's efforts to redeem himself in Patusan. Through
Marlow a number of other characters are introduced, many of
whom are foils to Jim or commentators upon his story. Each of
them throws a certain light upon Jim's case, but none of them
supplies the last word.

One of the first effects which Jim has upon Marlow is to shake
his faith in his fellows and his confidence in his own judgment.
Jim comes from the right place and stands for "all the parentage
of his kind." "He was the kind of fellow you would on the
strength of his looks, leave in charge of the deck—figuratively
and professionally speaking" (Ch. 5). But appearances are de-
ceiving: "it wouldn't have been safe." What Jim's case seems to
say is that we cannot be sure of others, no matter how sound their
training or lofty their principles, even if they are one of us.

Though Marlow repeatedly assures us that he has no exalted
conception of himself, like Brierly and Jim, he, too, cherishes a
set of beliefs which give an ideal value to his existence. He has
lost his romantic individualism, his youthful illusions of personal
grandeur; but he glorifies the community of which he is a part and
clings powerfully to his beliefs in "the solidarity of the craft" (Ch.
11), "fidelity to a certain standard of conduct" (Ch. 5), and the
superiority of the British racial character. Jim's case challenges all
of these beliefs and threatens to rob "our common life of the last
spark of its glamour" (Ch. 11); for Jim is a member of the craft,
he intends to be faithful to the fixed standard, and he comes from
the right place.

One of the chief reasons for Marlow's obsession with Jim's case
is his need to protect these beliefs and the glamor and security

which they provide. When he visits the chief engineer in the hospital, he hopes to learn that, despite all appearances to the contrary, Jim has been faithful, that the fixed standard has retained its sovereign power. The possibility that his cherished belief is illusory is "more chilling" to Marlow "than the certitude of death." In seeking "some exorcism against the ghost of doubt," he was, as he says, "looking for a miracle" (Ch. 5).

Jim's jump from the *Patna* threatens Marlow's belief in our common glory, just as it threatens Jim's belief in his personal glory. The question posed by Jim's jump is this: are "we" all really like Jim? Will we all succumb to the dark powers if the temptations are strong enough? Is our rectitude dependent upon circumstances? The French lieutenant says that we are all born cowards. Marlow does not want to believe this: " 'The fear, the fear—look you—it is always there.' . . .'I suppose I made some sign of dissent, because he insisted . . .' " (Ch. 13). The French lieutenant's unromantic version of human nature will do well enough for most men, but not for "us." It is almost as unpalatable to Marlow as it is to Jim, though he can entertain it, whereas Jim cannot. Jim clings fiercely to his belief in himself, refusing to admit the contrary evidence; but Marlow's convictions are deeply shaken. " 'Nobody,' " he tells Jewel, " 'nobody is good enough' " (Ch. 33). In his effort to comfort her, he says this "with the greatest earnestness"; but on the next page he confesses to his auditors that he "cannot say what [he] believed" (Ch. 34). The questions which Jim's case raises about our common nature are unanswerable.

Marlow's difficulty in arriving at definite answers to the questions raised by Jim's case is compounded by the fact that he is not sure that he understands the case itself. At first he sees Jim in the light of his racial theories, and concludes, like the omniscient narrator, that Jim is innately defective, that there is "some infernal alloy in his metal" (Ch. 5). If this is so, then Jim's jump may not say so very much about "us" after all; but it is impossible to determine whether Jim is typical or is simply an anomaly, a faulty sovereign.

Marlow is fairly certain, however, that Jim's moral essence has been revealed by his jump from the *Patna,* that his claims of courage and rectitude are self-deceptions, and that his hope of redemption can never be fulfilled. "He believed," says Marlow, "where I had already ceased to doubt" (Ch. 13). When he turns to Stein for help, his object is not to give Jim the chance he is looking for, but to "bury him in some sort. . . . it would be the best thing, seeing what he is" (Ch. 21).

After witnessing Jim's success in Patusan, Marlow no longer knows what he believes; perhaps Jim is good enough. But his doubts had begun much earlier. From the very beginning of their acquaintance, his confidence in his own judgments is shaken by Jim's confidence in himself. There is something in Marlow that yearns for the impossible, that wants to believe in Jim's innocence, in Jim's dream, in man's ability to master fate. Thus, despite his conviction that Jim is guilty and that he is hopelessly lost, Marlow cannot bring himself "to admit the finality": "The thing was always with me, I was always eager to take opinion on it, as though it had not been practically settled: individual opinion—international opinion—by Jove!" (Ch. 14).

Jim's career in Patusan produces a radical change in Marlow's view of him. Instead of seeing him mainly as a failure, he now sees him largely as a success. Jim seems to have realized his impossible dream. He achieves a "greatness as genuine as any man ever achieved" (Ch. 24). During his visit to Patusan, Marlow makes up his "mind that Jim . . . had at last mastered his fate" (Ch. 34). After he knows the whole story, he still speaks of Jim's "extraordinary success" (Ch. 45).

Despite his assertions that Jim is brave and true and that he has mastered his fate, Marlow is far from certain about any of these things. He has many more doubts about Jim's success than he had had about his failure. Marlow recognizes that Jim is motivated less by a sense of moral responsibility than by a kind of "idealized selfishness" (Ch. 16). As long as Jim is alive, moreover, he is subject to the vicissitudes of fate, and Marlow cannot be "certain of him" (Ch. 35). "While there's life . . . there is fear" (Ch. 16). Only in death is there "a sense of blessed finality": "End! Finis! the potent word that exorcises from the house of life the haunting shadow of fate. This is what—notwithstanding the testimony of my eyes and his own earnest assurances—I miss when I look back on Jim's success." At the end, however, after Jim's death, Marlow seems no more in possession of certitude. The last page is full of unanswerable questions and faltering affirmations. We are still in a world of doubts.

Jim's case remains enigmatic to Marlow not only because he can never understand Jim fully, but also because he cannot settle upon a univocal perspective from which to judge him. At first he sees Jim predominantly from a communal perspective, but he soon enters into Jim's own view of his case, and he also becomes aware of the cosmic perspective and is "made to look at the convention that lurks in all truth" (Ch. 8). In the second half of the novel he sees Jim increasingly in his own terms, from a phenomenological perspective; but he never loses sight of the communal perspective for very long and never stops judging Jim in its terms. As he oscillates between these three points of view, Marlow incorporates the perspectives of the more single-minded characters, feels their truth, and senses their limitations. He enters into the phenomenological perspectives of Stein and Jim, the communal perspectives of the French lieutenant and the privileged listener, and the cosmic perspective of Chester; but he finds that none of these perspectives is adequate for an understanding of this concrete and perplexed world. They provide answers which are too clear, too simple, too absolute. He can neither fully accept nor fully reject any of these perspectives; his view of each is conditioned by his awareness of the others.

In the early stages of their relationship, Marlow judges Jim largely in terms of communal values and understands him in terms of "our" common psychology. One of the reasons Jim is not clear to Marlow is that he is misperceiving him; he is trying to understand him not in Jim's terms, but in his own. He imagines Jim's feelings to be what his would be in a like circumstance, to be what one of us would (and should) feel. Jim is not entirely without the feelings which Marlow ascribes to him, but Marlow vastly exaggerates their importance. He comes to see that what Jim is taking to heart is not so much his guilt as his disgrace, not so much his "breach of faith with the community of mankind" (Ch. 14) as his failure to live up to his romantic conception of himself. Despite his dawning realizations, however, he clings to his view of Jim as a man stricken by his social conscience, perhaps because it re-enforces his belief in the power of the fixed standard. At the time of his visit to Stein he still sees Jim as "a straggler yearning inconsolably for his humble place in the ranks," a man who feels "confusedly but powerfully" the "severity" of the spirit of the land and "its secular right to our fidelity" (Ch. 21). It is "by virtue of his feeling" that he matters, that he has a claim to Marlow's brotherhood and a right to his assistance. Seeing Jim as an inconsolable straggler gives a moral sanction to Marlow's deep involvement with this irredeemable sinner.

Marlow protests so much, is so careful to insist that he saw Jim as lost, dead, virtually nonexistent, because there has been developing in him another view of Jim which is partly responsible for his loyalty and about which he feels uneasy. Marlow's close proximity to Jim gives him a concrete reality which threatens to escape the categories of the communal ethic. There is something in Marlow's psychology, moreover, which tempts him to share Jim's version of reality, to credit his excuses, and to participate in his dreams. Witnessing Jim's struggle to preserve his belief in himself precipitates a conflict in Marlow between the communal and the phenomenological perspectives. In Jim's presence he fears "being circumvented, blinded, decoyed, bullied, perhaps, into

taking a definite part in a dispute impossible of decision if one
had to be fair to all the phantoms in possession—to the reputable
that had its claims and to the disreputable that had its exigencies"
(Ch. 8).

Through most of Jim's narration, Marlow tries to hold on to
the communal perspective. Occasionally, however, Jim manages
to seduce him into accepting his version of reality. Jim does not
want "a judge," says Marlow; he wants "an ally, a helper, an
accomplice" (Ch. 8). Despite his strong efforts not to, Marlow
cannot help slipping into this role. Even away from Jim's presence, he shows signs of an identification with Jim's perspective.
When Jim tries to evade his responsibility, Marlow pokes at him
with his barbed shafts; when others are hard on him, Marlow
tends to take Jim's part.

This is what happens in his conversation with the French lieutenant. When Marlow points out that Jim did not have "the
example of others" to support him on the *Patna,* the French
lieutenant responds sympathetically:

> He raised his eyebrows forgivingly: 'I don't say; I don't say. The
> young man in question might have had the best dispositions—the
> best dispositions,' he repeated, wheezing a little.
>   'I am glad to see you taking a lenient view,' I said. 'His own
> feeling in the matter was—ah!—hopeful, and . . .' (Ch. 13)

But the lieutenant is not taking a lenient view; he insists that
" 'the honour is real' " and that Jim has lost his. The conversation
ends in an atmosphere of suppressed conflict, with the two men
facing each other "mutely, like two china dogs on a mantlepiece."
Marlow is "disconcerted"—"Hang the fellow! he had pricked the
bubble"—and he sits down "again alone and discouraged—discouraged about Jim's case." He is discouraged because he wants
to believe, like Jim, that having "the best dispositions" counts for
a lot, but he cannot dismiss the French lieutenant's judgments,
which are very close to many of his own. Under the influence of

the communal perspective, which the French lieutenant has insisted upon, Marlow proceeds to tell the story of little Bob Stanton, whose behavior on a sinking ship was all that Jim's should have been on the *Patna*. The phenomenological perspective reasserts itself a few pages later when Marlow observes, quite satirically, that the Frenchman's "pronouncement was uttered in the passionless and definite phraseology a machine would use, if machines could speak" (Ch. 14).

The French lieutenant is invested with great authority, and his judgment of Jim is never really shown to be invalid. It is clear, however, that both Marlow and the implied author find his perspective to be too definite, too simple, and too inflexible. He is one of the good, stupid kind who never go wrong, but who are not suited to deal with the complexities of human experience: ". . . he reminded you of one of those snuffy, quiet village priests, into whose ears are poured the sins, the sufferings, the remorse of peasant generations, on whose faces the placid and simple expression is like a veil thrown over the mystery of pain and distress" (Ch. 12). This associates him with Jim's father, the parson, who writes to his son that "there is only one faith, one conceivable conduct of life, one manner of dying" (Ch. 36).

The French lieutenant and Jim's father both belong to that impeccable world which is unthinkingly committed to the communal perspective and to which Jim can never return. Marlow has his roots in this world, but he possesses enough scepticism and enough imagination to entertain other points of view. The effect of his receptivity is to generate intense inner conflict: "I can't explain to you who haven't seen him and who hear his words only at second hand the mixed nature of my feelings" (Ch. 8).

Contributing to the mixed nature of Marlow's feelings is the fact that at times he sees both the communal ethic and Jim's struggle to save "his idea of what his moral identity should be" (Ch. 7) from the perspective of cosmic absurdity. From the cosmic point of view Jim's certificate is, as Chester puts it, " 'A bit

of ass's skin' " (Ch. 14). Jim's sufferings over "this precious notion of a convention" are, in Marlow's eyes, both "solemn, and
a little ridiculous, too" (Ch. 7). He has not violated an absolute
commandment, after all, but "only one of the rules of the game."
From the cosmic perspective, Marlow's fixed standard of conduct
and Jim's idea of what his moral identity should be are equally
phantasmal. Chester's hero is Holy-Terror Robinson, who, after
having been caught in cannibalism, "didn't allow any fuss that
was made on shore to upset him; he just shut his lips tight, and
let people screech" (Ch. 14). Marlow recoils from the utter amorality of Chester's point of view, but he shares Chester's vision of
a valueless universe, and there are times when he sees Jim
through Chester's eyes: "He was really taking too much to heart
an empty formality which to Chester's rigorous criticism seemed
unworthy the notice of a man who could see things as they were"
(Ch. 15).

The cosmic perspective is never negated in *Lord Jim*, but neither is it offered as the only reality. Marlow is aware that it has
its truth, but he feels that it is not a truth by which we should be
guided in our feelings or our conduct. Unlike Camus, who urges
a constant lucidity, Conrad feels that an awareness of the absurd
can be handled only in small doses. Jewel's description of the
death of her mother drives Marlow "out of [his] conception of
existence" and confronts him with cosmic chaos. He returns
quickly, however, to "the sheltering conception of light and order which is our refuge": ". . . it was only a moment: I went back
into my shell directly. One *must*—don't you know?" (Ch. 33)

Conrad values the man who is aware of the absurd, who does
not live out his life in blind ethnocentricity, but who is able to
recognize, as Marlow does, that the communal perspective is also
valid. Seeing the "convention that lurks in all truth" (Ch. 8) must
not blind us to the truth that inheres in conventions. It is a truth
for man, a truth that has grown out of human experience and that
has a "saving power." The spirit of the land has a "right to our

fidelity, to our obedience" (Ch. 21). It is a "secular right," one
which has no sanction in the cosmic order and which can never
be demonstrated to the reason. The important thing is that we
feel "the demand of some such truth or some such illusion." It is
his perception that our cherished beliefs are, from the cosmic
point of view, illusions, that makes Marlow so distrustful of ideas
("Hang ideas!") and "the vagaries of intelligence" (Ch. 5). The
communal ethic will not stand much intellectual scrutiny. The
"good, stupid kind" in whose presence we feel so secure are
those for whom the communal perspective is an absolute. Conrad's attitude toward them is always ambivalent. A higher being ·
in his scale of values is a man like Marlow, who sees and still
believes.

The mixed feelings which govern Marlow's reactions in the
first half of the novel are no less operative in the second half, in
which the central issues become how good and how bad it is to
be a romantic and whether or not Jim has achieved greatness in
Patusan. The cosmic perspective diminishes in importance, but
Marlow continues to oscillate between the communal and the
phenomenological perspectives in his response to Stein's philosophy and in his reaction to Jim's career.

Like the French lieutenant, Stein, too, has a definite view of
Jim's case; and, like Jim's father, he too feels that " 'there is only
one way' " to be (Ch. 20). Stein's philosophy, however, is not one
of moral responsibility and communal honor; he is a spokesman
for romantic individualism and is concerned almost wholly with
the individual's relation to himself. He does not see Jim as a
traitor to the human community or a man who has cut himself off
from his fellows by crime. The " 'real trouble' " is not in Jim, but
in the human condition; everyone longs for some absolute fulfillment, but no one is " 'strong enough' " to conquer reality.
We are all subject to " 'world pain' " when our eyes are forced
open. The solution lies not in communal effort and identification with the human enterprise, but in keeping our eyes closed,

in following the dream of our own glory on to the end.

Stein professes to " 'understand' " Jim's case " 'very well,' " and when he diagnoses Jim as romantic, Marlow is "at first . . . quite startled to find how simple it [is]." As Stein talks, however, his "assurance" diminishes; and when he concludes, Marlow is, as usual, full of doubts. Stein's philosophy is an exaltation of the phenomenological perspective; it urges us to cling to our personal version of reality no matter how destructive this may be or how much it may be controverted by experience. If we immerse ourselves in the dream and follow it on to the end, our lives will be suffused with poetry; and we will be able to retain our youthful freshness, our perpetual hopefulness, our illusion of invulnerability. Marlow is alive to the appeal of this philosophy which is so flattering to our wishes; its "charming" light may signal the presence of dawn, the promise of new beginnings. His dominant response, however, is to judge it from the communal point of view. From this perspective, Stein's philosophy is clearly inimical to our survival. Its light is "deceptive," obscuring as it does the dangers of existence; and it signals not dawn, but the coming of night. The "great plain on which men wander amongst graves and pitfalls [remains] very desolate under the impalpable posey of its crepuscular light" (Ch. 20).

As it does here, the imagery of the novel tends throughout to favor the communal perspective. The cosmic order is associated with darkness, death, hidden dangers, elemental furies, violent and menacing uproars. When we confront the cosmos directly, the world seems "to wear a vast and dismal aspect of disorder," and we lose "all [our] words" in a "chaos of dark thoughts" (Ch. 33). In contrast to the cosmic process, the humanized world is consistently associated with daylight, sunshine, safety, order, and all the products of human consciousness, including language. When we look at the world from within "the sheltering conception of light and order" to which our "words . . . belong," we see that "in truth, thanks to our unwearied efforts, it is as sunny an arrangement of small conveniences as the mind of man can conceive." The phenomenological perspective is associated predominantly with dusk, obscurity, moonlight, gloom, shadows, dreams, phantoms, ghosts, caverns, graves, self-destruction, and burial alive. There is more positive imagery ("light of glamour," "impalpable poesy," "magnificent vagueness", "glorious indefiniteness"); but it, too, has an aura of insubstantiality.

One corner of Stein's room is strongly lighted by a reading lamp; "the rest of the spacious apartment [melts] into shapeless gloom like a cavern" (Ch. 20). As Stein expounds his philosophy, he moves "into the shapeless dusk" and becomes a "shadow prowling amongst the graves of butterflies": "It had an odd effect —as if these few steps had carried him out of this concrete and perplexed world. His tall form, as though robbed of its substance, hovered noiselessly over invisible things . . . ." As he proclaims that " 'there is only one way' " to be, his "voice [leaps] up extraordinarily strong, as though away there in the dusk he [has] been inspired by some whisper of knowledge." But when he re-enters the bright circle of light, his gestures become tentative, "his twitching lips [utter] no word, and the austere exaltation of a certitude seen in the dusk [vanishes] from his face." He utters his "conviction," finally, in "a subdued tone," in a "whisper." "The light had destroyed the assurance which had inspired him in the distant shadows."

Stein's simple view of Jim's case, his "certitude seen in the dusk," is highly congruent with Jim's career in Patusan; for, in following Stein's advice, Jim, too, steps out of this concrete and perplexed world into a dimly lit realm of phantoms, shadows, and dreams. When he jumps from the *Patna*, Jim falls into an abyss, into "an everlasting deep hole" (Ch. 9), out of which, it seems, he can never climb. In Patusan he rises from the grave; but he is reborn as "a disembodied spirit" into a "world of shades" (Ch. 45). He is identified with the moon, which seems to have fallen "from its place in the sky" to the bottom of a precipice and to be ascending with "a leisurely rebound" (Ch. 34). It floats "away from the chasm between the hills like an ascending spirit out of a grave" (Ch. 24). The light of the moon under whose aegis we are to see Jim's rebirth is "cold and pale, like the ghost of dead sunlight." "It is to our sunshine," says Marlow, "which—say what you like—is all we have to live by, what the echo is to the sound: misleading and confusing. . . . It robs all forms of matter—which, after all, is our domain—of their substance, and gives a sinister reality to shadows alone."

On this occasion Jim looks "very stalwart" to Marlow; "not even the occult power of moonlight" can "rob him of his reality." Later, however, as Jim tells Marlow of the "ever so many experiments" he is going to try, "nothing on earth [seems] less real . . . than his plans, his energy, and his enthusiasm" (Ch. 34). Raising his eyes, Marlow sees the ascending moon, which throws "its level rays afar as if from a cavern." In "this mournful eclipse-like light" everything is heavily shadowed, including "the solitary grave" of Jewel's mother. Marlow thinks of the living who, like Jim, are buried alive, "buried in remote places out of the knowledge of mankind." Patusan is "one of the lost, forgotten, unknown places of the earth." At times it seems to Marlow that when he leaves it will "slip out of existence, to live only in [his] memory" till he, himself, passes "into oblivion." Jim's success partakes of the insubstantiality of Patusan. By following his dream he escapes life's perplexities; but, in doing so, he sacrifices its concrete reality.

Marlow's view of Patusan is intelligible, of course, only in the light of his racial attitudes. "We exist only in so far as we hang together" (Ch. 21). Patusan is a "lost corner of the earth" because of its "utter isolation" from Western civilization. The natives don't count, and nothing that Jim does there really matters. His success has a phantasmal quality because it lacks "externals" (Ch. 22). Its materials are fit "for a heroic tale," but "thirty miles of forest shut it off from the sight of an indifferent world." The communal view of Jim's career in Patusan is summed up by the privileged listener:

> "You prophesied for him the disaster of weariness and of disgust with acquired honour, with the self-appointed task. . . . You said also . . . that 'giving your life up to them' (*them* meaning all of mankind with skins brown, yellow, or black in colour) 'was like selling your soul to a brute.' You contended that 'that kind of thing' was only endurable and enduring when based on a firm conviction in the truth of ideas racially our own, in whose name are established the order, the morality of an ethical progress. 'We want its strength at our backs,' you had said. 'We want a belief in its necessity and its justice, to make a worthy and conscious sacrifice of our lives.' . . . In other words, you maintained that we must fight in the ranks or our lives don't count." (Ch. 36)

Here is another definite view of Jim, one with which Marlow has great sympathy. He can make no stronger assent, however, than "Possibly!" He immediately switches to the phenomenological perspective and offers a very different interpretation of Jim's career: "The point . . . is that of all mankind Jim had no dealings but with himself, and the question is whether at the last he had not confessed to a faith mightier than the laws of order and progress." Again, Marlow is uncertain: "I affirm nothing."

Despite his sympathy with the privileged listener's attitudes and his committment to the communal perspective, there is a part of Marlow which responds positively to romantic individualism and which sees Jim as an immense success. "Immense! No doubt it was immense; the seal of success upon his words, the conquered ground for the soles of his feet, the blind trust of men, the belief in himself snatched from the fire, the solitude of his achievement. All this . . . gets dwarfed in the telling" (Ch. 27). Marlow is Jim's historian, his epic poet. One of his objects in telling Jim's story is to save it from oblivion, to provide some externals for the heroic tale. His rhetoric is designed to rouse us from the "safe," "profitable," and "dull" habits of mind which keep us from appreciating the glamor of Jim's achievement. Jim has fanned the spark of Marlow's youthful romanticism, has claimed "the fellowship of those illusions you had thought gone out, extinct, cold" (Ch. 11). Marlow tries to fan the same spark in his auditors: "Yet you, too, in your time must have known the intensity of life, that light of glamour created in the shock of trifles, as amazing as the glow of sparks struck from a cold stone —and as short-lived, alas!" We must note, of course, that the romantic attitude is undercut by the very imagery which is employed to arouse it.

Jim's pursuit of his dream leads to the downfall of the order he has built in Patusan and to the betrayal of his promises to Jewel. His amorality is clear when he proclaims that " 'nothing is lost' " (Ch. 44). But the price that he pays, and that he makes others pay, for the fulfillment of his dream seems overshadowed in Marlow's mind by the glamor of his triumph, which is "romantic beyond the wildest dreams of his boyhood" (Ch. 36). Jewel says that Jim was false, and Marlow can appreciate her feelings; but his primary response is once again to defend Jim from his detractors. "She . . . said he had been driven away from her by a dream,—and there was no answer one could make her—there seemed to be no forgiveness for such a transgression. And yet is not mankind itself, pushing on its blind way, driven by a dream of its greatness and its power upon the dark paths of excessive cruelty and of excessive devotion? And what is the pursuit of truth, after all?" (Ch. 37). This is Marlow's most impassioned defense of romanticism; and his last question makes it clear that he is defending not only Jim, but himself as well. His dream is the pursuit of truth.

It is not the pathos of Jim's death that Marlow emphasizes at the end, but its poetry. Like Julien Sorel, Jim proves himself, by the manner of his death, to be an unflinching hero. His death provides a "blessed finality" which exorcises, once and for all, "the haunting shadow of fate" (Ch. 16). Marlow, himself a pursuer of absolutes, has consistently been envious of those who have claimed certitude or invulnerability, who have not been crushed down by the perplexities of this concrete world. He cannot help being in awe of a man who has truly mastered his fate.

In the process of examining any one set of reactions, there is a danger of making Marlow appear more single-minded than he ever is. It must be understood that he oscillates between the various perspectives from moment to moment and that often his mixed feelings are to be found within individual sentences. On the last page, everything is still tentative and uncertain. Jim's success is extraordinary, but his fame is obscure. The communal perspective is very much in evidence: he tears "himself out of the arms of a jealous love . . . at the call of his exalted egoism. He goes away from a living woman to celebrate his pitiless wedding with a shadowy ideal of conduct." Even so, Marlow is not sure that he "was so very wrong" when he answered "for his eternal constancy." Marlow oscillates between seeing Jim as more real and as less real than other men: "Now he is no more, there are days when the reality of his existence comes to me with an immense, with an overwhelming force; and yet upon my honour there are moments, too, when he passes from my eyes like a disembodied spirit astray amongst the passions of this earth, ready to surrender himself faithfully to the claim of his own world of shadows." The final paragraph begins with the question which has haunted Marlow throughout the novel: "Who knows?"

The conflict between the communal and the phenomenological perspectives remains, up to the end, a dispute impossible of decision. This does not mean, however, that the novel is thematically unresolved. Excepting the first four chapters, what the novel as a whole seems to be saying is that there is no absolute perspective available to man in this life. Every claim of certitude turns out to be an illusion. Each perspective has its truth, and also its limitation, its error. It enables us to see some things clearly, but it blinds us to others. We come closer to the full truth if we can combine the partial truths which each perspective affords. The greatest error is to make a partial truth into an absolute.

Each of the perspectives we have been examining gives us a partial truth. From the cosmic perspective, life is absurd. The fixed standard of conduct is a convention, one of the rules of the game; and Jim's anguish over his disgrace is ridiculous. From the communal perspective, Jim is a traitor to the human community, a lost soul whose life outside of the ranks does not count. From the phenomenological perspective, Jim's fate is of immense importance, to himself; and, in his own terms, he achieves an extraordinary success. What the novel seems to be saying is that these are all truths, but that each is incomplete, inadequate, in need of qualification by the others.

Once Jim goes to Patusan, the central questions seem to be: Does Jim redeem himself? Does he achieve greatness? The novel shows that these questions cannot be answered yes or no. The answer is yes *and* no. Stein says Jim was true; Jewel says he was false. They are both right; and both, of course, are partly wrong.

From the communal perspective, Jim does not redeem himself nor does he achieve greatness. By fleeing to Patusan, he cuts himself off from the possibility of any meaningful redemption, which can come only through staying in the ranks and keeping stroke. Jim's service to the community of Patusan does not count, not only because Patusan itself does not count, but also because he serves for his own glory rather than as an agent of Western civilization. The privileged listener had contended that " 'that kind of thing [is] only . . . enduring when based on a firm conviction in the truth of ideas racially our own, in whose name are established the order, the morality of an ethical progress' " (Ch. 36). His words prove prophetic. Patusan is based upon a conviction of Jim's invulnerability. When that is shattered, so is the community. Brown is a symbol of the dark powers, the hidden dangers, against which a morally founded order is designed to protect us. From the communal point of view, Jim clearly fails his people—in fact, though not, of course, in intention. And he fails Jewel, to whom he has made such solemn promises. Those who have depended on Jim for their safety or well-being are left devastated.

From Jim's own perspective, or from that of Stein, things look quite different. Jim has snatched his belief in himself from the fire. The "honour and . . . Arcadian happiness" he captures for himself "in the bush" are "as good to him as the honour and Arcadian happiness of the streets to another man" (Ch. 16). The blind trust of men is a "testimony to [his] faithfulness which [makes] him in his own eyes the equal of the impeccable men who never fall out of the ranks" (Ch. 43). Even when the awful thing happens, Jim feels that "nothing is lost"; for he has, in his own mind, been true to his people. By his death he proves both his faithfulness and his courage; he masters his fate. He has followed his dream to the end and has made it come true.

We can never make sense of *Lord Jim* thematically if we attempt to identify any one character or perspective as *the* moral norm. It is Marlow, of course, who comes closest to embodying the perspective of the novel as a whole. But the novel achieves something which Marlow cannot quite manage. Marlow cannot come to rest in any one position. The more embracing his vision becomes, the more uncomfortable he is. Seeing the world through his eyes gives us the baffling quality of life as experienced. The novel as a whole rises above Marlow's painfully mixed feelings and makes the ambiguities which so trouble him available to our contemplation. It is not torn between the conflicting perspectives, as Marlow is; it embraces them all, affirming and qualifying at the same time.

IV

As we have seen, from a thematic point of view Jim's story is not wholly intergrated. Conrad seems to present two somewhat different Jims, and the two halves of the novel focus on somewhat different issues. From a psychological perspective, Jim's behavior is completely consistent, and his story is perfectly unified. His central motivation throughout is the protection of his pride; and his story is that of a man who lives without being cured, who follows his neurotic solution on to the end. Its major episodes involve threats to his idealized image, his maneuvers in its defense, and his final vindictive triumphs.

In Horneyan terms, Jim is an expansive person of the narcissistic type:

> the person is his idealized self and seems to adore it. This basic attitude gives him the buoyancy or the resiliency entirely lacking in the other groups. It gives him a seeming abundance of self-confidence which appears enviable to all those chafing under self-doubts. He has (consciously) no doubts; he *is* the anointed, the man of destiny, the prophet, the great giver, the benefactor of mankind. All of this contains a grain of truth. He often is gifted beyond average, early and easily won distinctions, and sometimes was the favored and admired child.
>
> This unquestioned belief in his greatness and uniqueness is the key to understanding him. His buoyancy and perennial youthfulness stem from this source. So does his often-fascinating charm. Yet clearly, his gifts notwithstanding, he stands on precarious ground. He may speak incessantly of his exploits or of his wonderful qualities and needs endless confirmation of his estimate of himself in the form of admiration and devotion. His feeling of mastery lies in his conviction that there is nothing he cannot do and no one he cannot win. (*NHG*, 194)

We are given scant information about Jim's childhood, and hence we know little of the sources of his narcissism. His father "seemed to fancy his sailor son not a little" (Ch. 7), and Jim's anxiety at the thought of returning home indicates that he cannot face a lowered estimate of his worth. His development seems to have followed a typical pattern: "The individual may first have relatively harmless fantasies in which he pictures himself in some glamorous role. He proceeds by creating in his mind an idealized image of what he 'really' is, could be, should be" (*NHG*, 109). Jim's idealized image is crystallized by a course of holiday reading in "the sea-life of light literature" (Ch. 1); but his fantasies of heroism seem to have begun much earlier: "Ever since he had been 'so high'—'quite a little chap,' he had been preparing himself for all the difficulties that can beset one on land and water. . . . He must have led a most exalted existence. Can you fancy it? A succession of adventures, so much glory, such a victorious progress! and the deep sense of his sagacity crowning every day of his inner life" (Ch. 8).

Whatever the etiology of Jim's neurosis, by the time his "vocation for the sea" (Ch. 1) declares itself, he is entirely committed to his search for glory and has a fully developed defense system. He is to be "always an example of devotion to duty, and as unflinching as a hero in a book." This idealized image feeds his pride, determines his claims, and dictates his shoulds. Any threat to it produces intense anxiety; and any violation of it generates self-hate, a need for self-punishment, and impulses of self-destruction. The meaning of life for Jim lies in being able to believe that he really is his idealized self. He will do whatever is necessary to protect this belief. Its loss is worse than death.

The first threat to Jim's idealized image occurs in the training-ship episode. Having fully identified himself with his idealized image, Jim looks down upon the ordinary life of men "with the contempt of a man destined to shine in the midst of danger." His real life is not in the prosaic here and now, but in the glorious future: amidst "the babel of two hundred voices he would forget himself, and beforehand live in his mind the sea-life of light literature." The special pride of the narcissistic person, says Horney, lies in his claim of "effortless superiority" (*NHG*, 314); and this is one of the reasons why Jim is so given to dreaming. In his dreams he can enjoy the glory of heroic achievement and noble suffering without the stress, effort, and pain which accompany

these things in real life. Though he has been preparing himself
for difficulties ever since he has been " 'so high,' " his prepara-
tions have been for a display of effortless superiority and not for
actual coping with harsh realities. When the gale strikes and he
is confronted by "the brutal tumult of earth and sky," he is truly
unprepared, just as he is later on the *Patna*. The real emergency
is not at all like his dreams; and he is awe-struck, paralyzed, by
a force so much more powerful than himself and so much beyond
his control.

Jim's experience in the gale threatens his pride system in several ways. The fact that he flinches while other men act is a
flagrant violation of his idealized image and its corresponding
shoulds. His fear is deeply humiliating, undermining as it does
his claim of invunlerability, his feeling that nothing can touch
him. One of his chief claims is that fate is on his side; he is "a man
destined to shine in the midst of dangers" (Ch. 1). The gale, by
"taking him unawares," seems to be denying this claim and, with
it, his special destiny.

Jim's initial reaction to his failure is to feel "the pain of conscious defeat" and to be filled with remorse, a desire for vindication, and, possibly, an impulse toward self-destruction. He sal-
vages his pride and assuages his self-hate in a variety of ways, all
of which Conrad sees through and treats ironically. He projects
his self-contempt onto both the elements and the boys who have
effected the rescue. The "spurious menace of wind and seas
. . . seen dispassionately . . . [seems] contemptible," and the boys'
pride in such an ordinary achievement is "a pitiful display of
vanity." By minimizing the achievement Jim minimizes the importance of his failure and, indeed, turns it into a reaffirmation
of his specialness: ". . . he was rather glad he had not gone into
the cutter, since a lower achievement had served the turn." He
disowns responsibility and blames external forces for his failure
to perform. He reaffirms his claims: ". . . the final effect of a
staggering event was that . . . he exulted with fresh certitude in

his avidity for adventure, and in a sense of many-sided courage."

A more severe threat to Jim's pride occurs during the storm at sea. Once again he encounters the kind of situation he has been dreaming of, and once again the reality is far different. Instead of being invulnerable, he is disabled by a falling spar. Instead of "cutting away masts in a hurricane" (Ch. 1), he is confined to his cabin and feels "secretly glad" that he does not have to go on deck. After spending "many days stretched on his back, dazed, battered, hopeless, and tormented," Jim is so demoralized that he does "not care what the end [will] be" (Ch. 2). His indifference is an escape from feelings too painful to bear, but even this defense does not work very well: ". . . now and again an uncontrollable rush of anguish would grip him bodily, make him gasp and writhe under the blankets, and then the unintelligent brutality of an existence liable to the agony of such sensations filled him with a despairing desire to escape at any cost."

Jim's anguish is not simply the fear of death; its chief source is self-hate and a despair of ever becoming his idealized self. His injury, his helplessness, and his battered state all mock his dream of a special destiny. He is overwhelmed by the "unintelligent brutality of an existence" which treats him so cavalierly and which exposes him to the agonies of self-hate. His fear and his relief at not having to go on deck mean that he is not an unflinching hero. Jim is not unusually cowardly. He places such high demands on himself for courage that he panics when he cannot live up to them and then becomes quickly demoralized. If he is not an unflinching hero, he is nothing. His agony is the agony of confronting his despised self, and his desire to escape at any cost is a defense against intolerable self-loathing. He would rather be dead than live without his dream. When the fine weather returns, Jim thinks no more about this experience; but it continues to affect him profoundly and is the major reason for his decision to enter the Eastern service.

Recuperating from his injury in an eastern port, Jim at first despises but eventually becomes fascinated by the men who have become officers of country ships. He despises them because they are not heroic adventurers; but "at length he [finds] a fascination . . . in their appearance of doing so well on such a small allowance of danger and toil" (Ch. 2). In many ways their temperament is akin to his own: "They had now a horror of the home service, with its harder conditions, severer view of duty, and the hazard of stormy oceans. . . . They shuddered at the thought of hard work, and led precariously easy lives. . . . They talked everlastingly of turns of luck. . . ."

Jim has not, in fact, found life in the home service what he dreamed it would be. The "regions so well known to his imagination" are "strangely barren of adventure"; and he has, moreover, "to bear the criticism of men, the exactions of the sea, and the prosaic severity of the daily task . . . whose only reward is in the perfect love of the work. This reward eluded him" (Ch. 2). The narcissistic person has a special aversion to work, especially if it is routine: "It is the glory of the dramatic, of the unusual that captivates [his] imagination while the humble tasks of daily living are resented as humiliating" (*NHG*, 314). Since he does not identify with the communal enterprise, there is nothing in the home service to feed Jim's pride. Even though he is disenchanted he cannot "go back"; he is enticed by the promise of adventures to come and enslaved by the compulsions of his search for glory. What else is he to do?

The Eastern service seems to provide what he is looking for. The "good deck chairs," the "large native crews," and the easy "distinction of being white" are very appealing, as is the reliance upon luck to make one's fortune. The "smiling peace of the Eastern seas" promises an "unbounded safety" (Ch. 3), a refuge from the horrible sensations he has just experienced. Nature here does not display an unintelligent brutality which threatens to crush his pride, but a benign aspect which is "like the certitude of fostering love upon the placid tenderness of a mother's face."

Even though he has so far experienced his idealized self almost wholly in imagination, Jim has had every expectation that fate would favor him with opportunities to prove his greatness and that he would really perform heroic deeds. His experience during the storm produces a major re-orientation. Before he was to realize his destiny in the future; now he realizes it wholly in his dreams. By joining the Eastern service, Jim attempts to protect his dream from the elemental furies, which have twice now reduced him to insignificance. The "invincible aspect of the peace" permits him once again to be "audacious." He becomes completely identified with his idealized image and is once more convinced of the validity of his claims. He experiences moments of great exaltation, as his dreams carry "his soul away with them and [make] it drunk with the divine philtre of an unbounded confidence in itself. There was nothing he could not face." The chief threat to his idealized image is his association with the sort of men he had formerly despised. He defends himself by muting his criticisms ("they weren't bad chaps though") and by disclaiming any kinship with them in his own mind.

When Jim explains to Marlow that he was not ready, he is not just fabricating an excuse. His dreams of "valorous deeds" have not prepared him for the situation which he now faces. Daydreams can be a useful device for preparing to cope with reality; but Jim's daydreams are all fantasies of omnipotence, of effortless superiority. Jim is overwhelmed at once by a profound feeling of helplessness. There are realistic reasons for this, of course, which Jim uses brilliantly in his own defense; but his sense of helplessness also has a subjective source. The thwarting of his claim of omnipotence drains him of strength and reduces him to a state of hopelessness. His rage at his powerlessness makes it all the more demoralizing. If he could have envisioned a way to save these people, he might have been able to act. But though his imagination can picture all the details of the upcoming disaster, it can discover no way to perform an heroic rescue. As he had done during the storm, Jim once again withdraws from a situation which can bring him only pain. He is not afraid of death; nor is he, as Marlow claims, afraid of the emergency. He simply gives up, taking refuge in the numbness of resignation. He does not want to do his possible (that is not a dictate of *his* shoulds); he wants "to die without added terrors, quietly, in a sort of peaceful trance" (Ch. 7).

Jim has other reactions, too, of course, the chief of which is anger. He is angry with fate for putting him in such an impossible situation. The actions of the officers, at once comical and base, intensify his sense of outrage:

> "Was ever there any one so shamefully tried!"
>
> He took his head in his hands for a moment, like a man driven to distraction by some unspeakable outrage. . . . In this assault upon his fortitude there was the jeering intention of a spiteful and vile vengeance; there was an element of burlesque in his ordeal— a degradation of funny grimaces in the approach of death or dishonor.

The "brooding rancour" with which Jim tells this part of his story is in large part the product of his thwarted claims: he has been treated so unfairly! Not only has fate failed to treat him as a favorite child, but it has mocked his dream of glory, has subjected him to unbearable temptation, and has fooled him into disgracing himself.

Jim must feel that he is the "victim" of an "infernal joke" if he is to hold onto his pride at all; to see his plight as accidental would reduce him to utter insignificance. In seeing himself as a victim of infernal powers, Jim is also defending himself against self-hate. He is disclaiming responsibility for his actions; and he is passively externalizing his self-mockery, feeling it as coming from without. His seeing the assault upon his fortitude as a kind of vengeance indicates feelings of guilt (perhaps for his earlier failures), even though he condemns the punishment as unfair.

His anger at the infernal powers reflects at once his outraged claims and an active externalization of his self-hate, which he directs at the crew and at fate rather than at himself.

In the moments preceding his jump, Jim experiences severe conflict between the demands of his pride and his urge toward self-preservation. He keeps his distance from his fellow officers, who are struggling with the life boat, in order to assure himself that "there [is] nothing in common between him and these men" (Ch. 9). His hatred of them is in part an externalization of the self-hate which he feels because they do in fact tempt him—so much that he stays at the opposite end of the ship and refuses to look at what they are doing. In a desperate effort to hold onto his dream, he resolves "to keep [his] eyes shut"; but when he feels the ship move, his eyelids fly open. He is convinced that the last moment has come. From this point until after the jump he seems to act in a daze, without conscious choice. He does not know what tore him out of his immobility, and he does not know how he came to jump: " 'It had happened somehow.' "

Given the fact that his desertion of the ship is a horrendous violation of all his shoulds, Jim must disown the act, not only afterwards, but while it is occurring. He is driven to jump, no doubt, by fear; but, even so, he can only behave this way because his pride system is in a state of collapse. His jump may, indeed, be motivated in part by a rebellion against his shoulds. He has struck an unconscious bargain with fate: if he holds onto his claims and follows his dream, fate will favor him with an heroic destiny. Since fate is not living up to its end of the bargain, why should he live up to his? The approach of the squall maddens him, and the movement of the ship knocks over something in his head. His anger is fully liberated and his restraining shoulds are swept away. Why sacrifice himself in this burlesque of an heroic ordeal?

Once Jim jumps, he is overwhelmed by self-hate and is kept from killing himself only by the presence of the other men. Their hatred, their abuse, their wish for his death, keep him alive by satisfying the demands of his self-hate and arousing an impulse of defiance: " 'I was not going to give them that satisfaction' " (Ch. 11). He externalizes some of his self-loathing by projecting it onto them, and his impulse toward self-murder becomes transformed into a murderous rage with the others.

The alleviation of his self-hate permits Jim to rebuild his defenses. He begins to disown his act. He equivocates on the moral issues in the ways which Marlow finds so offensive. In effect, Jim tries to escape self-condemnation through a variety of artful dodges and to restore his pride by holding on to his claims. Fate has been unfair to him this time, but if he maintains his belief in himself another opportunity is bound to come. Jim can no longer satisfy his pride through imaginary exploits; he must prove that his idealized image is his true essence by actualizing it in reality. This cannot be done immediately, however. He must be given another chance, a clean slate. What he can do in the meantime is to assert his claims, to defend them against all detractors. By doing this he will insure his eventual vindication. *"The claims are his guaranty for future glory"* (NHG, 62; Horney's italics). Hence Jim's pugnacity and resilience. Through his tenacity he will compel fate; his bargain is now out in the open.

Neither Brierly nor Marlow can understand why Jim undergoes the ordeal of public inquiry and formal condemnation; but there are a number of reasons why he "eat[s] all that dirt" (Ch. 6). Despite his rationalizations, Jim feels very guilty about the violation of his shoulds. His public disgrace permits him to externalize his self-hate and to feel abused because life is once again being unfair. Instead of feeling crushed by his guilt, he can feel defiant, self-righteous, scornful of the "fools" who stare at him in court (Ch. 6). His severe punishment also serves his need for expiation. His feelings of guilt affect the terms of his bargain with fate; he expects to undergo a series of ordeals before his clean slate is granted: " 'Something's paid off—not much. I wonder what's to come' " (Ch. 16). His voluntary submission to the legal process also feeds Jim's pride. It confirms his claim of moral superiority by separating him in an unmistakable way from the other officers; if he accepted Marlow's offer of escape, he would be one of them. By facing it out, moreover, Jim is living up to his idealized image: he does his duty; he does not flinch.

A further advantage which Jim hopes to gain from the public hearing is the confirmation of his version of reality. In this, of course, he is severely disappointed. As we all do, he needs consensual validation if he is to stabilize his belief system. He needs others to see that he was the victim of an infernal joke, that it really doesn't prove anything. But the court does not want his explanations; it wants facts—only facts; and Jim, discouraged, begins to doubt whether he will "ever again speak out as long as he [lives]."

It is Marlow who provides Jim with an opportunity to escape from his moral isolation. Telling his story to Marlow enables Jim to order his thoughts, to elaborate his defenses, and to perfect his strategies. Marlow's "understanding" confirms his version of reality and gives him the re-enforcement which he needs so badly. Marlow is often critical, of course; but Jim rarely sees this. He senses Marlow's underlying sympathy and succeeds more than once in casting upon him "the spirit of his illusion" (Ch. 9). He derives great moral support from the fact that he is being " 'believed' " by " 'an elder man' " (Ch. 11). He can " 'never face' " his father: " 'I could never explain. He wouldn't understand' " (Ch. 7). The board of inquiry seems to live in an equally simple world of moral absolutes. Marlow is an authority figure whose wide experience and imaginative sympathy enable him to enter into Jim's perspective. It is no wonder that Jim burrows "deep, deep, in hope of [his] absolution" (Ch. 8).

The remainder of Jim's career is profoundly influenced by his friendship with Marlow, who provides him with jobs as well as with moral support. Marlow's letter to Mr. Denver gives rise to

an excessive elation, which is bewildering to Marlow. Jim's identification with his idealized image is, at this point, very shaky. By
going out on a limb, by making himself "unreservedly responsible" for Jim (Ch. 17), Marlow treats Jim in a way which is appropriate to his claims, and thus restores Jim's "confidence" in himself. Jim becomes "another man altogether"—his proud self.
Marlow feels that he has saved Jim from starvation—"This was
all"—but Jim sees this good fortune as a change of luck, a sign
from heaven. His claims are being honored; he is once again
fortune's child. He marches out into the night with "the un-
hesitating tread of a man walking in broad daylight."

Jim's hopes are soon shattered. He leaves Mr. Denver when the
second engineer of the *Patna* shows up; he leaves Engström &
Blake when Captain O'Brien calls the *Patna* officers "skunks"
(Ch. 18); and there are many other incidents of the sort. Jim
tackles each new job "with a stubborn serenity" (Ch. 13), confident that he is expiating his guilt and insuring the eventual compliance of fate. He endures his "toil without honour. . . . very
well"—"except for certain fantastic and violent outbreaks" when
the *Patna* case crops up. Though he has proclaimed that he will
run " 'from no man,' " he is extremely vulnerable to insulting
behavior and the conventional judgments of men. Anything
which undermines his claims threatens his bargain and deprives
him of his future glory. Whether he fights or runs away, Jim's
motive is the same: the protection of his pride, of his dream.

As Horney observes, "any hurt to our pride may provoke vindictive hostility. . . . It goes all the way . . . from irritability to anger
to a blind murderous rage" (*NHG,* 99). From shortly after he
jumps until he finally releases his vindictive rage by shooting a
man in Patusan, Jim displays a barely controlled craving for violence. He wants to murder the chief, he would like to hammer
Marlow in the cur incident, and he frequently clenches his fists
and mutters threats against anyone who would dare to insult him.
In the cur incident Marlow observes that he is "amazingly angry"

(Ch. 6), and his anger finally issues in "the brutal violence" of his quarrel with the cross-eyed Dane. He takes great pleasure in killing the would-be assassin: "... he told me he was experiencing a feeling of unutterable relief, of vengeful elation" (Ch. 31). Afterwards he finds himself "calm, appeased, without rancour, without uneasiness, as if the death of that man had atoned for everything." In Patusan Jim is able to fulfill all his wishes, and without guilt. It is possible that earlier he runs away to keep himself from committing a crime that would surely destroy his chance of a clean slate.

Jim is willing to undergo his "period of probation amongst the infernal ship chandlers" (Ch. 16); but he is beginning to lose some of his "elasticity" when his faithfulness is rewarded at last by the offer of a clean slate in Patusan. He sees that this is the "chance he had been dreaming of," and within a few moments he attains a state of "exaltation" which Marlow finds "phenomenal, a little mad, dangerous, unsafe" (Ch. 23). " 'This is luck at last.' " The compliance of fate feeds his pride and bolsters his wavering identification with his idealized image. He becomes once again his proud self: " 'Don't you worry. Jove! I feel as if nothing could touch me. Why! this is luck from the word Go. I wouldn't spoil such a magnificent chance!' "

From the perspective of our psychological analysis, it is not difficult to understand Jim's courageous behavior in Patusan. His earlier failures were not really the result of an inborn cowardice; and now that he has a chance to make up for them, he is driven by his shoulds into the most reckless displays of courage. He feels that nothing can touch him in part because he is aware of the power of his shoulds and is confident that he will not violate them. His fear of violating his shoulds far outweighs his fear of death; if he spoils this magnificent chance he will have no further defense, and existence will be a living hell. If he fulfills his shoulds, on the other hand, he will be his idealized self, no matter what happens to his life. Hence he is not afraid of the Rajah and his coffee or of Cornelius. He disregards Cornelius "on general grounds": " 'I feel that if I go straight nothing can touch me. . . . The worst thing he could do would be to kill me, I suppose. . . . Well—what of that? I didn't come flying here for my life— did I?' " (Ch. 34). To safeguard his life would violate his shoulds and hence is unthinkable. Note that Jim does not seem concerned with the effect which his death would have on his people.

Jim's recklessness has many functions. It serves not only to prove that he is an unflinching hero, but also to disprove all past imputations of cowardice. It is an assertion of his claims, a testing of fate; if he is truly invulnerable, nothing can touch him. Finally, his recklessness is an expression of self-punishing impulses. By exposing himself to danger, he continues his expiation. This at once compels fate and proves his moral sensitivity. Instances of Jim's reckless behavior in Patusan are too numerous to mention. His disdain of Cornelius's open hostility ultimately costs him his life.

In Patusan Jim's dreams come true. Luck is on his side, he bears "a charmed life," and every reckless act redounds "to his glory" (Ch. 29). His relationships with Doramin, with Dain Waris, and with Jewel are "like something in a book" (Ch. 33). He is the bearer of the magic talisman, the true friend, the triumphant warrior, "the knight rescuing the damsel in distress." His "conquest of love, honour, men's confidence" is fit material "for a heroic tale" (Ch. 22). His fame is "tinged with wonder and mystery on the lips of whispering men" (Ch. 27). The sole representative of his superior kind, he becomes "the virtual ruler of the land" (Ch. 28).

It is no wonder that Jim is nearly satisfied. His neurotic solution is working to perfection, his claims are being honored, his pride is being fed. The narcissistic person "needs endless confirmation of himself in the form of admiration and devotion" (*NHG*, 194). Jim receives this from Jewel and from his people. The narcissitic person's "feeling of mastery lies in his conviction that there is nothing he cannot do" (*NHG*, 194). Jim can do everything. While he is being harassed at Cornelius's, he declares, in a moment of frustration and of candor, that he will "make them all dance to his own tune yet" (Ch. 30); and he does. Marlow is struck by the fact that he takes "a personal pride" in the rising of the moon, "as though he had had a hand in regulating that unique spectacle. He had regulated so many things in Patusan! Things that would have appeared as much beyond his control as the motions of the moon and the stars. It was inconceivable" (Ch. 21). Helene Deutsch thinks "that Patusan is a state of insanity with delusions of grandeur."[10] Jim's grandeur, of course, is real: ". . . it was immense! Immense!" (Ch. 27). The fantasy is Conrad's.

Jewel fears that Jim will return to the white man's world, but Marlow senses correctly that he will never go back. He is the captive not of the land or the people, but of his craving for reassurance and his need for glory. ' "I must feel—every . . . time I open my eyes—that I am trusted—that nobody has a right—don't you know?' " (Ch. 24). In Patusan, Jim can open his eyes and still remain in his dream: outside there is only world pain. He sometimes wishes that he could have the greater glory of being a hero to the impeccable world, but he realizes that he " 'can't expect anything more' " (Ch. 35). He has in Patusan what he has waited for all his life: he *is* his idealized self. He must remain " 'because nothing less will do.' " To give this up would be " 'harder than dying' " (Ch. 24).

Even in Patusan, Jim's self-hate continues to haunt him. He had hoped to wipe out the past, to start afresh, as though he had " 'never existed' " (Ch. 22). But he cannot forget why he came there; he cannot escape his despised self. He tells Jewel that he is not good enough; he suspects that Marlow " 'wouldn't like to have [him] aboard [his] own ship' "; and he feels that his people, who trust him, " 'can never know the real, real truth' " (Ch. 32). Because he is still so insecure, he must prove again and again that he is an example of devotion to duty and as unflinching as a hero in a book. " 'I must go on, go on for ever holding up my end, to feel sure that nothing can touch me' " (Ch. 35). He can never be " 'done with . . . the bally thing at the back of [his] head' "; but he has only " 'to look . . . at the face of the first man that comes along, to regain [his] confidence' " (Ch. 32).

It is evident that Jim's loyalty is not to the people who depend upon him, but to his shoulds. As Marlow says, he has "no dealings but with himself" (Ch. 36). The natives must never regret their trust in him not for their sake, but for his. He feels a heavy responsibility not to spoil his magnificent chance. It doesn't matter if Cornelius kills him as long as he is courageous. When he must choose between Jewel and his shoulds, he chooses the latter. He uses his great power to create an "orderly, peaceful life" in which "every man [is] sure of to-morrow" (Ch. 40), but everything depends on him, and he is content to have it that way. He takes satisfaction in the fact that there would be "Hell loose" (Ch. 35) if he should leave. His importance feeds his pride. The edifice which Jim raises could last only if he were truly omnipotent. Conrad indulges his delusions of grandeur for quite a while; but he is too much of a realist to let them prevail. Brown arrives, and Jim's edifice collapses "into a ruin reeking with blood" (Ch. 40).

Jim gives Brown a clear road, with his weapons, because he is at once too insecure to resist Brown's manipulation and too sure of himself to suspect the hidden danger. From the opening moment of their dialogue, when Brown asks him who he is and why he came there, Jim is on the defensive. The reminders of the past arouse his anxiety; he must once again confront and deny his despised image. The simplest solution would be to let Brown and his men starve to death. But Brown says that Jim is " 'too white' " to do this. He would rather have an open fight: " 'I am not a coward. Don't you be one' " (Ch. 41). Given Jim's uncertainty about being good enough for the white world and his horror of being thought a coward, he is compelled to relinquish this solution. The threats to his pride force him once again to prove himself.

His initial attitude toward Brown is severely punitive: " 'You don't deserve a better fate' " (Ch. 41). Brown's reply—" 'And what do you deserve?' "—gets "in," gets "home" (Ch. 41). Jim's claims make him feel deserving of special favors; but his self-contempt tells him that he deserves no more than Brown gets. Brown's allusions to the fear which made him run away, to the slightness of his offense, to his saving his life in the dark all foster a profound sense of identification in Jim and make it impossible for Jim to judge him. Jim relates to Brown henceforth as he relates to his own earlier self. He excuses; he indulges. He tells Jewel that " 'men act badly sometimes without being much worse than others' " (Ch. 43). In a sense he becomes Brown's providence, or at least Brown's Marlow: he gives him another chance.

Jim's pride requires that he give Brown at least an open fight; his identification makes it impossible to be so punitive. He has no choice; he must give Brown what he wants—a clear road. The welfare of his people has nothing to do with it. If they decide to fight, he will not lead.

Jim's identification with Brown and his belief in his own omnipotence combine to give him a false sense of security. He is unable to see Brown realistically or to consider the situation objectively. Brown is an evil-doer (like Jim's despised self), but he has had an evil destiny (like Jim the innocent victim). If he is treated well, he will behave decently. Jim comes to the council with his mind made up and offers no argument but the reliability of his judgment, which has never deceived them. Jim has his anxieties. He is afraid that "something might happen for which he would never forgive himself" (Ch. 43). But he *must* let Brown go; and the success of his every scheme, of his every reckless impulse, has so re-enforced his claims that he may well believe himself infallible. In any event, it is important that his people honor his claims, and they do. This proves his power to Brown (who is incensed by his confidence) and gives him some welcome reassurance after the "bitterness" of their confrontation. The natives associate this situation with Sherif Ali's war, and so does Jim. He once again takes the responsibility for success on his own head. This is to be one more proof of his greatness. He is, as usual, careless about Cornelius.

After his world falls "in ruins upon his head" (Ch. 45), Jim has no choice but to accept death. " 'There is,' " as he says, " 'no escape.' " If he lives "everything [is] gone"; but if he dies, " 'nothing is lost.' " To save his life is to lose his dream; his self-hate would be unendurable. By dying at the hands of Doramin, he satisfies his need for punishment, he expiates his guilt, and he saves his dream. He proves, once and for all, his faithfulness and his courage. Not only does he insure his glory among men, but he conquers "the fatal destiny itself." The dark powers have attempted once more to rob him of his peace; but he has proved that nothing can touch him. As he sends "right and left at all those faces a proud and unflinching glance," he is wedded forever to his idealized image.

V

Marlow, too, is a mimetic character. His reactions to Jim's case, his deep involvement in Jim's life, his celebration of Jim's success, and his manner of telling Jim's story are all inwardly motivated. His relationship with Jim is charged with intense emotion from start to finish, and his perceptions of Jim are often colored by his own needs. It is one of Conrad's great achievements that he manages to give us a clear picture of Jim through a narrator who has so many vested interests in the story he is telling. The first four chapters help, as does the dramatic quality of Marlow's narration, which seems clearly divisible at times into representation and interpretation. Marlow is a good observer; and he has, as a story teller, his own mimetic impulse which enables him to convey more than he can fully understand.

Marlow suffers from a combination of high standards and low self-esteem. After a period of youthful romanticism during which he had an exalted notion of his own greatness, he has been humbled by the might of nature, the uncertainty of fate, and a sense of his personal insignificance. He has transferred his pride from himself to his community, which he invests with glamor and which he counts on to protect and sustain him. As long as he lives up to its standards, he can remain identified with it and partici- pate in its glory. Should he fall, life would lose its meaning and he would be subject to intense self-hate. His idealized image is that of an humble man who keeps stroke, who does his duty and thereby holds on to his precious place in the ranks.

Marlow is uncertain of his ability to live up to his standards. "From weakness unknown," he feels, "not one of us is safe" (Ch. 5). It is difficult to say exactly why he is so insecure. He manifests guilt feelings and has kept some bad company, but there is no indication that he has even come close to losing his honor. One reason for his self-doubt is that his taboos against pride require him to be unsure of himself; his uncertainty is somehow reassur- ing. In his scheme of things the confident, the proud, are struck down by fate. Marlow must walk a fine line: he must shun self- righteousness while feeling, at the same time, that he has been faithful to his standards. His fears of weakness unknown helps him to accomplish this: he has the right to think himself good enough, but not the right to be satisfied. Through his rectitude he participates in our common glory; through his dependence on the community, his self-doubt, and his fear of fate, he hopes to avoid pride and retribution.

It is because of his own needs that Marlow reacts to Jim so intensely. He is "furious" with Jim and "sorry for him" (Ch. 5). His anger is partly an affirmation of his standards, but it is mainly a response to the threat which Jim's desertion poses to his safety and his pride. By undermining his faith in his judgment of men, in the steadfastness of his fellows, and in the sovereign power of the fixed standard, Jim's desertion exposes him to the dark powers, heightening an already strong feeling of vulnerability. It threatens his pride in the training of his boys, upon which he has built a sense of worth and a bargain with fate. He will train boys who are "fit to live or die as the sea may decree," and the sea will be good to him in return, as it has been. If his boys turn out like Jim, then he has *not* for "once in [his] life at least . . . gone the right way to work," and he has *not* earned favorable treatment. Jim's violation of the solidarity of the craft threatens to "rob our common life of the last spark of its glamour" (Ch. 11); and the fact that Jim is "one of us" calls into question our racial superiority. Marlow has given up the notion of a special destiny for himself, but he clings to the idea of his race as a chosen people who will be favored by fate because of their virtues. Jim's weakness and disgrace challenge this reassuring belief. The undermining of his pride and confidence heightens Marlow's anxiety and feeds his anger.

Jim's failure undermines most of all Marlow's confidence in himself. Because of their similarities in race, calling, and temperament, Marlow identifies very strongly with Jim. If Jim can go wrong like that, then so can he. Given Marlow's need to live up to his standards, the prospect of going wrong terrifies him; it is "the true shadow of calamity." Jim's case confronts Marlow with his despised self; what Jim has done is what Marlow is most afraid of doing. Because of his self-contempt Marlow has a fear, almost amounting to a conviction, that his hidden self is weak, cowardly, unrestrained. When he looks at Jim he sees what he, given a certain combination of circumstances, could easily become.

In addition to his anger, therefore, Marlow has an enormous pity for Jim's sufferings and a very great stake in his exoneration or redemption. If Jim is innocent, then Marlow may be good

enough; if Jim can redeem himself, then so could Marlow if
he fell. He invites Jim's confidence for the same reason that
he desperately visits the chief engineer; he hopes to discover
"some profound and redeeming cause, some merciful explanation, some convincing shadow of an excuse" (Ch. 5).

In his dealings with Jim, Marlow oscillates between aloofness
and empathy. He needs to keep his distance, to keep judging, to
stay angry, in order to uphold his standards and to maintain his
sense of rectitude. He is vulnerable to Jim's insinuations that he
might have jumped too, and he struggles against making any fatal
admissions. Just as Jim must insist that he is different from his
partners in crime, that he is not one of them, so Marlow must
continually assure both himself and his auditors that he and Jim
are distinct beings. He is afraid that his involvement with Jim
indicates a moral affinity, and he defends himself by attributing
it to various noble motives. By making his involvement a matter
of conscience and duty, Marlow assuages his guilt and justifies
himself both to his auditors and his shoulds.

He admits, however, that there is no moral impulse behind his
effort to help Jim escape. He wants to spare Jim the details "of
a formal execution" because he, like Brierly, is also on trial. As
Jim does with Brown, Marlow indulges and excuses his other self.
He gives Jim chance after chance, and he is often swayed by Jim's
rationalizations. It is Marlow, not Jim, who speaks of the "villainy
of circumstances" that cuts off the *Patna* officers "from the rest
of mankind, whose ideal of conduct has never undergone the trial
of a fiendish and appalling joke" (Ch. 10). Despite his talk of "the
Dark Powers" being "perpetually foiled by the steadfastness of
men," Marlow feels powerless in the hands of fate and fearful of
his unknown weakness. He does not need to be an unflinching
hero, but he is in dread of violating his standards. He is so
responsive to Jim's rationalization because he is preparing his
own excuses in advance.

Marlow is so sorry for Jim because he imagines Jim to be

suffering the self-contempt and hopelessness which he would experience in like circumstances. As we have seen, he misperceives Jim, who is not really "a straggler yearning inconsolably for his humble place in the ranks" (Ch. 21). He gradually becomes aware of Jim's narcissism and is prepared by the time he consults Stein to recognize Jim as romantic. He reacts to his glimpses of the true Jim with anger, dismay, disgust, and amazement. He is "oppressed by a sad sense of resigned wisdom, mingled with the amused and profound pity of an old man helpless before a childish disaster" (Ch. 9). He is alarmed, too. Not only has he long since outgrown the illusions of youth, but he finds them dangerous, threatening: "Why hurl defiance at the universe? This was not a proper frame of mind to approach any undertaking" (Ch. 23). Pride goeth before a fall. In a universe full of dark powers which seem out to cut men down to size, the proper attitudes are resignation, acceptance, devotion to duty. To be safe we must remain in our humble place in the ranks.

Marlow is disturbed by Jim's arrogance; but he is also attracted to it, very powerfully. It awakens his proud self; it reminds him of his youth: "Youth *is* insolent; it is its right—its necessity; it has got to assert itself, and all assertion in this world of doubts is a defiance, is an insolence." Like Jim, Marlow set out with magnificently vague expectations, with "a beautiful greed of adventures" (Ch. 11); but he has become disenchanted, subjugated, convinced of the power of external forces and of his own insignificance. His earlier confidence has been replaced by doubt, his conviction of invulnerability by a profound insecurity. His subdued self finds Jim's illusions to be dangerous, childish, absurd. They must be punctured (in Marlow's own mind, at least) if a mature world view is to prevail. But Marlow has another side, usually repressed, which admires Jim's pride, delights in his romanticism, and wants to see him triumph. He thought his youthful illusions had "gone out, extinct, cold"; but they are "rekindled at the approach of another flame" and "give a flutter deep, deep down somewhere, give a flutter of life . . . of heat!"

Marlow is afraid of pride in himself, but he is attracted to it in others. Anything which feeds his pride or feels like arrogance produces an immediate disclaimer. When Jim asserts that holding up his end in Patusan helps him to keep in touch with the impeccable world, " 'with—you, for instance,' " Marlow is "profoundly humbled by his words" (Ch. 35). He immediately reverses their roles and manages to become Jim's inferior: "I felt a gratitude, an affection, for that straggler whose eyes had singled me out, keeping my place in the ranks of an insignificant multitude. How little that was to boast of, after all! I turned my burning face away." Part of his attraction to proud people is that they subdue his pride, making him feel more comfortable with himself and safer in the world. The "good-natured and contemptuous pity" with which Brierly treats him confirms his modest estimate of himself and keeps him firmly in the ranks of the "twelve hundred million other . . . human beings" who also have no special destinies. Instead of being offended by Brierly's condescension, he finds "something . . . attractive in the man" (Ch. 6).

Another part of his attraction to proud people is that they embody an aspect of his idealized image which he has renounced but which he cannot entirely give up. He can experience his proud self vicariously, and hence innocently, through them, especially if he keeps reminding himself that he is not one of them and that they are heading for a fall. The other components of Brierly's appeal are his pride (he is "acutely aware of his merits and of his rewards"), his confidence (he is free of "indecision" and "self-mistrust"), and his good luck ("he had never . . . had an accident, never a mishap"). This is the way Marlow would like to be; and he has a secret hope that men like Brierly and Jim will prevail, will show that man, not fate, is the master. Their fall produces mixed emotions: it disappoints his hopes but confirms the wisdom of his own solution.

Marlow also likes romantics. In his mature wisdom he has

settled for a share of our common glory, but he is thrilled by heroic tales and the romantic's "gift of finding a special meaning in everything that happen[s] to him" (Ch. 32). He glories in Stein's destiny, which is rich "in all the exalted elements of romance" (Ch. 20). It is he who celebrates the pepper traders, who glorifies the romantic quest for Truth, who sees Jim and Jewel as knight and maiden. As we have seen, he becomes Jim's epic poet and tries to fan in his auditors the same spark of youthful romanticism which Jim has brought to a glow in him.

The fallen Jim confronts Marlow with his despised self, but the proud Jim stirs into life hopes and claims which he has long since abandoned. His feeling that we are what our biology—or, in one passage, God—has made us and that "the initial word of each our destiny" is "graven in imperishable characters upon the face of a rock" (Ch. 17) indicates a profound sense of resignation. Neither our behavior nor our destiny is in our own hands; we discover our character and suffer our fate. Jim is defiant. He refuses to give up his claims either for himself or his future; he will follow his dream to the end and make it come true. Marlow is deeply skeptical; but, with part of his being at least, he would like to believe. He becomes Jim's ally. If Jim is triumphant then he will have contributed to the mastering of fate. Marlow's conception of mankind, and of himself, is at stake.

Marlow has very mixed feelings about Jim's career in Patusan. "Romance" has "singled Jim for its own" (Ch. 29), and Marlow is enthralled by his success. Jim is what Marlow had dreamed and then despaired of becoming. His triumphs are "immense"; his "faith" is "mightier than the laws of order and progress" (Ch. 36); his glory surpasses any that can be gained in the ranks of an insignificant multitude.

At the same time, Marlow has his reservations, his anxieties. While his proud self exults in Jim's triumphs and wants to believe in his invulnerability, his subdued self distrusts Jim's moral character and is fearful of destiny. He is skeptical about Jim's redemption and vaguely guilty about his role as Jim's accomplice. His pride in Jim, his confidence, violate his taboos against such feelings; and he needs, almost superstitiously, to question "the fabulous value of the bargain" (Ch. 24) and to reaffirm his fear of the unknown. Since it is outside of the community which is the source of genuine glory, Jim's success has no substance. "While there's life," moreover, "there is fear" (Ch. 16). Jim is challenging fate. Marlow's subdued self is afraid of retribution; his proud self wants the contest to be over, with Jim triumphant.

The conclusion of Jim's story fulfills Marlow's hopes and confirms his fears. "There is," he explains to the privileged listener, "a sort of profound and terrifying logic in it, as if it were our imagination alone that could set loose upon us the might of an overwhelming destiny. The imprudence of our thoughts recoils upon our heads; who toys with the sword shall perish by the sword. . . . Something of the sort had to happen" (Ch. 36). There is a logic in Jim's downfall, as we have seen; but Marlow is referring here not to the dynamics of Jim's interaction with Brown, but to the logic of his own bargain with fate. He does not mean that the catastrophe was an "unavoidable consequence" of Jim's shutting his eyes and following his dream, but that the proud man is doomed to fall. Insofar as Jim's catastrophe is his own as well (he is "bitterly disappointed" [Ch. 37] when he hears of it), he, too, is being punished for allowing himself to imagine that a mere mortal had mastered his fate.

But, in a sense, Jim *has* mastered his fate, as much as a man can. "Our common fate" is to be "deserted in the fullness of possession by some one or something more precious than life" (Ch. 28). By the sacrifice of his life, Jim avoids this; the dark powers do not rob him twice of his peace. Thus, despite the disaster, Marlow sees him as having achieved "an extraordinary success" (Ch. 45). Of Brierly, Marlow asks, "Who can tell what flattering view he had induced himself to take of his own suicide?" (Ch. 6). He has such a powerful interest in seeing Jim's end as "romantic beyond

the wildest dreams of his boyhood" (Ch. 36) that he is incapable
of asking such a question in this parallel case.

Indeed, Marlow is incapable of seeing Jim clearly at all, except,
perhaps, from the inside. In his need to preserve his image of Jim
as a romantic hero, he ignores almost totally Jim's responsibility
for the debacle. As Jim had done in the *Patna* affair, Marlow
places all the blame on the Dark Powers and their "blind accomplice" (Ch. 38), in this case, Brown. Jim's conversation with
Brown is a "kind of duel on which Fate looked on with her
cold-eyed knowledge of the end" (Ch. 42). Brown manipulates
Jim by activating his anxieties and compulsions; but Marlow tells
us that "he didn't turn Jim's soul inside out"; he was simply "a
menace, a shock, a danger to his work." The "sad, half-resentful,
half-resigned feeling" which Marlow attributes to Jim makes little
sense in terms of Jim's psychology but a great deal in terms of
Marlow's. It is a pure projection. Marlow defends Jim against
Jewel's accusations and sees Jim's triumph in the council not as
a misuse of power but as a testimony to Jim's fidelity:

> From the moment the sheer truthfulness of his last three years of
> life carries the day against the ignorance, the fear, and the anger
> of men, he appears no longer to me as I saw him last—a white
> speck catching all the dim light left upon a sombre coast and the
> darkened sea—but greater and more pitiful in the loneliness of his
> soul, that remains even for her who loved him best a cruel and
> insoluble mystery. (Ch. 43)

Jim will not be alone and misunderstood as long as he has Char-
ley Marlow to do him homage. It is amazing, as I have said, that
we can see Jim so clearly through the mists with which Marlow
surrounds his story. Marlow himself is no mean artful dodger.

However much he glories in Jim's vindictive triumph, Marlow
returns, at the end, to his usual ambivalence. The final page is full
of doubts. His ambivalent response to the catastrophe is, like his
mixed feelings about every other aspect of Jim's career, a product

of his inner conflicts. His basic conflict is between his expansive and self-effacing trends. When his expansive trends are dominant, he is his proud self. He identifies with Jim's claims and sees him from his own perspective. When his self-effacing trends are dominant, he is his subdued self. He sees Jim from the outside and judges him in terms of communal values. There are strong elements of resignation, also, in Marlow's character. When his resignation is uppermost, he is his wise, old, detached self. Nothing seems to matter: the fixed standard is just one of the rules of the game, and he is alternately wearied and amused by Jim's romanticism.

When he first encounters Jim, Marlow is predominantly self-effacing, though he has many resigned attitudes and a history of youthful expansiveness. He never relinquishes his basic defenses, but Jim's defiance and seeming conquest of fate sweep away his resignation and give him an opportunity to experience his repressed expansiveness vicariously, in a way which is compatible with his self-effacing shoulds. By the end his expansive cravings have become so powerful that they seem, at times, to dominate. In the final paragraphs, expansive and self-effacing attitudes are finely balanced. Marlow cannot make a definitive comment on Jim's story not only because of the uncertainty of human knowledge and the relativity of human judgments, but also because he is in the grip of an inner conflict which is very far from being resolved.

VI

Our psychological analysis of Marlow and of Jim has a multitude of implications. In concluding, I shall look at its bearing on two things: theme and the character structure of the implied author.

Stein analyzes Jim's plight in existential terms: man cannot live without a dream, but to live within a dream is to live destructively.

From a psychological point of view, we see that Stein has diagnosed the case not of man, but of the neurotic who lives to actualize his idealized image and whose greatest enemy is reality. If Jim were to climb out of his dream, to live in reality, his life would be unbearable. The only alternative to living neurotically is getting cured; but Stein knows of no cure but death. Whether it means to be or not, the novel is a brilliant exploration of the plight of those who must live without being cured and of the destructiveness of neurotic solutions.

The implied author, too, seems to feel that a man who is born falls into a dream; but he distinguishes, as Stein does not, between private and communal dreams. All men idealize their existence, but the romantic follows a dream of his own glory, whereas those who stay within the ranks participate in a dream of our collective greatness. On a thematic level the novel does not, finally, choose between these two dreams; but its rhetoric clearly favors first one and then the other. For the first half of the novel, the communal dream seems preferable to that of the romantic individual. It has greater survival value, a concern for the common good, and a more realistic estimate of cosmic powers and human capabilities. The romantic individual is concerned only with his relation to himself; in the pursuit of his dream, he is likely to betray his trust and to destroy himself. The dominant feeling conveyed by the second half of the novel is that there is something heroic about the overreacher. Jim's adventures in Patusan are given an epic treatment, and his death is glorious.

In psychological terms, the romantic attempts an expansive solution, whereas the man who pursues the communal dream tends to embrace self-effacing values. Conrad is drawn to both solutions, criticizes each from the point of view of the other, and, at times, sees through them both. He attempts to allay his inner conflict through projection, intellectualization, and detachment.

Psychological analysis shows Marlow to be an individualized character whose story has its own fascination and whose responses to Jim have deeply personal meanings. While it invests him with a profound human interest, it also divests him of some of his authority and raises questions about the themes which he seems intended to illustrate. While the problem of uncertainty is a truly existential one, Marlow's responses to it are frequently overintense and reflect his individual psychology more than the basic needs of the species. Because of his personal insecurities, Marlow is incapable of a sustained world-openness. At bottom, he is afraid of life, of process; he has too much anxiety to live with any degree of comfort in this concrete and perplexed world. He is more closely in touch with reality, however, than is any other character. He is too caught up in his private needs to be a completely reliable index to the plight of man, but his suffering is not without foundation.

Marlow has a true perception of the limitations of our knowledge and the relativity of our judgments. Each of the perspectives which he entertains has its validity, and the conflict between them is genuine. From the cosmic point of view, both communal and personal values are illusions, rules of some arbitrary game. Communal values are valid for man, however, whatever their status in the cosmos. They are concerned with human survival and well-being, which are realities, even if the conventions which seek to insure them are not absolute and everlasting. The individual's sense of life and measure of success are truths for him, however phantasmal or destructive they may appear from the other perspectives. *Lord Jim* comes closer than any novel I know to doing justice "to all sides at once" of this "dispute impossible of decision" (Ch. 8).

Psychological analysis does not challenge the novel's juxtaposition of the three perspectives. It calls attention to the fact, however, that we can entertain these perspectives in more or less healthy ways and that Marlow's perceptions are often influenced by powerful subjective determinants. If he is intended to be a reliable narrator in Wayne Booth's second sense of that term (that is, a reliable guide to the world outside of the novel), he cannot be wholly trusted in that capacity.

It is difficult to say whether or not he is so intended. The opening chapters of the novel invite a thematic reading, and I have offered one. But *Lord Jim* can be seen, from the fifth chapter on, as basically an impressionistic novel which makes no claims for the reliability of the interpretations which it dramatizes. It deals with some major aspects of the human condition as they are experienced by a man of a certain temperament. It gives us Marlow's impressions with absolute authority; what we make of them is up to us.

The character structure of the implied author seems similar to Marlow's. In him, too, there is a movement from self-effacing to expansive attitudes which is accompanied by increasing inner conflict and a defensive detachment. His turning the narration over to Marlow may well have been a strategy for dealing with inner conflicts which he felt surfacing. In the first four chapters, he celebrates the communal ethic, satirizes Jim's expansive dreams, and emphasizes our dependence on others. The action which he contrives deflates Jim's pretensions and punishes him for his excessive claims. Jim's artful dodges are mercilessly exposed and his persistence in his dream is mocked through Marlow. Beneath Conrad's hostility, however, and perhaps in some measure responsible for it, there lies a wish that we could be like Jim and succeed, that we could conquer reality through the sheer force of desire.

This wish surfaces when, after Jim clings to his dream through a period of probation, he is given another chance in Patusan. Patusan is a land of dreams, of wish-fulfillment. The first half of *Lord Jim* resembles a moral fable; the second half is a fairy tale in which both Jim and his creator realize their expansive fantasies. The moral perspective which was so firmly established earlier never disappears; but, like Marlow, Conrad takes an obvious delight in Jim's triumphs. Patusan is, after all, *his* creation.

His shift in attitude is evident in the omniscient narrator's description of the privileged listener. This man, like Marlow, is an erstwhile romantic who has become a sober spokesman for the communal ethic. Despite his stern pronouncements, Jim's story excites his longing for a life of adventure and serves as a vicarious fulfillment:

> . . .his wandering days were over. No more horizons as boundless as hope, no more twilights within the forests as solemn as temples, in the hot quest of the Ever-undiscovered Country over the hill, across the stream, beyond the wave. The hour was striking! No more! No more!—but the opened packet under the lamp brought back the sounds, the visions, the very savour of the past. . . . He . . . read on deliberately, like one approaching with slow feet and alert eyes the glimpse of an undiscovered country. (Ch. 36)

The omniscient narrator speaks here with a distinctly different voice from that which we heard in the opening chapters. He seems to enter into the privileged listener's nostalgia and to have become, like Marlow, much more responsive to the appeal of romance. Even while he is introducing a communal judgment, he seems deeply sympathetic with those who find in Jim an embodiment of their adventurous dreams and their lost youth.

Conrad so structures the novel's action and its rhetoric that all of his conflicting attitudes are expressed and, in some measure, satisfied. The first half of the novel mocks Jim's expansive claims; the second half of the novel honors them. In Patusan, Jim's solution seems to be working like magic. The novel's conclusion affirms both the expansive and the self-effacing solutions. Jim is a triumphant hero, but the danger of pride is confirmed. The implied author gains distance from his inner conflicts and protects himself against their paralyzing effects by presenting them through Marlow. He turns a potential impasse into a rich source of characterization and controlled ambiguity.

Despite these protective devices, the implied author's conflicts

result in certain confusions of effect. The self-effacing value system is so firmly established at the outset that we are somewhat
bewildered by the implied author's indulgence of Jim's dreams in
Patusan. Jim is ultimately punished for his pride, but there is little
judgment of his failings or insight into his self-delusions. We
move from the great distance of the opening to an over-identification at the end. Marlow's fear and uncertainty are shown to be
well-founded, but the intrusion of reality into the fairy tale seems
like a sop to the implied author's self-effacing shoulds, a gesture
to keep up appearances. Jim is made to pay, but his triumph
seems to be well worth the price. The real force of the story, for
Conrad, as well as for Marlow, lies not in Jim's fall from the
heights but in his mastery of fate. There is a reaffirmation of
self-effacing and resigned attitudes, but what the story is really
about is vindictive triumphs and dreams come true.

Chapter VIII

Powers and Limitations of
the Approach

Realistic fiction is a genre with enormous strengths and, in its classical form, with certain built-in weaknesses. The psychological approach helps us to understand its problems and to appreciate its achievements.[1] It tends to bring out its weaknesses by calling attention to the conflicts between theme, form, and mimesis; but it also leads us to have more appropriate expectations of the genre and to see that its faults are often the defects of its virtues. Most important, it helps us to do justice to the genre's strengths by demonstrating the centrality of mimesis and the brilliance of its character creations.

The great characters have been there all along, of course, and have been appreciated by many readers. But without the conceptual system offered by an appropriate psychological theory, we have not been able to see them clearly and to talk about them in detail. We tend, as critics, to dwell upon those aspects of literature about which we can speak and to ignore those for which we have no vocabulary. The theories of Wayne Booth and Northrop Frye have been of immense value in helping us to appreciate the rhetorical and the formal aspects of fiction, but they have tended to obscure the importance of mimesis. Frye grants a mimetic pole to literature, but his own interest in the mythic pole and his fear of outside disciplines has led him to place it at the very fringe of literature and almost beyond the pale of literary criticism. Mimesis is a distinctly literary achievement. It requires great artistic skill, and there is nothing like it in any other mode of discourse. But the conceptual systems which will help us to appreciate it cannot be drawn from literature itself. We need a sociological approach to the imitation of social reality and a psychological approach to the imitation of man's inner life and behavior.

Fully realized characters tend, in E. M. Forster's words, to "kick the book to pieces."[2] This is particularly true when the characters are the protagonists in either a comic or a tragic education plot and when they are presented from a classical moralistic perspective. When we understand the characters psychologically, we find again and again that their "growth" is a delusion and that the author's interpretation is confused, too simple, or just plain wrong. Weakness of interpretation may reflect the author's inner conflicts, his neurotic values, or the limitations of his understanding (which are often those of his age); but it may also be the result of his genius in characterization. As Forster's remark suggests, if an author has succeeded in creating an autonomous character, "life" is almost bound to overwhelm "pattern," whatever his degree of health or wisdom.

Though the psychological approach gives us a powerful tool for relating the confusions of the work to the inner conflicts of the writing self, it also helps us to see that there are certain conflicts which belong to realistic fiction as a genre and which can be either exacerbated or reduced by the author's technical choices. The conflict between form and mimesis is built into the low mimetic mode. As Frye says, "the realistic writer soon finds that the requirements of literary form and plausible content always fight against each other."[3] Thematic confusions and disparities between representation and interpretation can often be traced back to the implied author and understood through an analysis of his psyche. But it is the genre's combination of the classical moralistic and the problematic existential perspectives which introduces the author's limitations into the work and which makes for inner disparities even when the author is self-consistent.

The conflict between the mythic and the mimetic components of fiction is difficult to resolve. In many novels it becomes most evident at the end, where plausibility and realistic detail are sacrificed to an aesthetically pleasing resolution. Happy endings almost always bring a raised eyebrow if we have truly understood the characters. Endings which try to be faithful to the mimetic impulse by suggesting the open-endedness or the ongoingness of life do not satisfy our aesthetic demand for completion, especially when the rest of the novel is highly patterned. The best kind of ending seems to be a death which is both realistically called for and aesthetically satisfying. Even such endings may not achieve a complete harmony, however, since the emotional effect of the mimetic portrayal may clash with that of the mythic structure.

There are technical solutions to the conflict between representation and interpretation which do not depend upon the psychological health or integration of the author. One solution is to avoid interpretation, as Dostoevsky does in *Notes from Underground;* another is to dramatize it, as Conrad does in *Lord Jim.* Conrad does not dramatize consistently; hence his novel does not achieve complete integration. But the large measure of success which he does achieve suggests that a highly mimetic novel can explore thematic concerns without sacrificing unity.

Notes from Underground is integrated because it subordinates aesthetic pattern to mimesis and almost completely eliminates theme. First person narration is an excellent device for revealing the workings of the underground man's mind and the quality of his experience. It makes analysis of theme impossible, but this is not a flaw in a novel which aims at character revelation, unless we apply some general rule that all novels should have themes. The novel does not provide many of the pleasures of aesthetic patterning, but this is the price we must pay for its fidelity to experience. It is not formless, however; for its details and the ordering of materials are intelligible in the light of its mimetic intention and the narrator's psychology. Its lack of theme and a traditional kind of structure may frustrate us somewhat, for we come to fiction with certain general appetites. But if we have correctly identified the work's "intrinsic genre" and have ordered our expectations accordingly, we will not be disappointed.[4]

There is, of course, a nontechnical solution to the problem we have been discussing, which is the one proposed by Wayne Booth. There would be no disparity between representation and interpretation in a highly mimetic work if the author were a wise and healthy man whose conceptions were adequate to his perceptions. This is certainly a possibility, but such authors are bound to be very scarce. Health is rare; past authors had no adequate conceptual systems available; and the artistic and analytical modes of thought are not usually found in the same person.

The techniques which I have labelled "solutions" are exactly the kind to which Wayne Booth objects in the modern novel. However we may feel about his moral anxieties, we must share Booth's concern for the epistemological problems which result from the disappearance of reliable narration. We are often left in uncertainty about the story itself. How do we know when an untrustworthy narrator is giving us accurate information about himself, about other characters, and about the course of events?

When the narrator is a fully drawn character, the psychological approach can provide helpful answers to these questions. In our analysis of *Notes from Underground* and *Lord Jim*, Horneyan theory enabled us to identify the defense systems of the narrators and to see through their distortions and misinterpretations, which then became important aspects of characterization. Such novels confront us with difficulties similar to those which we encounter in real life. We have no independent sources of information, as we often do in life; but we know much more about the fictional narrators than we know about most people. We may never be certain that we have detected all of their misrepresentations, but with the help of psychological analysis we can make some educated guesses and attain a reasonable degree of probability. What we lose in certainty through unreliable modes of narration we often gain in deep inside views and a phenomenological grasp of experience.

The psychological approach can help us, too, with some of the moral problems by which Booth is troubled. When we have understood the narrator psychologically, we are less likely to be influenced by his unhealthy values, unless they speak very powerfully to our own defensive needs, in which case no amount of authorial condemnation would make much difference. Psychological analysis shows that, from a moral point of view, the mode of narration is not as important as Booth makes it out to be. Omniscient narrators are not necessarily wise or even consistent. They are no more likely to be reliable guides to the moral issues in the book or to the world outside of it than are their characters or the narrators of more fully dramatized fiction. If the "reliable" narrator is employing his rhetoric to justify a neurotic solution, as he often is, we need just as much protection from him as we do from the dramatized narrator.[5] Whatever the mode of narration, we will judge the book's moral significance in terms of our own value system. For those who accept the Third Force view of human nature, human values, and the human condition, the psychological approach provides a sophisticated method for evaluating a book's interpretations of the experience which it portrays and the adequacy for life of the solutions which it affirms. It can help us to distinguish, as the author often cannot, between personal, historical, and existential problems.

Those who do not accept Third Force psychology may still wish to consider the perspective suggested by this book, which is that implied authors should be understood as fictional personae rather than venerated or judged as authoritative sources of values. The narrative technique of much realistic fiction invites us to regard the author as a sage. In addition, we want to see our great authors as god-like figures or as wise fathers; and we are disturbed by a critical perspective which frustrates that craving. But seeing them thus leads us to rationalize their inconsistencies, to ignore the psychological functions of their belief systems, and to remain unaware of the richness of their personalities.

Perhaps the greatest danger in regarding our authors as authorities, however, is not that we will ask only admiring questions, but that we will reject them as false prophets. If we judge them as authorities, we are likely to make much of the fact that they seem so often to be wrong. By calling attention to their inner conflicts, the psychological approach may seem to be dismissing our authors as neurotic; but that is not its intention. We naturally want to understand their inconsistencies, to evaluate the adequacy of their interpretations, and to determine the significance of their vision for ourselves. The psychological approach can help us to do these things; but it does not demand that our authors be wise men and reject them because they are not. It suggests, rather, that we can appreciate them best if we lay aside our own value hungers and needs for authority and see them allocentrically, as utterly fascinating objects of contemplation. If we see them as fictional personae, they offer us deep inside views of how the world looks to people with their personalities.

Our authors *are* great authorities, god-like figures, when it comes to creating characters. The psychological approach shows that the characterization in these novels is brilliant, awe-inspiring, beyond anything that we have dreamed of in our usual modes of criticism. It is the work of genius. It is also a sign of allocentric perception, of being-cognition, of the artist's ability to transcend his belief system and his defensive needs and to make his novel "a house fit for free characters to live in."[6] Iris Murdoch praises the great realistic novelists for their tolerance, their respect for reality, their "real apprehension" of other people "as having a right to exist and to have a separate mode of being which is important and interesting to themselves" (p.257). The "individuals portrayed" in their novels "are free, independent of their author, and not merely puppets in the exteriorization of some closely locked psychological conflict of his own." This is a very penetrating insight, though I cannot agree with Miss Murdoch's statement that "the great novels are victims neither of convention nor of neurosis." The neurosis is there, as we have seen; but the characters escape it. As Forster says, "they 'run away,' they 'get out of hand': they are creations inside a creation, and often inharmonious towards it."[7] It is to the great credit of our authors that, despite their own needs, preconceptions, and vested interests, they can allow their characters to rebel, to be themselves, to live their own lives. As Miss Murdoch observes, this is more than tolerance; this is love (p. 269).

It is because these characters are free (in Murdoch's sense) that we can study them for themselves and understand them in motivational terms, without reference to their aesthetic and thematic roles. It is their autonomy, moreover, which gives them their universality and perpetual relevance. However we may judge the author's views as truths *about* experience, we immediately recognize his mimetic characters as true *to* experience and as endowed with the human interest which real people always have. Works which seem rather dated when we study them thematically are quite fresh when we approach them psychologically. Different cultures tend to glorify different neurotic solutions, but people remain much the same. Their celebration of self-effacing values makes many Victorian novels seem old-fashioned; but the protagonists of these novels are intensely interesting when we see them as people. Their problems, character structures, and defense systems are still very much with us.

II

There are certain dangers, of course, in detaching characters from their aesthetic and thematic roles. A novel is not simply mimesis; it is a story told from a certain moral and intellectual point of view and from a certain emotional distance. It has a shape which gives its characters and actions certain mythical overtones. The author, through his dramatic and rhetorical ordering of materials, has told a certain kind of story. Psychological analysis seems not only to ignore this, but to tell an altogether different kind of story.

What the psychological approach seems to leave out is treatment. It is a commonplace of criticism that the kind of work we have and its impact upon us are determined less by the matter than by the artistic handling of the story. As Booth points out, Federigo's story in *The Decameron*, "could have been made into any number of fully realized plots with radically different effects" (*Rhetoric*, p. 9). This has general application. An action which is comic when presented from one distance will be pathetic when presented from another; a character who seems heroic when viewed from close up might, if seen from a greater distance, participate in an ironic or a satiric effect. In order to experience a novel as literature one must, in Booth's terms, allow oneself to become a "mock reader" whose attitudes are determined by those of the implied author. The kind of psychological analysis which I have engaged in sees characters and actions from a perspective of its own, a perspective which has nothing to do with that established by the aesthetic pattern or the rhetoric of the work. In a sense, the characters' stories as I have told them *are* different from the stories told by their authors. And yet they are not entirely different; for though they are not faithful to the authors' formal and rhetorical intentions, they are true to their representations of experience.

I do not mean to replace the experience of characters that we have when we are under the author's spell with the experience which is provided by psychological analysis. It is desirable to have both experiences; each discovers values denied to the other. It is best to see characters from a psychological perspective only *after* we have seen them from the novel's point of view. Otherwise, on our first reading we will feel a conflict between the intentions of the work and the direction of our own response, and certain values appropriate to our initial experience may be forever lost to us. Whether we use a psychological approach or not, it is difficult to experience a work emotionally and analytically at the same time, and it is unwise to analyze too soon. As Booth says, we need to formulate the laws of successive readings. Each successive reading of a novel makes some qualities more and others less prominent than they were in earlier readings. The sophisticated reader tries to respond in the ways which are appropriate to that particular reading, to remain aware of all the values which he has experienced, and to see how, and if, they fit together.

This is more easily said than done, of course. Some of my students have complained that they will never again be able to see Dobbin or Maggie from the author's point of view; and they fear that once they have become accustomed to looking at characters psychologically they will be unable to give themselves up to a novel's rhetoric and to experience its aesthetic effects. These are real dangers. My object has been to heighten our appreciation of mimetic values; but if the psychological approach is employed too early or looms too large, it may well be destructive of other important effects. Let me emphasize now that it is one perspective among many, and that it illuminates some, but not all, of a work's achievements.

The problems we have been discussing are not basically the fault of the psychological approach. There is a conflict of values within realistic fiction itself. Some of its effects are incompatible with others. The limitations of human perception are also a factor: to see one thing clearly requires relegating others to the background. The only solution is repeated acts of perception employing a variety of perspectives.

There are other problems which seem to be more inherent in the approach. I have argued that it is reductive to see characters only in terms of their aesthetic and thematic functions and that the psychological approach enables us to appreciate their individuality. Is it not also reductive to see characters in terms of the Horneyan categories? The psychological approach seems to replace one set of rubrics with another. To analyze the characters, and sometimes the implied authors, as "neurotic," moreover, seems to deprive them of interest and dignity, to reduce them to triviality. As one of my colleagues put it, "Who wants to take seriously the experience of NEUROTICS?"

Any mode of analysis is reductive, especially if it replaces the immediate experience of the work with its own abstract formulations. It seems to me that the psychological approach is no more reductive than any other, and it is less reductive than many, providing that it is used correctly. The Horneyan taxonomy lends itself to perfunctory classification, but this is a temptation which must be resisted if the approach is not to be self-defeating. The object of the approach is not to classify characters or to prove the value of the Horneyan system; it is to explain the characters in their complexity and to help us see them better. As Maslow observes, "we must not maneuver ourselves into the foolish position of stigmatizing theories and abstractions because of their dangers. Their advantages are great and obvious . . . ."[8] Horneyan theory permits us to see the significance of many details which we would otherwise ignore and to grasp puzzling inconsistencies as part of a coherent system.

One way of counteracting the dangers of rubricizing is to discuss characters in considerable detail, as I have done here. Dobbin, Amelia, Maggie, and Marlow all employ self-effacing strategies and hence have characteristic similarities; but I hope that they have emerged from my analysis as highly individualized human beings, with different histories, problems, inner lives, and human qualities. The best safeguard against reductiveness is, of course, to go back to the work and to assimilate the findings of analysis into direct experience. The critic can only point to this as the next step; the reader must carry it out. The object of analysis is not to replace immediate experience, but to enrich it.

Seeing characters and implied authors as neurotic may lead some readers to dismiss them, but this is neither a necessary effect nor one which I intend. As the Third Force psychologists use the term, almost everybody is more or less neurotic. The word, I know, is a red flag. What it means is that the person so described has not been well gratified in his basic needs, is not relatively free of anxiety and defensiveness, and is not able to employ his abilities in a predominantly self-actualizing way. Unfortunately, this describes most of us; but it does not mean that we have no admirable qualities, no high achievements, no strivings for health, or that we are devoid of dignity, worth, and interest. At the core of Third Force psychology is a great and unpalatable truth: frustration of our basic needs damages us and our compensatory strategies are destructive. The psychological approach refuses to accept the glorification of neurotic solutions; but it does not dismiss the human beings whose hardships have hampered their growth and forced them to live defensively.

Nor does it look upon them with condescension, as beings of another and a lower species. If I am able to recognize certain neurotic processes in fictional characters and to talk about them with insight, it is because I have found them, or the possibility of them, in myself. When Alyosha Karamazov explains to Lise why Captain Snegiryov will accept the gift of money tomorrow which he has rejected today, Lise asks, " 'aren't we showing contempt for him, for that poor man—in analyzing his soul like this, as it were, from above, eh?' " Alyosha replies: " 'No, Lise, it's not contempt. . . . How can it be contempt when we are all like him, when we are all just the same as he is. For you know we are all just the same, no better. If we are better, we should have been just the same in his place. . . .' "[9] To those who ask Lise's question about the analyses in the preceding chapters, I can only make Alyosha's reply. Understanding a character need not lead us to scorn or reject him; it can bring us close to him and form a basis for love and compassion.

I must admit that the kind of analysis in which I have engaged tends to invite judgment rather than sympathy and to break down reader identification. One reason for this is that I have had, frequently, to quarrel with a character's interpretation of himself or with an implied author's glorification of neurotic solutions. Another reason is that the very act of analysis involves a standing back, a detachment. Instead of feeling with, it attempts to account for the other person and his version of reality. The movement away from empathy which is inseparable from analysis must be counterbalanced by a return to the phenomenological grasp of experience which literature affords. As I have said, psychology helps us to talk about what the novelist knows, but fiction helps us to know what the psychologist is talking about. The marriage of these two ways of apprehending experience is essential if we are to have both empathy and insight.

In a certain way, of course, we do take a character or an implied author less seriously when we have understood his neurosis. When his attitudes, judgments, and world views are seen as expressions of his defense system, they lose weight as truths about the human condition and as guides to life. This will seriously diminish the value of a work if we are going to it for a picture of Man rather than for portraits of men, for truth about experience rather than for truth to it. I hope I have persuaded my readers that these are inappropriate demands. If we are to appreciate their mimetic achievements, we, like the great realists, must rise to allocentric perception, must see their creations for what they are and not for what we need or want them to be.

III

In this book I have employed Third Force psychology to approach five novels and a limited set of literary problems. I have been tempted to display the much wider range of its powers, but each new application has so many implications that I have thought it best to confine myself to the issues which I could handle responsibly in this context and at this time. I realize, however, that readers must have wondered from time to time about the applicability of the approach to concerns which have been ignored here. In closing, I shall suggest the range of interests to which Third Force analysis can be profitably applied. It is of value to biographers, to students of culture, and to psychologists of art, as well as to literary critics.

To begin with, the novels studied here represent only a sampling of the literary works to which Third Force psychology brings a remarkable illumination. Other works include a wide range of realistic novels, plays and narrative poems with mimetic characters, and thematic works which explore conflicting value systems or affirm one or another of the defensive strategies. These works belong to a variety of genres, periods, and national literatures.

We have seen that psychological analysis can help us to understand the psyche of the implied author. It can also illuminate the writer's artistic personality[10] and the relationships between his writings, his life, and his culture. When I began to develop this psychological approach to fiction, my plan was to write a book on Thackeray which would show how the conflicts evident in the implied author of *Vanity Fair* reappear in Thackeray's other writings, in his life, and in his culture. This would be a very delicate undertaking, requiring an elaborate theoretical apparatus, immense knowledge, and the resolution of many difficult problems; but I believe that it could be done with reasonable success, with the help of Third Force psychology. Giving all due weight to the autotelic quality of the work, the importance of generic conventions, and the distinction between the man and the artist, it is still possible to learn a great deal about the historical person from his work and a great deal about the culture from both. An understanding of these relationships would shed considerable light upon the creative process and the relation between art and neurosis.

Some of the most important advances in literary criticism in recent years have been in the area of genre study. We have come to see that genres have evolutionary histories, that verbal meaning is genre-bound, that correct identification of genre is a prerequisite of valid interpretation, and that genres must be described in highly specific rather than in general terms.[11] The contribution of Third Force psychology to this area of criticism is that it can help us to go beyond description to an understanding of the emotional significance of various generic patterns. In some cases, at least, generic patterns seem to embody the conflicts, the solutions, the world views, and the fantasies associated with particular defensive strategies. When we see this, the history of literature and the preference of authors, readers, and cultures for certain literary forms take on new significance.

Like Freudian theory, Third Force psychology can tell us a great deal about audience response. To begin with, it can identify the conflicts, solutions, and values to which the audience is responding. Then, it can account for partial, biased, or conflicting responses. If a character or a work embodies an aggressive, a detached, or a self-effacing solution, or a particular structure of inner conflicts, readers will respond in terms of their own predominant solution or their own structure of conflicts. Criticism often tells us as much about the critic as it does about the work of art. It would be extremely interesting to analyze the whole body of criticism on a work from a psychological point of view. Not only would we learn much about the work and about the dynamics of literary response, but we would also gain insight into the subjectivity of perception and the inevitability of conflicting interpretations.

The psychological study of characters, implied authors, biography, genre, and audience response can be very helpful in the analysis of culture. The applicability of Horneyan theory to characters from Antigone to Herzog convinces me that human beings have remained much the same; but each age has its characteristic attitudes toward the various defense systems, its own formulations of and variations upon them, and its particular structure of conflicts. The prevalence of self-effacing protagonists in Victorian literature and the growing importance of detached characters in modern literature are good indicators of cultural movements. The response of an age to its own literature and to the literature of the past can tell us much about the Zeitgeist.

The psychological approach to fiction has its contribution to make not only to students of art, culture, and biography, but also to students of psychology. I have learned much from Horney; but I like to think that she would have learned some things about her own theory from this book. My findings suggest that she was not simply describing the neurotic personality of our time; her theories have very wide applicability. She gave us few detailed analyses of individuals. My analyses of characters flesh out her categories and reveal, perhaps, some variations and combinations which she would have recognized but did not spell out. Students of psychology have much to learn, I propose, from the application of her theories to literature and to the other areas which I have been discussing. One thing which they can gain is, as I have suggested, an empathic understanding of the inner experience of Horney's "types." Clinicians may have acquired this from their practical experience; but clinicians, neophytes, and non-clinicians alike can find in literature a rich source of individual variations and phenomenological insight.

In Third Force psychology we have a major contribution to human understanding. This theory is as powerful a tool of literary, biographical, and cultural analysis as any which we have. If the potential of the theory is to be actualized, the Third Force psychologists need what Freud and Jung found: co-workers in other disciplines who will apply their theories to a variety of phenomena, showing how wonderfully well they work, and testing, refining, and extending them in the process. This book was conceived as a contribution to our understanding of realistic fiction; but, if it has been at all successful, it must suggest the potency of Third Force psychology and the promise which it holds for other tasks, both in literary criticism and in related disciplines.

Notes

Chapter I

1. *Psychoanalysis and Shakespeare* (New York, 1966), p. 151. Whenever the source is clear, page numbers will be given parenthetically in the text.

2. There is a slight modification of Holland's position in *The Dynamics of Literary Response* (New York, 1968), Chapter 10 ("Character and Identification"): "Psychoanalytic critics regularly apply psychological concepts from the world of everyday reality to characters who exist in a wholly different kind of world—it should not work but it does" (p. 267). My contention is that it should work, and it does.

3. (Ithaca, 1965), p. 192.

4. See especially, Robert Scholes and Robert Kellogg, *The Nature of Narrative* (New York, 1966); Northrop Frye, *The Anatomy of Criticism* (Princeton, 1957); Wayne C. Booth, *The Rhetoric of Fiction* (Chicago, 1961); and Sheldon Sacks, *Fiction and the Shape of Belief* (Berkeley and Los Angeles, 1964).

5. There is an element of interpretation in all representation, of course, in that representation is not mere copying but involves artistic selection for the purpose of creating a more effective mimetic portrait. When I distinguish between representation and interpretation, I am using "interpretation" to mean analysis and judgment.

6. "The Art of Fiction," in *Myth and Method, Modern Theories of Fiction,* ed. James E. Miller, Jr. (Lincoln, 1960), pp. 24, 5.

7. Arnold Kettle, *An Introduction to the English Novel* (Harper Torchbook

ed., New York, 1960), Vol. 1, p. 21.

8. (Berkeley and Los Angeles, 1965), p. 30.

9. *Mimesis, The Representation of Reality in Western Literature*, trans. by Willard Trask (Anchor Book ed.: New York, 1957), pp. 433–434.

10. "Myth, Fiction, and Displacement," in *Fables of Identity* (New York, 1963), p. 36.

11. *Studies in European Realism* (New York, 1964), p. 10.

12. *Aspects of the Novel*, (London, 1927), Chapter 4.

13. *The Dehumanization of Art* (Anchor Book ed.: Garden City, 1956), p. 92.

14. Cleanth Brooks and Robert Penn Warren, *Understanding Fiction* (New York, 1959), xvii.

15. *Understanding Fiction*, p. 81.

16. Merleau-Ponty, quoted by Herbert Spiegelberg, *The Phenomenological Movement: A Historical Introduction* (The Hague, 1960), Vol. 2, p. 416.

17. *Anatomy of Criticism*, p. 5.

Chapter II

1. C. G. Jung, *Modern Man in Search of a Soul*, trans. W. S. Dell and Cary F. Baynes (Harvest Book: New York, n.d. [1933]), p. 118.

2. Karen Horney, *Neurosis and Human Growth* (New York, 1950), p. 15. Hereafter cited as NHG.

3. Abraham Maslow, *Toward a Psychology of Being* (Princeton, 1962), pp. 3–4. Hereafter cited as PB. The leading exponents of this position, in addition to Horney and Maslow, are Kurt Goldstein, Otto Rank, C. G. Jung, Erich Fromm, Rollo May, Carl Rogers, Gordon Allport, and Ernest Schachtel. For a fuller listing of the groups which, in the last twenty years, "have . . . been coalescing into a third, increasingly comprehensive theory of human nature," see PB, vi.

4. There are two other needs which Maslow defines as basic, but which he does not integrate into his hierarchy of prepotency. They are the needs to know and understand and the aesthetic needs. For a fuller discussion of each of the basic needs, see Maslow, *Motivation and Personality* (New York, Evanston, and London, 1954), Chapter 5. This work will be cited hereafter as MP.

5. For a fuller discussion of peak experiences, see PB, Chs. 6 and 7.

6. I am indebted here to Erich Fromm's discussion of "The Existential and Historical Dichotomies in Man," *Man for Himself* (New York and Toronto, 1947), pp. 40–50.

7. For a valuable collection of essays on the relation between psychological theory and value theory, see *New Knowledge in Human Values*, ed. Abraham Maslow (New York and Evanston, 1959).

8. For an application of Maslow's hierarchy to the study of culture, see Joel Aronoff, *Psychological Needs and Cultural Systems* (Princeton, 1967).

9. "A Theory of Metamotivation: The Biological Rooting of the Value Life," *Journal of Humanistic Psychology*, VII (1967), p. 124.

10. For a discussion of B-values, see *Religions, Values, and Peak Experiences* (Columbus, 1964), Appendix G, and "A Theory of Metamotivation."

11. Carl Rogers, *On Becoming a Person* (Boston, 1961), p. 51. Hereafter cited as BP.

12. *Metamorphosis* (New York, 1959), p. 167. Hereafter cited as M.

13. See M, p. 226, for a discussion of the relation between allocentric interest and love. See also, Erich Fromm, *The Art of Loving*.

14. *New Ways in Psychoanalysis* (New York, 1939), p. 305. Hereafter cited as NW. For a full scale account of Karen Horney and her ideas, see Harold Kelman, *Helping People: Karen Horney's Psychoanalytic Approach* (New York, 1971).

15. This process is vividly described in a letter from a patient which Horney published in *The American Journal of Psychoanalysis*, IX (1949), 4–7.

16. The term "false-self system" is used by R. D. Laing in *The Divided Self* (Baltimore, 1965). Though Laing is an existential-phenomenological analyst, who seems unaware of Horney and Maslow, his findings, and sometimes even his language, are amazingly close to theirs. It is in Laing that I find the best description of how defense systems such as those which Horney analyzes operate in psychosis.

17. Horney's conception of basic anxiety is very close to and can be enriched by Laing's notion of "ontological insecurity." See *The Divided Self*, Ch. 3.

18. *The Neurotic Personality of Our Time* (New York, 1936), p. 68. Hereafter cited as NP.

19. I am combining the terminology of Horney's last two books. For a discussion of this see note 22 below.

20. *Our Inner Conflicts* (New York, 1945), p. 20. Hereafter cited as OIC.

21. For a description of the typical course of such a relationship, see NHG, 247–258.

22. There is a problem in Horney's system which should be discussed at this point. In *Our Inner Conflicts* Horney classifies defense systems as compliant, aggressive, or detached; in *Neurosis and Human Growth* she

classifies them as self-effacing, expansive, or resigned. On the one hand, her typology is derived from inter-personal strategies; and intra-psychic dynamics (the nature of the idealized image, the content of the claims and shoulds, the sources of pride and self-hate) are determined by the inter-personal defense system. On the other hand, the typology is derived from the intra-psychic processes (the individual's relation to his idealized image, his shoulds, etc.) which seem to be details of the system rather than seminal principles. It is evident, moreover, that "self-effac- ing," "expansive," and "resigned" refer not only to intra-psychic solu- tions, but also to many of the phenomena described under the rubrics "compliant," "aggressive," and "detached." In Chapter I of NHG, Hor- ney accounts for the evolution of the idealized image, the shoulds, etc. in much the way she did in OIC; but in later chapters she fails to integrate this perspective with her emphasis on the intra-psychic deriva- tion of the major types.

My view is that in NHG Horney was caught up in the exploration of intra-psychic processes and that she tried to derive her whole system from them, much as in OIC she derived everything from inter-personal moves. Her thought was constantly evolving, she did not see every- thing at once, and she never got to the point of establishing clearly and in a balanced way the relationships between the inter-personal and in- tra-psychic processes. Her best statement is that we cannot understand the dynamics of neurosis from either intra-psychic or inter-personal conflicts alone, "but only as a process in which interpersonal conflicts lead to a peculiar intra-psychic configuration, and this latter in turn depends on and modifies the old patterns of human relations" (NHG, 237). But this statement is not really in keeping with the organization of her theory in the book as a whole. In my applications of Horney, I use both sets of terms interchangeably.

Chapter III

1. *An Essay on Man*, Anchor Book ed. (New York, 1953) pp. 182–183.
2. All quotations from *Vanity Fair* are from the Riverside edition, ed. Geoffrey and Kathleen Tillotson (Boston, 1963). Chapters will be cited in the text. When there is no chapter given, the quotation is from the last chapter cited.
3. By "Thackeray" I always mean the implied author of *Vanity Fair*.
4. Gordon Ray, *Thackeray, The Uses of Adversity*, 1811–1846 (New York, 1955), pp. 421–422.

5. "The Degradation of Becky Sharp," *South Atlantic Quarterly*, VIII (1959), 605.

6. Russell A. Fraser, "Pernicious Casuistry: A Study of Character in *Vanity Fair*," *NCF*, XII (1957), 142.

7. See especially, Sister M. Corona Sharp, O.S.U., "Sympathetic Mockery: A Study of the Narrator's Character in *Vanity Fair*," *ELH*, XXIX (1962), 324–336.

8. See especially, Mark Spilka, "A Note on Thackeray's Amelia," *NCF*, X (1955), 202–210.

9. It is beyond the scope of this study to explore the biographical and cultural implications of our psychological analysis; but, if Thackeray the man is similar to the implied author of *Vanity Fair*, our interpretation of the novel will be of as much value to the student of his life as it is to the critic of his art. The relations of the writing self to the historical author and of the novel to its time are complicated matters which cannot be explored here, but it is evident that the neurotic patterns manifested in *Vanity Fair* may be traceable both to Thackeray's character and to his culture. In the present study we are concerned with the novel as a work of art. The biographer and the cultural historian will, of course, want to use the novel as a source of insight into its creator and its age; and the mode of analysis employed here can, I think, be very useful to them.

10. The formistic aesthetic, as described by Stephen Pepper in *The Basis of Criticism in the Arts* (Cambridge, Mass., 1946), pp. 96–113, also insists that when unhealthy characters, values, and attitudes are represented, a mature point of view should prevail in the work as a whole.

Chapter IV

1. I am using the C. K. Scott Moncrieff translation. Chapters will be cited in the text. When there is no chapter given, the quotation is from the chapter last cited.

2. See F. W. J. Hemmings, *Stendhal: A Study of his Novels* (Oxford, 1964), Ch. IV. The relevant passages can be found in the Norton Critical edition of *The Red and The Black* (New York, 1969), edited by Robert M. Adams, pp. 524–526.

Chapter V

1. *The Great Tradition* (London, 1950), pp. 41–42.

2. "Toward a Revaluation of George Eliot's *The Mill on the Floss*," *NCF*,

XI (1956), 18–31; and *Experiments in Life: George Eliot's Quest for Values* (Detroit, 1965), Chapter 8.

3. In the present chapter I shall focus upon a psychological analysis of Maggie. For a full sense of the education pattern of the novel and of the ways in which George Eliot's interpretation of Maggie differs from her mimetic portrait, the present analysis should be read in conjunction with the studies cited in note 2. Chapters 7, 8, and 12 of *Experiments in Life* are especially relevant. There is further discussion of my changed view of George Eliot in the concluding section of this chapter and in my review of U. C. Knoepflmacher's *George Eliot's Early Novels: The Limits of Realism*, in *Journal of Modern Literature*, I (1970–1971), 272–277.

4. All quotations from *The Mill on the Floss* are from the Riverside edition, ed. Gordon S. Haight (Boston, 1961). Book and chapter numbers will be cited in the text. When there is no number given, the quotation is from the last chapter cited.

5. There are striking parallels between Karen Horney's description of the typical childhood situation and psychological evolution of the self-effacing person and George Eliot's dramatization of the life history of Maggie Tulliver; see NHG, 221–222.

6. For a Freudian interpretation of the Maggie-Tom relationship, see David Smith, "Incest Patterns in Two Victorian Novels," *Literature and Psychology*, XV (1965), 144–162. The Freudian approach yields some good insights, but I find it less adequate to the complexities of the text than Horneyan psychology.

7. For a thematic interpretation of Maggie's search for calm, see "Toward a Revaluation of George Eliot's *The Mill on the Floss*," *NCF*, XI (1956), 25–30.

8. See especially George Levine, "Intelligence as Deception: *The Mill on the Floss*," *PMLA*, LXXX (1965), 402–409, and William R. Steinhoff, "Intent and Fulfillment in the Ending of *The Mill on the Floss*," in *The Image and the Work* (Berkeley, 1955), pp. 231–251. Steinhoff feels, as I do, that Maggie at the end is "giving in to her weakness: a fatal timidity toward life"; but he finds it "impossible to believe that George Eliot was unaware of this weakness, since she herself had been forced to a decision in similar circumstances and had chosen otherwise" (p. 241). This argument from biography is of dubious validity in the absence of evidence of awareness *in the novel*.

9. I engaged in such criticism myself in *Experiments in Life*, where I not

only expounded, but also tacitly assented to George Eliot's theory of fiction and valued her novels—in part, at least—for the soundness of their moral vision.

10. *The George Eliot Letters,* ed. Gordon S. Haight (New Haven, 1954–55), VI, 216–217.

11. Ibid., VI, 216–217.

Chapter VI

1. For typical thematic readings of *Notes,* see Joseph Frank, "Nihilism and *Notes from Underground,*" *Sewanee Review,* LXIX (1961), 1–33; Edward Wasiolek, *Dostoevsky: The Major Fiction* (Cambridge, Mass., 1964), Ch. 4; Konstantin Mochulsky, *Dostoevsky: His Life and Work,* trans. Michael A. Minihan (Princeton, 1967), Ch. 12; Isidore Traschen, "Dostoevsky's 'Notes from Underground,' " *Accent,* XVI (1956), 255–264; and Robert Louis Jackson, *Dostoevsky's Underground Man in Russian Literature* (The Hague, 1958), Chs. 1–3.

2. On this point, see James Lethcoe, "Self-Deception in Dostoevskij's *Notes from the Underground,*" *SEEJ,* X (1966), 9–21; Scavan Bercovitch, "Dramatic Irony in *Notes from Underground,*" *SEEJ,* VIII (1964), 284–291; and Ralph E. Matlaw, "Structure and Integration in *Notes from the Underground,*" *PMLA,* LXXIII (1958), 101–109.

3. The rationale for a psychological approach is stated very well by both Lethcoe and Matlaw, though neither really provides the psychological analysis which he calls for. "The problem," says Lethcoe, "might be formulated thus: Is the paradoxical character of the underground man to be evaluated in the light of his philosophical theories about the nature of man, i.e., that man is free, arbitrary, many-sided, and irrational; or are we to see such theories as the kind of theories such a character as the underground man would naturally hold in order to rationalize his existence." Lethcoe concludes that "a shift in critical emphasis is in order. *Notes from the Underground,* which is usually approached as a philosophical work, is perhaps best approached as a psychological study" (p. 17).

4. The most interesting psychological analysis of the underground man to date is Mark Spilka's "Playing Crazy in the Underground," *Minnesota Review,* VI (1966), 233–243. There are some good observations also in R. L. Jackson, Ch. 3; in Herbert Walker, "Observations in Fyodor Dostoevsky's *Notes from the Underground,*" *American Imago,* XIX (1962), 195–210; and in Bella S. Van Bark, "The Alienated Person in Litera-

ture," *The American Journal of Psychoanalysis*, XXI (1961), 186–189.

5. Part II, section ii. I am using the Constance Garnett translation. Part and section numbers will be cited in the text. When there is no number given, the quotation is from the last section cited.

6. For Horney's discussion of the dynamics of this character type, see *NHG*, 270–272.

7. Horney's discussion of "impairment of morale" is highly relevant to the underground man:

> A person neglects his appearance; he lets himself become untidy, sloppy, and fat; he drinks too much, sleeps too little; he does not take care of his health—does not, for instance, go to the dentist . . . he neglects his work, or whatever serious interest he has, and becomes slothful. . . . These conditions occur when people are so flooded with self-contempt and hopelessness that their constructive forces can no longer counteract the impact of self-destructive drives. The latter then have free sway and express themselves in a mostly unconscious determination to demoralize themselves actively. . . . The neurotic's response to this inner process varies. It may be glee; it may be self-pity; it may be fright. (NHG, 152)

8. See OIC, 77–78.

Chapter VII

1. To avoid excessively complicated punctuation, I shall use double quotes for Marlow's narration except when there is internal quotation.

2. By "Conrad" I mean here not only the implied author of *Lord Jim*, but also the artistic personality whose belief system can be inferred from the whole corpus of his fiction.

3. The phrase is Herbert Spencer's. For a fuller account of the evolutionary theories underlying Conrad's beliefs, see Bernard J. Paris, *Experiments in Life: George Eliot's Quest for Values* (Detroit, 1965), Chapter 3.

4. Morton Dauwen Zabel, ed., *The Portable Conrad* (New York, 1952), p. 140.

5. Ibid., p. 547.

6. G. H. Lewes, *Problems of Life and Mind*, Third Series: *The Study of Psychology* (Boston, 1879), p. 144.

7. Ibid., p. 145.

8. "Heart of Darkness," p. 560.

9. Ibid., p. 540.

10. *Neuroses and Character Types* (New York, 1965), p. 356.

Chapter VIII

1. When I speak of *the* psychological approach in these concluding remarks, I am simply referring, in a convenient way, to the approach developed here. There are, of course, other psychological approaches.

2. *Aspects of the Novel* (London, 1927), Ch. IV.

3. "Myth, Fiction, and Displacement," in *Fables of Identity* (New York, 1963), p. 36.

4. For a discussion of the concept of "intrinsic genre," see E. D. Hirsch, *Validity in Interpretation* (New Haven and London, 1967), especially Chapter 3.

5. It should be noted that the majority of the "reliable" narrators in eighteenth and nineteenth century fiction were employing their rhetoric on behalf of the compliant solution. This solution moves in the direction of humanitarian values and is conducive to the social virtues; hence we may not feel a need of protection against its supporting rhetoric. In terms of individual development, however, this solution is destructive; and the glorification of it is not conducive to emotional well being.

6. Iris Murdoch, "The Sublime and the Beautiful Revisited," *Yale Review*, XLIX (1959), 271. Subsequent references to this essay will be given in the text.

7. *Aspects of the Novel,* Ch. IV.

8. *Motivation and Personality* (New York, Evanston, and London, 1954), p. 287.

9. Fyodor Dostoevsky, *The Brothers Karamazov,* Book V, chapter i.

10. By the artistic personality I mean that personality which is implied by the author's total production. When we study a writer's corpus with the object of tracing his development, identifying his recurrent interests, and understanding the inner logic which holds together his entire created world, we are dealing with his artistic personality.

11. See E. D. Hirsch, *op. cit.*

Index